From the OTHER SIDE:

Women, Gender, and Immigrant Life in the U.S., 1820-1990

DONNA GABACCIA

Indiana University Press
Bloomington and Indianapolis

The paper used in this publication meets the minimum requirements of American
National Standard for Information Sciences—Permanence of Paper for Printed
Library Materials, ANSI Z39.48-1984.

Manufactured in the United States of America

Library of Congress Cataloging-in-Publication Data

Gabaccia, Donna R., date
    From the other side : women, gender, and immigrant life in the
U.S., 1820–1990 / Donna Gabaccia.
        p.   cm.
    Includes bibliographical references and index.
    ISBN 0-253-32529-3 (alk. paper). — ISBN 0-253-20904-8 (pbk. :
alk. paper)
    1. Women immigrants—United States—History.   2. Women alien
labor—United States—History.   I. Title.
    JV6601.W7G33   1994
305.48′8—dc20   94-5613
    2   3   4   5   00   99   98

For my beloved grandmother, supportive parents, and scribbling sisters

CONTENTS

Acknowledgments

The list of friends and colleagues who have offered me support, advice, and criticism over the years I've worked on this book is a long one. The project began when Dirk Hoerder gave me the chance to teach a seminar on immigrant women during my Fulbright year at Bremen in 1985–86. He and his coworkers on the Labor Migration Project encouraged me to think about female migration, resulting in an essay that eventually became chapter 3 of this book. I'm especially happy to have the chance to thank Christiane Harzig, who organized the October 1990 Bremen conference on "Women in the Migration Process" and who shared the results of her own innovative research project on Chicago's immigrant women. Leslie Moch, friend and author of *Moving Europeans*, also offered sage advice on matters both scholarly and personal.

This book reflects seven years of discussions at a wide variety of conferences and scholarly sessions. I've learned much from comments, queries, and challenges from Elliot Barkan, Julia Blackwelder, Caroline Brettell, Kathleen Conzen, Mary Cygan, Hasia Diner, Randy Dodgen, Susan Glenn, Nancy Green, James Grossman, Marilyn Halter, Wanda Hendricks, Isabel Kaprielian-Churchill, Hartmut Keil, Joy Lintelman, Deirdre Mageean, Yolanda Prieto, Fraser Ottanelli, Sibylle Quack, Vicki Ruiz, Maxine Seller, Rita Simon, Suzanne Sinke, Diane Vecchio, Rudy Vecoli, Susan Watkins, and Sydney Weinberg. I wish especially to thank the many on this list who read early drafts of the manuscript.

Suellen Hoy and Walter Nugent discussed book titles with me and gave me courage through the ups and downs of the job search I started as I began writing this book. My new colleagues in Charlotte in turn helped ease my transition from old multiethnic New York to the new South.

A National Endowment for the Humanities Summer Stipend and a German Marshall Fund of the United States Distinguished Lectureship in spring and summer 1991 provided necessary financial help. For personal support, I thank also my mother, Marjorie Krauss Gabaccia, my father, Remo Palmo Gabaccia, my sisters, Julie Gabaccia McKenna and Linda Gabaccia, and my friends Brian Wasileski, Linda Pawlowska, Dorothy Kachouh, and Jeanne Chiang. Of course, the biggest thanks are saved for last: I have been nurtured by Thomas and Tamino Kozak through some very trying times while conceiving and bringing forth this book. I hope only that, in the end, what I make is equal to what I take.

Introduction

'I am old-fashioned from the other side. . . . American women . . . they got different manners. . . . But the young Italian girls, my daughters, they're up to date, just as good, just as polite. . . .'[1]

The speaker is Maria Zambello, an Italian immigrant living in the United States. This book explores the lives of foreign-born women who, like her, entered the United States from what many of them called "the other side."[2] Where was the other side? And how did a person like Zambello know when she had crossed over the boundary between it and the United States? In thinking about her own life, Maria Zambello compared herself only to other women; she disparaged herself as "old-fashioned" and less "good" than American women, rather than merely as poor. For Zambello, polite "modern" behavior—not her nativity or ethnicity—excluded her from American womanhood. The younger girls she saw as up-to-date and "just as good" had—in her view, at least—crossed the boundary from the other side while remaining Italian. Her daughters, however, almost certainly thought of themselves as Italian Americans.

Zambello's comments remind us of the centrality of gender—in a world divided between powerful and less powerful regions, and in the lives of immigrants who had moved from one to the other by migrating to the United States. Zambello could not easily isolate gender from other dimensions of her life. Immigrant women like her carried with them not merely Italian or German or Japanese ways, but also the distinctive female traditions found within their native cultures. To become American, these women invented "ethnic" female identities. Most immigrant women—like most men—creatively blended old and new in doing so. Most women welcomed the challenges and economic opportunities of a dynamic American economy; yet, like men, they also exhibited some ambivalence about accepting unmodified the individualism and voluntarism they associated with American modernity.

In one very significant way, too, immigrant women's confrontation with American life differed sharply from men's. Both ethnic conservators and Americanizers who wanted to "go after the women" saw women's loyalties as central to cultural transformation.[3] Associated symbolically with cultural identity—indeed, with the very "heart" of a culture—immigrant women and their daughters became markers of the line dividing Americans from outsiders; as a result, they found their lives subjected to intensive scrutiny both from other immigrants and from Americans.

While most histories of immigrants in the United States begin with the experiences of migratory men disguised as genderless humans, *From the Other Side* instead begins with the experiences of migratory women.[4] But though centered on women, its analysis does not stop with them. Immigrant women cannot be studied apart from men of their own backgrounds, nor apart from American women. As mobile and culturally distinctive outsiders, foreign-born women shared key experiences with foreign-born men, as well as with native-born women who migrated from country to city, poor women who struggled to survive and prosper, and native-born minorities seeking dignity and acceptance as Americans. Immigrants' daughters, in turn, encountered elite majority women eager to guide them toward American-style womanly behavior.

Not all immigrant women were alike, of course, and *From the Other Side* demonstrates how class, ethnicity, and time of migration shaped important variations in women's experiences, whether on the other side, in the process of migrating, or in the United States. A woman's starting place on the "other side" of an international economy proved the greatest influence. Whether in subsistence farming, humble wage-earning classes, or elite society, a woman's origins opened a specific range of migration choices and of opportunities for adjusting to life in the United States as an immigrant. Ethnic culture worked its influence through distinctive family, kinship, and communal traditions which gave women precise ethnic identities but also masked work, community, and cultural tensions shared by women of many backgrounds. Thus, even though each wave of immigrants originated in different regions around the globe, continuities in the experiences of the female and foreign-born are striking. For all these reasons, *From the Other Side* may strike the reader as slighting ethnic variation at times. When it does so, however, it is in order to highlight how the lives of women from the other side resembled, intertwined with, and departed from both the lives of immigrant men and the lives of other groups of American women—especially middle-class women and women of the "racial" minorities of the United States.

From the Other Side works outward from its focus on immigrant women, along with their interactions with foreign-born men and native-born women, to develop a general but also gendered interpretation of linkages among world development, migration, and American immigrant life.[5] Although woman-centered, it can be read as an alternative to general studies that have privileged men's experience as immigrants.[6] The boundary linking the United States to the "other side" was global in dimension; it was defined by economic inequalities under capitalism and by the inequalities of political centralization through colonialism and nation-building. *From the Other Side* begins by pointing to parallels between migration and nation- or empire-building as organizers of an integrated but hierarchical world economy in the nineteenth and twentieth centuries. Hierarchical integration continued within multiethnic nations of immigrants such as the United States. Incorporation into both the global economy and multiethnic polities proceeded differently for men and for women. But rather than contrasting the successful integration of women immigrants into an American mainstream from which racial minorities (groups subordinated as expanding nations and empires conquered them) have been excluded, *From the Other Side* suggests how migration has repeatedly challenged the American notion of biological difference, in both its "racial" and its "sexual" varieties.[7] As foreign women crossed over from the other side, they did not simply adjust to American life—they redefined the meaning of American womanhood.

From the Other Side focuses on change and continuity in migration and immigrant life between 1820 and 1990. It does not tackle the complex and fascinating story of the European and African settlement of the Western Hemisphere; there seemed no sensible way to treat the settlement of the United States separately from that of other colonies prior to its existence as a nation-state. It was in 1820 that an independent United States, acknowledging the resurgence of immigration following the Napoleonic Wars, began to count and to monitor migration over its borders, thus providing a logical starting date for this study.

Working within this 170-year period, *From the Other Side* offers an interpretive synthesis of several large multidisciplinary literatures on immigrant women. As such, it draws large strokes on a large canvas in order to attract the reader's attention to common themes across the disciplines. Some readers will miss in this method the cacophony of individual women's voices, and specialists may find the book does not advance debates on female difference or specific time periods. The broad approach of *From the Other Side* is, however, intended to highlight the connections of many groups of women to global transformations, as well as reinforcing the linkages among scholarly agendas.

From the Other Side was undertaken with several other goals in mind as well. One was to encourage scholars to write more monographs on immigrant women of particular backgrounds; another was to identify topics that beg for comparative study. The book should stimulate scholars in immigration studies to consider gender more systematically, by introducing them to issues central in women's studies. And it may encourage scholars in women's studies to continue submitting key concepts—from modernization and race to emancipation and patriarchy—to ever more intensive cross-cultural scrutiny.

Demographically and culturally, women immigrants closely resembled men of their own backgrounds. At work, at home, and in their communities, however, their lives diverged from men's: regardless of their exact origin, women's and men's responsibilities were more often complementary than shared. Sharing experiences instead with other females, immigrant women initially found common ground with their "own kind," especially with female kin, neighbors, and workers of immigrant backgrounds.[8] Initially, older women like Zambello had few contacts with native-born women. However, as the population of middle-class immigrants increased in the twentieth century and as the daughters and granddaughters of immigrants grew to maturity in considerable numbers, their contacts with Americans of a wide variety of backgrounds proliferated, changing how class and ethnicity defined American womanhood in the process.

From the Other Side tells this tale in three parts. "Coming to the United States" examines the changing location of the other side, its mutable relationship to the United States, evolving gender roles on the other side, and the influence of gender on migration patterns. "Foreign and Female" compares nineteenth (1820–1930) and twentieth (1930–1990) century women immigrants in the United States, identifying continuities among immigrant women of differing ethnicity and nationality. (Note that I am considering 1930 the watershed between the two centuries because of massive legal and economic changes in the 1920s, as described below.) A third section, "Changing," shows how class and cultural change in the twentieth century have redefined both immigrant women's adaptation to U.S. life and the identities of their female descendants.

From the Other Side imitates immigrants in starting "on the other side," for it is there that scholars have found the origins of modern migratory patterns. Chapter 1 identifies the changing backgrounds of immigrants to the United States: in the nineteenth century, northern and western Europeans gave way to southern and eastern Europeans and Asians; in the twentieth century, "third world" immigrants from Latin America, the Caribbean, and Asia have replaced most Europeans. While culturally diverse, women of these many backgrounds nevertheless shared key experiences on the margins of a changing global economy. For though the U.S. economy drew alternately on labor from abroad and on its own racial minorities to swell its labor pool, many of its immigrant workers had themselves begun their lives as colonized, racial minorities in other empires or nations around the world.

Subsequent chapters explore the paradox of cultural diversity and shared economic positions for women of the other side. Chapter 2 examines gender relations on the other side, as capitalism, commerce, and political centralization provoked defensive and adaptive strategies of response to changes in rural and subsistence-oriented economies around the world. Strategies for dealing with change increasingly assigned subsistence production to older, married women, while pushing growing numbers of younger, unmarried women along with men into wage labor: prior to migration, significant numbers of immigrant women, past and present, had already worked as domestic servants, market traders, and factory operatives. Both women's families and women's position within those families changed in response to worldwide change; for younger and older women, migration offered important, if differing, ways to pursue hopes fostered at home.

Migration, however, was no simple reflection of women's growing individualism. Chapter 3 demonstrates how both wage-earning and political turmoil (sparked by the formation or collapse of nations and empires) produced closely linked patterns of male and female migration to the United States. For most women, family and economic motives for migration remained inseparable. Past and present, women migrants have come most often from the dynamic corners of the other side, where wage-earning motivated female mobility. In the twentieth century, however, the United States introduced ethnic discrimination and class-specific provisions to migration policy, forcing women to enter the country as family dependents rather than as autonomous wage-earners. Thus a switch from male- to female-dominated migrations around 1930 reflects more than a growing demand for women wage-earners in the United States (or a diminishing demand for males).

Once they had arrived, immigrant women's starting places—notably their previous work experiences, age, and marital status--shaped their contacts with capitalism, both as waged workers and as housewives and consumers. Chapter 4 shows that women immigrants with the greatest autonomy often took the most traditional jobs in the United States, while women in family migrations pioneered newer forms of employment. Until recently, few immigrant women shared the jobs of their foreign-born brothers or husbands, and most clustered in the humblest of American jobs. Foreign-born women in the North had the kinds of jobs performed by women of the racial minorities in the South and Southwest—mainly in domestic service. Immigrant women also dominated factory work, a field which excluded African American women until World War II. Married women earned money at home, too, and continued older patterns of subsistence production; although they were called housewives, their domestic work little resembled that of middle-class American women.

Over time, patterns of employment converged among women of foreign and native birth, regardless of race or ethnicity. Foreign-born women today are still somewhat more likely than native-born women to find low-skill jobs in service and industry, but they are also significantly overrepresented in professional positions. In the twentieth century, too, middle-class and native-born women's juggling of multiple responsibilities at home and in waged work has come to resemble that of immigrant and minority women of the nineteenth century. Domesticity, as it was understood among the American middle classes in the nineteenth century, has virtually disappeared as a class marker in the United States. American womanhood has changed significantly as immigrants became American women, so that the female American models confronting immigrant women today are far different from those of the past.

Chapters 5 and 6 establish that immigrant women interacted primarily with people of their own backgrounds. Thus, while many groups shared broadly similar family configurations, immigrant women's distinctive languages, cultures, and traditions shaped identities unique to them. Women shared an understanding of their cultural distinctiveness with men of similar background. Immigrant women resembled women of America's racial minorities in viewing family ties as resources supporting female power and ethnic solidarity. Kinship also facilitated women's struggles against culturally specific traditions of misogyny.

In common with African American women, immigrant women worked together with men to build social worlds beyond their families. Although immigrant women created female ethnic organizations, their collective action fostered community solidarity, not female autonomy. Chapter 6 demonstrates further that waged work became the most important basis for immigrant women's solidarity with women from outside their group: immigrant daughters played a major role in building female labor and working-class organizations. Their activism simultaneously fostered cooperation and conflict—both with working-class men and with middle-class American women.

Class divided immigrant women among themselves, and these divisions became especially visible in the twentieth century. Chapter 7 shows that the proportion of well-educated and elite immigrants has increased substantially over the last fifty years. Not uncommonly, their reception has been a discouraging one. Professional refugee women, in particular, have often shared with men of their groups years of disheartening downward mobility after migration to the United States. In the past, upwardly mobile and professional women of foreign birth, like men, sought leadership and influence primarily within their ethnic communities. In the past, too, immigrant women differed from native-born white professionals and very much resembled educated African American women in combining careers with marriage and child-rearing. Today, by contrast, middle-class immigrant women professionals less frequently work in ethnic enclaves, and they often pursue careers in traditionally male fields.

Change in this century has also characterized the descendants of earlier generations of immigrant women. Chapter 8 explores the complex cultural transformations that accompany migration, showing how women's choices came to epitomize the successful integration of immigrant minorities into the American mainstream or, alternatively, the successful survival of ethnic identity. In women's lives, however, the two alternatives intertwined, especially in domestic work, which had been urged on immigrant women and their daughters by both Americanizers and ethnic preservationists. Exercising greater control over their individual marriage choices and children, immigrants' daughters gradually assumed responsibility for maintaining, adapting, and transmitting ethnic identity through their domestic labor. Today, the descendants of nineteenth- and twentieth-century European immigrants scarcely differ from other American women in their everyday behavior, yet they—far more than men—believe that ethnicity influences their lives. As a result, they have sometimes regarded the new wave of feminist activism with some skepticism. Ironically, these modern-day "jugglers" share more in common with the work lives of their own immigrant grandmothers than with the middle-class American female professionals of bygone decades whom feminists often claim as their foremothers.

From the Other Side shows how the women from the other side altered American notions of womanhood from the nineteenth to the twentieth century. Nineteenth-century migrations redefined the meaning of "American," as first Catholic and Jewish, then southern and eastern European immigrants claimed the label for themselves and broadened the ethnic range subsumed within it. In the twentieth century, the children and grandchildren of Asian and European immigrants became ethnic Americans at the same time that the United States began to acknowledge and seek to redress its history of discrimination against its racial minorities. The descendants of Asian, Mexican, and West Indian immigrants have rightly pointed to the peculiar difficulties they have faced in "becoming American." At the same time, studies that control for nativity and generation in studies of racial minorities usually reveal striking differences between native- and foreign-born, especially in education and occupational choice. Surprisingly, the foreign-born sometimes seem closer to general American patterns of employment, attitude, or family life than the native-born minorities they may seem to resemble "racially."

In American eyes, immigrants of Asian, African, or Native American descent become Americans by becoming racial minorities. Recently arriving elite, well-educated immigrants from the third world contemplate this road with much ambivalence. Many prefer to become ethnic Americans—Korean Americans or Jamaican Americans—rather than "blacks" or "Asian Americans." The coming of large groups of middle-class immigrants of color will, I feel, fruitfully challenge American assumptions about class and race. In like manner, immigrant women employed in engineering, medicine, and other scientific and technical professions will undermine firmly held American notions about gender.

Perhaps these predictions seem overly optimistic. But given the history of immigrant women in the United States, current definitions of race, Americanness, and American womanhood will unquestionably be hard put to survive the challenge of this country's most recent arrivals.

PART I.

Coming to the United States

ONE

Where Is the Other Side?

Immigrant women came to the United States from the same corners of the earth as immigrant men, and they traveled via the same routes. The location of the corners from which they came, however, changed remarkably during the three great waves of migration (1830–1860; 1880–1920; 1965–present). The nation receiving them also changed during these years. One challenge in studying men and women immigrants is to document their diversity while recognizing what they shared as migrants.

Angela Spoo Heck, a German speaker, represents the first great nineteenth-century wave of immigrants from northern and western Europe.[1] Born near Trier, Heck was twenty-eight and newly married when she left her native land in 1854; she accompanied her migrating husband Nikolaus, an unemployed journeyman tailor. The couple traveled to Antwerp, then boarded a sailing ship for New York. Heck had neither applied for permission to leave home nor received a cash grant from her town's mayor, eager though he was to be rid of poor "creatures" crowding local welfare lists. A devout Catholic, Heck found she could not pray during the terrifying transatlantic voyage. In her first letter home, she joked with her brother-in-law about the million lice that had joined the immigrants on their voyage over.

By the end of the nineteenth century, Asians and southern and eastern Europeans heading for the United States outnumbered Irish, Scandinavian, British, and German immigrants like Heck. Typical was Jennie Grossman. Born into a Jewish family in Lulieniec in Russian Poland around 1904, she left with her parents and brother just before World War I.[2] Grossman's father was an itinerant carpenter who returned to his three-generation household for Sabbath each week. At times Russian soldiers were billeted at his house, but they offered no protection during pogroms. Grossman's father suffered recurring nightmares of anti-Semitic violence; Grossman and her brother several times hid beneath their barn to avoid attack from Gentiles. Still, the departure from Lulieniec proved traumatic for Grossman's mother. Her elderly father had traveled along as far as Warsaw, but en route to the port city of Danzig, train personnel pushed him away from the emigrants. Shocked, and unable to say good-bye, Grossman's mother dropped a mirror she was holding: she carried the pieces for years afterward.

Since 1965, immigrants from Asia, the Caribbean, and Latin America have become the majority. Martha Vásquez de Gómez, for example, traveled to the United States from her rural Mexican home in 1973.[3] She was just sixteen, the eldest of ten children, and accustomed to heavy household work. Her widowed father had been ill, so when a friend of an aunt offered to take her to San Antonio, where she knew a family that would employ her, he readily agreed to let her go: he would have one fewer to feed. Vásquez de Gómez traveled by bus, with her aunt's friend and a counterfeit passport. Curious to see the United States, she worked there for a number of years and then returned home to see her father one last time. Soon thereafter, she married a young man in Guadalajara. She never returned to the United States.

Culturally diverse, these three women shared origins on "the other side," in regions of the world connected to the United States through economic and political ties, yet also economically and politically far less powerful than it. As the United States changed from an ex-colony within the British Empire to an independent and expanding nation-state, an international capitalist giant, and—ultimately—a world leader, its international connections continuously redrew the location of "the other side."

IMMIGRATION IN A CAPITALIST WORLD ECONOMY

If there were no inequality in the world, there would be far less migration. For the past 400 years capitalism and political centralization, most visibly through colonialism and through the expansion of nation-states such as Italy and Russia, have been key generators of inequality and of opportunity, and thus of migration. According to John Bodnar, "most of the immigrants transplanted to America . . . were in reality the children of capitalism."[4] While important, Bodnar's view misses how political subordination, too, sparked human mobility. Political change cannot be neatly divorced from the history of the capitalist world economy.[5] State policies have influenced human migration from the mercantilist empires of the seventeenth century, with their organization of the slave trade and of colonial investment, through the restrictive immigration laws of nations in the twentieth century.[6] The experiences of minorities like the Grossman family cannot be understood apart from their subordination during periods of national or imperial consolidation or collapse. In fact, politics may be the most important determinant of the way understandings of race and ethnicity change over time.

Capitalism and political centralization cannot tell us all we need to know about emigrants. Economic inequalities occur within nations and within empires, too; most migrations cross no international boundaries. And while economic inequality may be an important precondition for much migration, the very poorest are usually too poor to take advantage of economic opportunities elsewhere.[7] World view, age, and gender matter. A prospective migrant has to recognize her problems, to know something of worlds beyond her own and to perceive them as better—and attainable.[8] And a prospective emigrant has to have the power to move. Adults and men have often known more of the wider world than children or women; they have also enjoyed cultural support in making decisions for others in their families.

Not all the problems immigrants hope to solve by migrating are economic or political in origin. A contemporary of Jennie Grossman left home because she did not want her father to arrange her marriage;[9] the fictional Swedish heroine of Moberg's *The Emigrants* repeatedly argued against her husband's desire to emigrate until one of her children died.[10] Personal and familial events can spark migrations, but cannot easily be measured.

It is true that from their points of view, Heck, Grossman, and Vásquez de Gómez did not become migrants in response to a "capitalist world system" or to "political centralization," but to individual and immediate opportunities. Pragmatically, however, each moved through a world shaped by capitalist development and by nation- and empire-building. Each experienced personally the ways in which immigration and international politics had integrated two widely separated regions of the world into a state of hierarchical interdependence. As immigrants met Americans and as subordinated minorities confronted their rulers, distorted social, cultural, and moral distinctions emerged; we call these views of difference ethnocentrism and racism. They made differences between developing and "backward" regions appear natural.[11] For Grossman, ethnocentrism meant the daily fear of pogroms; for Vásquez de Gómez and Heck, it meant instead hearing complaints about them from elite Americans, earlier German arrivals, and Chicano employers in San Antonio.

In contrast to immigrants, the "racial" minorities of the United States were created as first European empires, and then the independent and expanding United States, gained varying degrees of control over Africa, North America, the Caribbean, and parts of the Pacific.[12] But when viewed from a global perspective, colonized or racial and immigrant minorities appear as overlapping and intertwined groups. Ambitious and competing dynasties in Europe had made colonies of their neighbors (England of Ireland, Spain of Sicily, Russia of Poland, and Turkey of Serbia) before or at the same time as they sought colonies elsewhere in the world.[13] Ethnic or racial minorities, the colonized, the enslaved, the partially free, and the formerly colonized have figured prominently in international migrations from 1492 down to the present. Empires seem always to "strike back" through mobile minorities.[14]

Few nations, furthermore, have sought economic development or political influence *only* as receivers of immigrants or *only* as "world powers." Great Britain built the world's largest colonial empire, but it was an empire characterized by high internal mobility. And while the United States became known as a nation of immigrants, it also acquired new territories and minorities in the nineteenth century and exercised political influence over a far-flung groups of allies after World War II. To this day, Great Britain's tradition of Empire and Commonwealth shapes its immigration policies.[15] In the United States, too, the history of immigration should be viewed in tandem with the histories of racial minorities and the expanding American "empire."

FROM COLONY TO AMERICAN EMPIRE:
IMMIGRANTS AND OTHER MINORITIES

From a collection of colonies marginal to the Spanish, French, and English empires of the seventeenth century, the United States emerged as an independent nation, committed to growth through migration, yet destined also to struggle with colonialism's legacy of creating racial minorities of conquered peoples. The population of the United States in 1790 still reflected the imperial policies of the British and French.[16] As in the rest of the colonized world, populations of Native Americans had declined precipitously. But unlike Africans in the Caribbean or in parts of Spanish and Portuguese America, Africans on the North American mainland, both slave and free, were outnumbered almost everywhere by Europeans and their descendants. England had started late in the competition for colonies, and it coaxed and coerced migrants to secure its colonies from Spanish and French encroachments. It opened its colonies to religious dissenters (Puritans in Massachusetts, Catholics in Maryland, Presbyterians in frontier areas from New York to North Carolina) and permitted foreigners, like the Germans of the middle colonies, to live under English laws and become citizens through naturalization.[17]

Most of the Europeans who had traveled to settle in British North America were humble people, hardly free themselves. England sent prisoners, convicts, and poorhouse residents to its colonies. Impoverished English men and women also sold themselves into temporary slavery as indentured servants in order to cross the Atlantic.[18] By 1790, however, the descendants of these European settlers had clearly distinguished themselves through law and custom from slaves and other Africans. Like its "mother" country, the United States quickly established its intentions to limit full citizenship to European men: its constitution enshrined the property rights of slave owners; it treated Native Americans as belonging to separate nations.[19]

Women had formed but a small part of colonial migrations to the Americas. Slave traders and plantation owners preferred male laborers, as did urban and rural employers of indentured labor.[20] Women's numbers equalled men's only among the most prosperous free migrants who traveled to North American colonies to farm the frontier or to establish religious settlements. By 1790, however, demographic increase had balanced sex ratios everywhere but on the western frontier of settlement. Most free white women, of course, remained men's dependents under law.

From the time of its first complaints (in the Declaration of Independence) about the British king limiting migration to the colonies, the United States had announced its intention to encourage immigration. In its constitution, however, it also proclaimed its right to limit access to residence and citizenship.[21] The Constitution provided for the abolition of the slave trade (which occurred in 1808), and plans to resettle emancipated slaves to Africa coexisted with Congress's decision to restrict citizenship through naturalization to whites.

Even after its independence, the United States remained firmly embedded in an Atlantic economy dominated initially by Great Britain.[22] Though it was no longer a colony, its trade ties and its continued need for foreign capital maintained conduits through which mass European migrations traveled after the end of the disruptive Napoleonic Wars. Encouraging immigration, however, was of little importance to the Founding Fathers at first. They looked not toward Europe but westward, committing the new nation to expansion as far as the Pacific and to the dispossession of American Indians and European colonizers on its borders. After the Louisiana Purchase and the conquest and purchase of a large part of Mexico's territory,[23] Easterners expected that Americans—that is, free, white English-speaking Protestants—would populate the west and southwest, outnumbering if not completely replacing the indigenous American Indians and mestizo Catholic Spanish-speakers of the region.[24]

The settlement and development of these western territories provoked a national crisis that clarified the relationship of immigrant and racial minorities in the United States and the position of the U.S. in the world. Wealthy southern planters looked forward to bringing slaves and slavery westward with them,[25] while opponents of slavery argued instead for free labor in populating and developing the United States. Increasingly, free labor came to mean labor from abroad, and opponents of slavery ultimately supported an open-door immigration policy.[26] By the 1850s, immigrants and racial minorities seemed positioned as conflicting sources of labor for national economic development. The Civil War established the nation's commitment to industrial growth by means of free rather than slave labor. Free men would labor on free soil or work as free wage-earners. Immigrants—not former slaves—would become wage laborers in the country's expanding industries.[27]

Industrial expansion in the United States opened new questions about the country's relationship to the rest of the world. President Monroe had announced U.S. opposition to European expansion in the Western Hemisphere. Industrial growth inevitably transformed the United States into a competitor with European empires for worldwide markets, and U.S. employers eagerly sought more and more laborers for expanding industries until World War I. Interested in trade with Asia and the Pacific, the United States sometimes saw carefully regulated immigration as an alternative to empire-building along European lines. In 1877, for example, Congress moved to guarantee that immigration brought only free laborers to the country. It excluded first "coolies" and "slave girls"—Chinese men and women who traveled to the United States on American trading ships as indentured servants and contract laborers—and then in 1885 all immigrant contract laborers, including those from Europe.[28] Determined to exclude all coolies and unwilling to view the Chinese as free migrants, Congress ended the migration of all Chinese laborers in 1882.[29] During the same years, however, the United States acquired its own subordinated racial minorities in colonies—only one of which (Hawaii) eventually entered the Union as a state.[30]

Overall, 95 percent of nineteenth-century immigrants came from Europe.[31] But despite their European origins, their large numbers drew shocked attention. After the turn of the century, almost a million immigrants a year strode off boats to find homes or work in the United States. Between 1880 and 1924, their numbers accumulated to impressive totals: four million Germans and almost as many Italians; three million Irish; two and a half million English, Scots and Welsh, and almost as many eastern European Jews; over one million Poles, and almost as many Scandinavians. Although small in numbers, the Chinese, Japanese, and Koreans continued to attract special, and negative, attention.[32]

In their poverty, nineteenth-century European immigrants resembled the indentured servants and redemptioners of the colonial era more than the Puritans and Cavaliers that Anglo-Americans proudly claimed as their country's founders. Most were of modest means or poor, and many had required assistance from home-villagers, illicit labor agents, or emigrated relatives to finance their trips to the United States.[33] Immigrants seeking jobs in industry heavily outnumbered settlers on the land. Many were "sojourners" with little intention of remaining in the United States.[34]

Few native-born Americans saw these new arrivals as followers in the footsteps of the original European settlers. Although Scandinavian, English, and some German immigrants shared the Protestantism of earlier English colonizers, most immigrants by the end of the nineteenth century worshiped in synagogues, in mosques, or in Catholic, Greek Orthodox, or Russian Orthodox churches. Because U.S. economic development drew on the hinterlands of nations and empires that could not match its rate of growth, many new arrivals (notably Irish, Poles, and South Slavs) had been colonized minorities—already disparaged for their backwardness and racial difference—at home. Fears of immigrant minorities mounted as southern and eastern Europeans—viewed as "dark" peoples from alien cultures—replaced the English, Scottish, and German newcomers of the pre–Civil War migrations.[35] But unlike immigrants from Asia or Africa, most could at least claim citizenship through naturalization if they so chose.

Not surprisingly, demands for racial discrimination in United States immigration policy increased.[36] Immigrants from China and Japan first bore the brunt of racist policies against foreigners, but discrimination did not stop with them. Mass migrations from Europe sparked intense debates about the racial status of European immigrants. Were the Irish white? Were the Italians? Could either ever successfully become Americans? Surprisingly often, the initial answer to all these questions was no.[37] Social-Darwinist racial theories roughly resembling those we today associate with Hitler found an official place in U.S. immigration policy in 1899.[38] Overnight, immigration officers declared northern and southern Italians two different races; they labeled most British West Indians as Africans; and they reclassified Polish or Russian Jews as "Hebrews," in order to emphasize their Semitic (and thus "Oriental") origins.

Migration had increased irregularly across the century, peaking just before World War I. Though the war put a clamp on immigration, the drop proved temporary; after the Armistice, demands for more restrictive laws grew. Over a presidential veto, Congress first excluded immigrants who could not read or write. When that law did not succeed in lowering immigration totals, new laws passed in 1921 and 1924 banned all Asian immigration and assigned tiny numerical quotas (albeit on a national, not a racial basis) to southern and eastern Europeans, while allowing large numbers of western and northern Europeans to enter. Clearly emerging from racial fears, these laws nevertheless did not attempt to restrict immigration from Africa (it was small in any case), from Mexico, or from any other nation in the Western Hemisphere, no matter what its peoples' "race."[39]

By banning small Asian immigrations and restricting sizable southern and eastern European migrations, Congress accomplished its overarching goal, reducing the total number of immigrants entering the United States in the 1920s to about 150,000 annually. By restricting immigration while demand for labor in the United States remained strong, however, Congress also practically guaranteed that new migrants would replace excluded ones in U.S. agriculture and industry.

With the restriction of European migration after World War I, the racial minorities of the United States and the peoples of its own colonies moved to replace immigrants from Europe. African-Americans abandoned rural homes in the South for northern cities, as did the Mexican-Americans of the Southwest. Unrestricted, migrations from south to north in the Western Hemisphere grew, especially across the land border separating the United States from Mexico. Puerto Ricans and Filipinos also left their U.S.-colonized homes to experiment with work in the United States. Supporters of racist immigration laws had argued that they would "take the pressure off an overheated melting pot" in industrial cities; instead, restrictive laws merely encouraged new peoples to try their luck in the pot.[40]

The Great Depression of the 1930s temporarily interrupted these new migrations. As jobs became scarce, the United States tightened its control of immigrants and resisted efforts to revise the quota laws of 1921 and 1924.[41] Racial prejudice continued an important influence on U.S. immigration policy: authorities deported Mexican workers from the Southwest, failing even to differentiate between legal and undocumented immigrants or between citizens and foreigners.[42] And the United States held firm against humanitarian demands that it suspend discriminatory quotas in order to allow Jews to escape persecution in Europe.[43] Still, Hitler's racial policies, leading to incarceration and murder of Jews and other minorities, attracted such negative attention that discrimination against racial minorities and southern and eastern Europeans in the United States became harder to defend. By World War II, Italians had become as indisputably white as the Irish before them. Filipinos gained their independence soon after the war, and campaigns against racial discrimination in all its legalized forms—from the segregated U.S.

Army and the drinking fountains of the South to prohibitions against Asian naturalization—gained momentum and support.

Modest changes initially exacerbated the contradictions inherent in U.S. immigration policy.[44] Congress lifted racist bans against its Chinese allies during World War II, and it gave its blessing to farms that actively recruited Mexicans as temporary "bracero" workers.[45] But it left in place discriminatory nationality quotas aimed at Asians and southern and eastern Europeans until 1965. Cold-war fears of foreign radicalism may have helped sustain discriminatory quotas through the economic boom of the 1950s.[46] But the cold war also worked to undermine immigration policy in practice, since anti-communism moved the United States to admit small groups fleeing Communism, first in the late 1940s from eastern Europe, then in 1956 from Hungary and in 1961 from Cuba.[47]

Only with a new Immigration Act in 1965 did the U.S. Congress finally attempt to provide a more permissive and racially neutral immigration policy. The law raised the number of immigrants admitted yearly to 290,000. It created numerical quotas and uniform visa requirements ("preferences") for all nations of the world.[48] The Immigration Act of 1965 can thus be seen as complementing its legislative contemporaries, the civil rights laws that ended legal racial discrimination against the country's racial minorities.

The new immigration laws of the late 1960s did make migration from the Western Hemisphere and from northern Europe relatively more difficult, since people from both had effectively enjoyed unregulated migration since the 1920s.[49] However, preferences for immediate relatives of naturalized immigrants and for skilled and professional workers guaranteed that older immigrant groups enjoyed particularly good access to visas, at least initially.[50] And the visa status of refugees remained problematic under the new legislation;[51] throughout the 1960s, 1970s, and 1980s, Congress and President responded periodically with special legislation and executive acts to allow carefully selected refugees, usually fleeing Communist countries or the Middle East, to enter the United States, notably from Cuba, southeast Asia, and the Soviet Union.

Patterns of immigration into the United States changed significantly under the new laws. Legal immigration totals rose well above the ceilings established under the 1965 law, to about half a million yearly in the late 1970s and 1980s, largely as a result of special provisions for relatives and refugees. As immigration increased, earlier migrations of African Americans to northern cities waned, and then reversed direction somewhat with the rapid economic development of the New South and the Sunbelt.[52]

European interest in migration to the United States declined as northern European economies rebounded from World War II and attracted southern and eastern European migrant guest workers of their own.[53] Italians, Portuguese, and Yugoslavs often preferred migration to northern Europe to migration to the United States, and the number of immigrants from these groups dropped to about 60,000 yearly in the 1970s.

The majority of immigrants entering the United States under the new law came instead from Asia (roughly 250,000 yearly in the 1970s and 1980s) and from Latin America and the Caribbean (upwards of 300,000 yearly during the same period).[54] In the 1970s and 1980s, Mexico, China, Korea, Cuba, Vietnam, and the Philippines regularly ranked among the top five countries sending immigrants to the United States. Spanish-, English-, and French-speaking immigrants from the Caribbean also rapidly increased in numbers.[55] The United States no longer draws new workers from the minorities of other nations, from its own racial minorities, or from its colonized territories. Instead, its immigrants now originate in the far-flung military and trade empire the United States has built as world leader since World War II. Many new immigrants, furthermore, are well educated and professional workers in their homelands.

As in the nineteenth century, however, today's new migrations challenge Americans to reconsider their definitions of race and racial minorities. Native-born Americans often see immigrants from the third world as Hispanics, African Americans or Asians, yet new immigrants rarely identify with such categories. Shared origins in Africa do not automatically make the French- or Creole-speaking, Catholic Haitian the soul sister of a native African American Protestant from Atlanta. Newly arrived Colombians contrast their supposedly pure Castilian Spanish to the "Spanglish" of Puerto Ricans; new arrivals from Japan and Korea are unlikely to feel much mutual solidarity as Asians. The United States in the 1990s seems to face again a period of fundamental transformation in its racial assumptions as new immigrant minorities undermine the racial categories created centuries ago by colonialism and national expansion in this hemisphere.

CONCLUSION

The history of immigration, past and present, begins in the changing margins—or other side—of the capitalist world economy. As conquest, capitalist investment, and ties of commerce disrupted subsistence production around the world, they generated first regional and then global markets for settlers and workers from developing nations. Unfortunately, analyses of global capitalism have rarely attended in any detail to women. This chapter, too, has downplayed the importance of gender and ethnicity in a world organized hierarchically through capitalism and political centralization into developing and backward regions. Still, a growing literature on women and economic development, supplemented by studies of women under colonial rule, does shed some light on immigrant women's early lives on the other side.

The next chapter will show that trade, investment, nation-building, and colonialism proceeded in patterned ways, forcing men and women of the other side to devise strategies for coping with change. But while capitalism and centralizing governments introduced fairly uniform changes in the hinterlands of the world, people's responses varied considerably with culture and gender. Initially, many rural peoples chose defensive strategies to protect their kin-based households from the atomizing influence of capitalism and its system of individual wage-earning and consumption. To limit capitalism's inroads, families assigned wage labor to particular family members—most typically young men, older men, and younger women. Over time, however, more people of the other side sought to make their peace with capitalism or empire through fulltime wage-earning. And whether one embraced or rejected these changes, migration became an important mechanism for securing a future in a changing world. In this respect, too, the history of immigrant women in the United States begins on the other side.

The Women of the Other Side

"A map of the city would show more stripes than on the skin of a zebra, and more colors than any rainbow," Jacob Riis wrote of New York's immigrant neighborhoods in 1890.[1] Riis would have found the other side even more colorful. Irish immigrants came to the United States as Cork- or Connaughters; Germans came as Bavarians or East Prussians; Italians came with village identities as Sambucese or Palermitani; even Jewish immigrants distinguished Galizianer from Litvak and Chasid from Maskilim. Today's "Latina" or "Hispanic" arrives thinking of herself as Cubana, Quesqueyana, or Norteña. The local identities of the other side defied bureaucratic efforts to categorize it on Ellis Island; it defies contemporary affirmative action guidelines.

Still, regardless of their precise origin, women began their transformation from the female half of the other side to female immigrant in response to the demands of capitalist expansion and national and colonial governments, demands involving only limited variations on a very small number of themes. Manipulating traditional gender ideologies in a changing context, the people of the other side responded not with hundreds of culturally distinctive coping strategies, but rather with only a few. For this reason one need not treat the experiences of Chinese, Italian, and Scandinavian women as wholly unique (although in other respects, of course, they were): these three groups of women shared key experiences in subsistence agriculture on the other side. Their experiences can be contrasted with those of Irish, Jewish Russian, and Japanese women, whose migrations are traceable instead to the spread of female wage-earning in the nineteenth century. Moreover, despite their very different backgrounds, one can usefully note how much today's immigrant women from Cuba, Cambodia, China, Antigua, or Mexico resemble this second group of women. On the other hand, both earlier groups of migrants included women uprooted at least partly by the disruptive effects of colonialism and state formation. For contemporary migrants, too, political conflicts emerging from state formation and the end of colonialism remain an important influence.

IN TRANSITION TO CAPITALISM: SUBSISTENCE PRODUCTION IN THE NINETEENTH CENTURY

Scholars agree that few migrants permanently leave economies based exclusively on subsistence production, where family groups work together to provide for most or all of their own needs. International migrants instead emerge from homelands in transition to capitalist production.[2] Most also leave regions which are either being integrated into newly forming political units or connected with disintegrating ones. The lives of women who left the other side as migrants are thus intimately bound with the histories of economic and political development of their homelands.

In rural northern Europe, Ida Lindgren married Gustaf, a large-scale tenant farmer in Skane, Sweden, in the late 1850s. The two initially prospered, and ate well—Ida would later miss the sweet-sour rye bread she baked and the drink she brewed of fruit from her own trees—but after a few years, poor harvests ruined prospects for a family that had grown to include five children. In 1870, the Lindgrens migrated to Kansas. Most of Ida's first reactions to life in the United States revolved around changed weather conditions, natural phenomena, crops, and food.[3]

Lalu Nathoy, a member of one of the many ethnic minorities of the Chinese empire, also worked on the land from an early age. Laboring beside her father, Lalu planted soybeans, covered over sweet potato plantings, and picked peanuts. After her father returned from a temporary emigration to Manchuria circa 1870 with sufficient cash, he risked all his savings to become a commercial wheat-raising farmer. Perhaps trying to emulate the mores of bourgeois China, he also ordered his daughter out of the fields and bound her feet. Unfortunately, poor weather destroyed his entire wheat crop. Perhaps sensing the vulnerability of this upstart (and now impoverished) family, a bandit gang led by one of her father's disgruntled hired hands attacked the Nathoy farmstead. They kidnapped and raped Lalu, and then sold her to an international trader who did not care that she still had feet "like dragon boats."[4] She was approximately 14 years old at the time.

About the same age as Lalu in the 1930s, Emma Ciccotosto lived in Italy's mountainous interior. Her father had made several trips to the United States, and he was in America at the time of her birth; later he migrated again to Australia. Emma's mother, with the help of her three children, farmed a bit of land during her husband's absences. She and the children lived in a house of baked mud brick and raised grain to bake into the pizza crust they ate with home-grown vegetables and oil. They cared for chickens and a cow and, working together with neighbors and kin, cut and threshed wheat for bread. Their farm and their labors fed and clothed them: Emma's mother raised flax to spin and then weave into cloth for her daughters' "treasure boxes," or dowries.[5]

Growing up in opposite corners of the world, the lives of all three women nevertheless reflected the rhythms of agricultural life and family ties to the soil. Divisions of labor by gender varied considerably in each place, as did the family and kinship beliefs of each of the women. In the early nineteenth century, the peasants of chilly Scandinavia wrung a difficult existence from the land by combining grain cultivation with animal husbandry and small-scale crafts. A typical farm passed from father to eldest son, but most men managed to acquire at least a small amount of land. An eldest son took over from his father when the older man retired; the son would bring his wife into a common extended "stem" household. Until their children could work, the son and his wife would hire farm hands and maids for room and board or for small payments in cash and kind. As the older generation died and growing children replaced outside workers, the household would turn into a "nuclear" one.[6]

Peasant women's work included care of the animals, the children, and the house; the processing and preparation of food; and the production of cloth and clothing. Men's responsibilities included building, grain cultivation, and provision of adequate fuel and forage. Men shared their agricultural tasks, albeit in carefully defined ways, with the women of their households. Thus at haying time, men cut while women raked. At harvest time, men reaped and threshed while women gleaned. Men less frequently took part in women's chores.[7]

Education, too, began and sometimes ended at home. Lutheran and Pietist Norwegians and Swedes believed the religious education of the family lay in the father's hands, but both boys and girls learned to read. Some continued for a few years in a local government-sponsored school, but not many enjoyed education beyond basic literacy and figuring.[8]

Farm households more frequently required the help of farm maids than male farm hands. Young women left their own families to work caring for animals on other farms. During the summer months, the farm maids took the animals to upland pastures; the farm wife supervised the production of butter or cheese. If the wife sold either at market, she controlled the cash she earned.[9]

The independent work of farm maids seems also to have given Swedish women some control over sexuality and marital choices. Farm hands often visited farm maids in their sleeping quarters, and as a boy's expectations of inheriting a farmstead increased, courting couples often began sexual relations. Although Protestant Scandinavians scarcely sanctioned premarital sex, and the male and female gossips of their small villages cruelly stigmatized illegitimate children and their mothers, few objected—or remembered—when marriage followed quickly upon pregnancy.[10]

In Italy in the nineteenth and twentieth centuries, agricultural organization, family structure, and the division of labor by sex differed considerably by region. As in Emma's family, subsistence production for a smallholder's nuclear family often was women's work, while men produced industrial goods for sale, or worked for wages in construction, or performed paid seasonal harvest work for commercial agriculture. In other areas, however, women spun or wove while men farmed. In some areas, commercial farms engaged the labor of extended family groups; in others they hired only men or only women.[11]

Italian fathers and mothers perceived daughters as heavy financial burdens, since daughters needed dowries before they could marry. After their marriage, however, women controlled the family purse and arranged their children's marriages. In this way women exercised considerable family influence. Mothers became the emotional centers of their immediate families; they were idealized through comparison to the Virgin Mary.[12] But they also created and helped sustain the kin networks upon which Italians depended for cooperative production and for social and economic security.

Strained by the new Italian state's accelerating demands for taxes after 1860, Italian peasants periodically revolted. Women figured prominently in the crowds that murdered tax collectors, threatened draft officials, sacked local grain merchants' storerooms, and burned down city halls. Nevertheless, women were excluded from many self-help organizations founded by men, notably friendly societies (fraternal orders).[13]

On the other side of the world, Chinese women did not belong to the lineage of their fathers, yet they lived in a world organized around extended groups of patrilineal kin, and Confucian respect for patrilineal ancestors provided their spiritual grounding as well.[14] In China, peasants hoped to prosper by farming in multi-generational patrilineal households. A father, his married sons and grandsons, and their wives and children shared a household, a farm, an economic destiny, and a common reputation. As in Italy, the division of labor by sex varied considerably by region. Among the Chinese poor, women commonly worked in the fields and fished in flooded rice fields or rivers. In the south, ambitious or more prosperous women worked instead in and around their homes—producing cloth and clothing, processing and preparing food, and caring for and rearing children.[15]

Because patrilineal clans needed sons to survive, Chinese attitudes toward female children, and their marriage customs, differed from Western ones, though misogyny was common to both areas.[16] Hard-pressed mothers neglected unwanted girl children.[17] To avoid the payment of expensive dowries and bride prices, poor women gave up their own small daughters for adoption into the families of the little girls' future husbands. Such adopted daughters-in-law bore surprisingly small numbers of children, perhaps because marital ties between men and women raised as siblings were sexually weak. Adopted daughters-in-law, however, enjoyed better relations with their mothers-in-law than older brides, who found it difficult to transfer obedience and emotional loyalty from their own mothers.[18] Within the patrilineal descent group and household, Chinese women created mother-centered, "uterine" families in which mothers determined the emotional climate of family life for their subordinates.[19] Women cultivated strong ties above all to their sons, but also to favored daughters-in-law and grandchildren.

Families without sons faced grave economic problems. Since children were expected to support their parents in old age, unmarried and only daughters in poorer families frequently worked as prostitutes; being regarded as fulfilling their filial obligations, they enjoyed community and cultural support in doing so. Most prostitutes eventually married, although usually as minor wives or concubines in large households.[20]

Similarities between women of the other side and those of the racial minorities of the United States seem particularly obvious among groups engaged in subsistence agriculture. In the Southwest, for example, Hispanic men became increasingly involved as hired hands in commercial agriculture and as seasonal labor in mining and construction, while Hispanas took over the responsibility for feeding their families back in the home village. By continuing to cultivate land collectively with their female neighbors and maintaining longstanding exchange networks in labor and food, they also sustained communal traditions in the face of capitalist demands for individual wage-earners.[21]

In subsistence areas around the world, family and kin groups worked together to feed, shelter, and clothe their members with no more than limited recourse to wage-earning and the market. Strongly held ideals of a collective family economy dictated the lives of all. In each case, a family economy required all family members to contribute to the family's needs; in return, the family functioned to meet the needs of its members.[22] Protestant, Catholic, and Confucian beliefs all sanctioned the sacrifice of individual needs for the good of the kin group, though patterns of kin relations varied considerably in the three regions.

Productive and reproductive work were indistinguishable in subsistence agriculture; peasant lives were not divided between a female private and a male public world, between female reproducers and male producers, or between "work" and "life."[23] Still, it is clear in all the three cases we have examined that gender determined the nature of a person's obligations and rights—and often to women's disadvantage. In all three cases, however, women contributed crucially and materially to group well-being; many gained influence through motherhood, though they worked longer hours than men.[24] Typically, too, women of limited resources could build kin networks to support their emotional and material well-being. Finally, among all the peasants described here, men shared with women a joint subordination to government power-wielders that was just coming under challenge in the nineteenth century.

Clues to women's status in subsistence economies are contradictory and inconclusive.[25] Generally, subsistence producers valued men more than women, and they welcomed the births of boys more than girls. In Latin societies, furthermore, men believed they had to control women's sexuality (their potential for incurring "shame") or all in the family lost honor and social status.[26]

Thus subsistence production in family economies encouraged male-female cooperation but also left room for gender conflict. The dynamics of this "cooperative conflict" or "interdependence" can scarcely be teased out of historical documents.[27] Evidence of virulent misogyny in European and Asian folklore and religious teaching is easy to find but very hard to interpret: we cannot know if it principally reflected social reality, functioned as an ideological sop to politically powerless men, or bolstered male esteem in the face of women skilled as manipulators of kin resources.[28]

Throughout the world, subsistence producers responded to the increasing pressures of capitalism and political centralization by adjusting gendered divisions of labor within family work groups, assigning women and the old more to subsistence production and food-raising, and men and the young more to wage-earning. We do not know how decisions like these were made, nor just how to interpret them in terms of their effects on women's situations. Viewed from one perspective, peasant men are seen as having begun to modernize and innovate while subsistence-oriented peasant women lagged behind, preserving older tasks. When the change is considered, however, in combination with national and colonial initiatives to empower men through military training, political rights, and land reform, it is easy to understand why anthropologist Barbara Rogers relates the beginning of women's "domestication"—their relegation to a distinctive, home-centered world apart from men's—to the decline of subsistence production.[29]

INDUSTRIALIZING HOMELANDS: WOMEN AND DEVELOPMENT IN THE NINETEENTH CENTURY

In parts of Europe and Asia in the nineteenth century, early capitalist incursions into subsistence-production economies generated further economic development, culminating in industrial production, wage-earning, and the rapid proletarianization of peasants. Industry developed in extremely localized fashion, and regional economic development spurred migrations to areas with jobs, making industrial metropolises out of cities like Tokyo, Shanghai, Berlin, Stockholm, Liverpool, Milan, Budapest, Moscow, or Lvov almost overnight. In response, women increasingly dedicated themselves to wage-earning and the search for a cash income.

In a small town near Warsaw in Poland early in the twentieth century, Beatrice Pollock's parents operated a tiny store in the Jewish ghetto of 200 families. Beatrice's father traveled, purchasing groceries, while her mother managed the store. Beatrice received home schooling because Jewish children had been barred from the public schools. By age five, Beatrice began helping out in her parent's store. The job consumed ever more of her time as she grew older, and she chafed under the harsh supervision of a stepmother after her mother died.[30]

More prosperous, Pollock's contemporary Michiko Sato was the third daughter, and one of eight children, of a sugar merchant family in Hiroshima City, Japan. Both of her parents managed the family business, which employed twelve people. Her mother—the "real boss," according to Michiko—insisted that the children go to school, but she did not otherwise supervise their lives; she was too busy at work. Servants cooked meals and cleaned their house. Michiko worked in the family store until an emigrant asked to marry her.[31]

Norah Joyce grew up in a family of seven children, five of them girls, on the Aran islands off the Irish coast. Like most island families, the Joyces supported themselves by combining farming, fishing, herding, and handcrafts.

At twelve, when Norah had finished parish school, she began doing house-work for summer vacationers on the island; at fifteen she went off to Dublin to work as a servant in one of their homes. A native speaker of Gaelic, Norah learned English in Dublin. Then in 1928 she emigrated to the United States.[32]

The choices of Irish women like Norah Joyce reflected Ireland's colonial status, within easy reach of Great Britain's expanding cities and industries. In the 1840s Ireland had suffered one of the most severe crises of subsistence agriculture in all of Europe, as over a million died during an extended potato blight. In the aftermath of the famine, Irish life changed in all essential details. Partible inheritance, youthful and universal marriage, and high fertility dis-appeared; primogeniture, late marriage, high rates of celibacy, and sharp de-clines in marital fertility replaced them. Without land, no one could marry in the countryside, and regardless of sex, they had to seek their fortunes else-where.[33] While Ireland itself offered few jobs for women, domestic service and textile jobs beckoned in England (or in colonial administrative centers such as Dublin).

Irish Catholicism and traditions of sex segregation made domestic service particularly attractive to Irish women, who saw work in middle-class homes as a protection against undesired contacts with men.[34] Moreover, like women in Scandinavia and Germany, Irish girls saw work in a middle-class urban kitchen as a step up from farm labor. It introduced women to bourgeois do-mestic practices and to the rudiments of genteel womanhood.

Unlike other Catholics, furthermore, the Irish did not disparage life-long celibacy. Indeed, Ireland stands out as one of the few European countries where late marriage and high celibacy rates did not result in climbing rates of illegitimacy. Burgeoning Irish Catholic sisterhoods offered unmarried women a world apart, where they could support themselves as religious workers.[35] Given a high degree of gender hostility in Irish culture, Irish women weighed wage-earning spinsterhood and convent life against mar-riage and sometimes found the latter too risky.[36]

After the famine, Irish women defined themselves in strikingly economic terms.[37] Whether married or single, they assumed they ought to earn money whenever possible. Women viewed waged work as a necessary form of so-cial security, since the outlook for marriage was limited, and the prospects of widowhood for wives (who married late) quite high.

Jewish women of eastern Europe also defined themselves in economic as well as familial terms.[38] In Russia, Poland, and Austria, Jews had always been excluded from agriculture. Russian economic development and the growth of industry further reinforced Jewish concentration in commercial and in-dustrial pursuits, as petty peddlers, as small-scale or marginal artisans, and, eventually, as early factory wage-earners.[39]

A religious faith based on adherence to and interpretation of written laws covenanted with God, Judaism exalted the learned man and scholar. All Jew-ish boys received the rudiments of training for religious scholarship. By con-trast, few girls received much religious education beyond the domestic rituals that were women's responsibility. Most learned to read and write. Because marriage to a young scholar might require women to become breadwinners, girls more often trained for a life of work.[40]

Settled in small market towns throughout the Russian Pale, Jewish women figured prominently in local commerce and exchange.[41] Jewish market traders bought and sold from the Gentile peasants among whom they lived and worked. Unlike Beatrice Pollock's mother (who was sickly), many traveled the countryside, maintaining contacts with peasant suppliers and purchasers. Wives who did not peddle or trade worked beside their shoemaker or tailor husbands.

As a religious minority in a Russian Orthodox empire, *shtetl* Jews often bore the brunt of violent peasant attacks, or pogroms. The Russian state provided Jews little or no protection, and in some cases even encouraged ethnic violence.[42] Peasants' hatred of Jews focused mainly on men, whom they falsely charged with murdering Christian children for religious rituals. But the Christians' violence did not stop with males, and both Jewish men and women especially feared for women during peasant attacks, since women might be raped as well as killed.[43]

Fleeing pograms and poverty, poor, single Jewish women gravitated toward cities offering factory work.[44] There, urban life and separation from their natal families sparked further change. They learned of the Jewish enlightenment and of the secular pursuit of justice for oppressed peoples. Inspired by such ideas, girls began to demand secular education for themselves.[45] In the early factories of eastern Europe, Jewish girls also encountered the first rumblings of the Jewish labor movement.[46]

Industrialization had also begun in Michiko Sato's homeland. In rural Japan, as in post-famine Ireland, peasants maintained family farms (called *ie*) big enough to sustain family life only by strict adherence to impartible inheritance. Most children had to leave their home community.[47] New taxes demanded by the Japanese state in the 1870s plunged farm households into debt and crisis; as in Italy, China, and eastern Europe, violent peasant revolts followed, as did the search for new sources of cash.[48] While Michiko Sato worked in a prosperous family business, a much larger population of newly proletarianized Japanese female wage-earners were attracted by humbler jobs in Japanese cities.

As in China, the place for girls in rural Japanese villages was tenuous.[49] Not only were poor girls subject, like their brothers, to being abandoned or being "sold" (indentured) into service, but they were much more likely than boys to be killed in infancy.[50] And, as in China, it was girls who were "to be sold"—that is, turned over to the kin group of their grooms-to-be. (Commercial language was employed in both societies because marriages required the groom's family to pay a "bride price," while the bride brought a dowry with her into her marriage). In strong contrast to China and much of southern Europe, however, Japanese women received as much education as sons, averaging six years of elementary school.[51]

As Japan's rulers encouraged industrial development in order to protect the country from Western exploitation, new jobs drew Japanese girls beyond their rural homes and family circles. Unmarried women found work in inns and in traditional industries (tea processing, paper-making). Farmers' daughters also made up the vast majority of workers in Japan's new and rapidly growing textile industry. Other girls worked in construction and mining. Overall, in 1900, women were 60 percent of Japan's industrial labor force. Parents received the wages of their indentured daughters who worked in mills far from their northern, mountainous homes. Living in dormitories, mill workers suffered constant surveillance and discipline, even in their free time.[52]

Factory girls fared better, however, than daughters contracted into lives as entertainers or prostitutes in official urban brothels. While some daughters dedicated themselves to paying off their family's debts in this fashion, others rebelled and sought to escape. But few who began work as prostitutes could return to rural life or to other jobs.[53]

Japanese daughters did not escape rural traditions of courtship and marriage. Mill workers continued to depend on their parents to arrange their marriages into the twentieth century. These arranged marriages eventually facilitated the migration of Japanese women like Michiko Sato to the United States.[54]

With further capitalist development and urbanization, the lives of the women of the other side increasingly revolved around the search for wages as the best means to "a living." Polish women migrated to Germany;[55] northern Italian women migrated to Swiss textile towns.[56] Swedish women went to Stockholm to work in middle-class kitchens, while Czechs and Slovaks headed for Vienna or Budapest in search of similar jobs.[57] In Europe, young girls moved cityward in larger numbers than their brothers as demand for domestic servants in middle-class households skyrocketed.[58] Thus women's migration began with wage-earning on the other side.

In some ways, wage-earning supported female autonomy. Young women earned individual wages, far from the immediate supervision of parents or brothers. Factory operatives shared the company of other girls much like themselves—an experience which could encourage both labor militancy and the creation of urban youth cultures.[59] But in other respects, old loyalties to family economies survived mobility and wage-earning. Many young urban workers, male and female, returned their wages to mothers or fathers remaining behind in the countryside.[60] In still other ways, new job options obviously created new forms of female subjugation. The farm maid in Scandinavia's summer pastures with her cows did not eat as well as the urban domestic servant in Stockholm, and her environment offered few new or exciting entertainments. But she undoubtedly enjoyed more independence.[61]

As women's work lives changed, so too did their options for marriage and family life. The age at marriage increased for both men and women; with the delay of marriage, rates of illegitimacy often rose as well.[62] Concerns about the sexuality and morality of domestic servants and factory girls, and more generally about any unmarried women living apart from their families, strongly colored discussions of female autonomy and the formation of the urban working classes on the other side.

For the men of the other side, capitalist development, proletarianization, and their insistence on acquiring political power went hand in hand. New national or imperial governments called upon men to serve in their armies; former peasants and serfs demanded that their voices be heard, too—as male citizens. As this "nationalization" of common men proceeded, the status of ordinary women seemed to decline relative to men's. But the most daring women also began claiming the rights of full citizenship for themselves.[63]

Industrialization required new coping strategies of rural peoples no longer able to grow their own food or return to the land that had fed, housed, and clothed them. Young female wage-earners' move beyond the immediate supervision of parents, kin, and home community brought dangers as well as new opportunities. Even among daughters like Beatrice Pollock or Michiko Tanaki—who still worked at home in family groups—contact with the marketplace and the city introduced women to a wider world and to new ways of thinking about it. These were important preconditions for the migrations that extended outward from the developing areas of the other side to the United States.

WOMEN AND THE OTHER SIDE
IN RECENT DECADES

Today's migrants to the United States also typically begin their lives in the developing parts of the third world.[64] For example, Thann Meng ("Celia") Vann Noup was born into an educated middle-class family in Cambodia, where her father was principal of a primary school. After finishing college in Phnom Penh, Vann studied for six months in Michigan, then returned to Cambodia in 1955 to marry and teach. Her husband, a soldier, became commander of anti-Communist forces opposing North Vietnamese incursions into Cambodia. Together, the couple had four daughters. After the United States left nearby Vietnam, Vann knew the Khmer Rouge would triumph, so she sent two daughters to her sister in Paris. With her other children, Vann attempted to flee, leaving her husband in a city under siege; she never saw him again. A number of harrowing years of starvation in Khmer Rouge camps followed, then escape to refugee camps and the United States.[65]

Mrs. Rosalyn Morris was born in Jamaica in the 1930s. Her mother had died young, and her father had gone away, so a grandmother raised her. At thirteen Rosalyn left school to begin work caring for young boys in a boarding school for thirty cents a week, plus her room and board. Later she moved on to a better job in the capital, Kingston, where she lived in as servant for a white family. By 1958 she had five children and worked as a cleaner in a Chi-

nese store. With many of her children growing up, however, Mrs. Morris decided to go to New York, leaving her youngest child with an aunt.[66]

Maniya "Honey" Barredo was a child star on Philippine television by the
time she was eight. The daughter of a former ballerina, she began dancing as
soon as she could walk. Raised in a comfortable but troubled large family in
Manila, the capital of the Philippines, Honey came to the United States at
eighteen in order to audition for the American Ballet Center, the school for
the Joffrey Ballet.[67]

Some immigrant women still leave lives in subsistence agriculture. Asy-
lum-seekers Isabela Ramírez and her husband Francisco, Kanojobal Indians,
grew up in the mountains of Guatemala. After a number of years of courtship,
they began a common-law marriage. Together the two managed a herd of
seventy sheep, but could raise little other food for their children, who rarely
ate more than three tortillas a day. When government troops annihilated
nearby Indian villages in 1981–1982, Isabela and Francisco, with many fellow
villagers, decided to follow cassette-tape messages sent by emigrated kin to
the United States.[68]

Like Beatrice Pollock from Jewish Russia and "Celia" Vann Noup from
Phnom Penh, refugee women entering the United States since the 1930s have
often enjoyed middle-class lives in their homelands. Typical are the many urban and middle-class women of Cuba who fled political repression after the
Communist revolution in 1960. The earliest Cuban exile women were solidly
middle- to upper-class, often well educated by the standards of their home
country. Nevertheless, a sharp cultural divide between the "street" and "the
house" had defined their lives; in Cuba "respectable" women led domestic
lives. To enter the street or public sphere as a wage-earner reflected negatively both on a woman's sexual morality and on the masculinity and breadwinning capabilities of her husband; it also carried with it the stigma of a fall
in class status, since only poor Cuban women worked outside the home.
Thus, though daughters raised in wealthy Cuban families received education
as a mark of their class, they understood that their futures would revolve
around marriage, family, and the complex social world of the Cuban elite.
Families celebrated a daughter's coming of age with elaborate ritual, but carefully protected her virginity.[69]

Refugees from rural Laos—predominantly Buddhists—were, like Isabel
Ramírez, among the poorer refugees. Until the 1970s subsistence agriculture
organized by large extended households persisted in Laos, and material standards of living were extremely low. Families raised rice and vegetables to eat;
fish from flooded rice fields supplemented their simple diets.[70] Women's education was even more limited than men's. Lao kinship principles encouraged Lao daughters to bring their husbands to live with or near their parents'
households. Typically the youngest daughter then inherited parental property. As a result, women lived and raised their children semicommunally
among groups of women kin they had known since infancy. Men (who, if

wealthy, might take more than one wife) seemed peripheral to life in an extended Lao household.[71]

In the third world today, as in rural Europe and China in the nineteenth century, domestic division of labor by gender has changed as capitalist production, foreign trade, and colonial bureaucrats have expanded their influence.[72] Initially women limited wage-earning in order to continue subsistence production and childrearing.[73] Substantial numbers of Latin American peasant women found themselves labeled "unemployed" as a result.[74] Yet state-supported agrarian reform transferred land titles only to men, and trained only them in new agricultural techniques.[75]

For most third world immigrants, however, work for wages and in small business ventures replaced subsistence production long before they left for the United States. Among the intelligentsia of the former Soviet Union and eastern Europe, in South America, and even in the Moslem Middle East, for example, education and training for professional employment are elite privileges shared by men and women, rather than male prerogatives. Many women of elite third world families pursued advanced study and professional training in Europe, the U.S.S.R., or the United States. Although some entered "women's professions" (defined differently in the Communist world, the Middle East, and Latin America), their education prepared them for a life of wage-earning.[76]

The same is true of humbler third world women, for whom wage-earning and money have become essential considerations. The search for wages, as in the past, first spurs their migration to developing cities.[77] But the exact nature of poor women's urban work differs by region and culture. In large parts of South and Central America and the Caribbean, urban demand for domestic servants draws huge numbers of rural women toward the slums of rapidly expanding new cities, from Medellín to Santo Domingo or Port-au-Prince.[78] (In Lima, 90 percent of women migrants become domestics.)[79] Women migrants to Latin American cities outnumber men. But migrants with children often find that market work as buyers, sellers, and traders allows them to continue familial responsibilities more easily than domestic service. (Female trading in the Caribbean and Latin America also builds on long-standing cultural traditions with roots in American Indian and African practices.)[80]

Although their work is similar, the family patterns of servants and market traders in Latin America and the Caribbean differ significantly from those of their Asian and European counterparts of the nineteenth century. It is true that in Latin America and the Spanish Caribbean, the middle classes remain influenced by Spanish traditions: the family ideal is monogamous, lifelong, and religiously sanctioned marriage, with child-rearing carried out within nuclear family households.[81] Many Afro-Caribbeans and poorer women throughout the Caribbean and Central and South America, however, prefer informal, short-term common-law marriages. Women form households with their mothers, young children, grown daughters, and grandchildren; they may or may not invite their current male partners to join them. Female relatives help care for and house the children of women working in domestic service or marketing.[82] These women believe that casual liaisons limit their exposure to male violence and allow them greater economic flexibility in providing for their children, whom they regard as their main source of emotional support.[83] A rapid rise in the number and proportion of female-headed households has accompanied economic development throughout the Caribbean and the mushrooming cities of South America.[84]

In parts of Southeast Asia and Mexico, new "global factories" have become the primary employers of city-bound rural women. Often built by Western investors, factories locate where labor is inexpensive and unorganized; most produce for highly competitive consumer markets in the United States and Europe.[85] Young unmarried women work for very low wages in these electronics, plastics, clothing, and food-processing factories.[86] In Southeast Asia, women make up forty percent of the industrial workforce.[87] Their parents see factory employment as a new and better way for girls to contribute to family economies,[88] and many working girls return substantial portions of their wages to their parents. Mexican girls working in factories gain slightly more control over their wages in time, but they too usually begin work to contribute to family economies.[89]

How much autonomy Asian or Mexican girls gain through their work remains controversial. Asian parents fear that girls living in dormitories and working in factories will reject traditional courtship and marriage rituals. Dating has increased among factory workers, as has the average age of marriage among the young women workers in Taiwanese global factories. Arranged marriages, however, have not disappeared, and most girls leave factory life to become daughters-in-law in complex extended patrilineal family households, which depend on wage-earning by several members.[90]

The homeland experiences of today's third world women do reveal some striking similarities to those of the developing parts of the other side in Europe and Asia in the late nineteenth century. In both these "other sides," we find wage-earning work, migration to nearby cities, and experiments with life beyond parental families becoming important female experiences—and ones that facilitate further migration.[91] Still, the similarities between nineteenth- and twentieth-century other sides should not be overstated. Third world women, especially in the Caribbean and in Central and South America, are accustomed to a degree of economic self-reliance that few Asian and European women enjoyed in the late nineteenth century.[92]

CONCLUSION

Every culture on the other side used gender to assign differing tasks and responsibilities, but precise notions of appropriate female behavior nevertheless varied significantly around the world, especially in regard to women's place in family systems. For the last two centuries, differing traditional notions of proper womanly behavior within families have confronted broadly

similar economic transformations introduced by capitalism, along with political changes sparked by the demands of nations and empires for taxes and
loyalty. Subsistence producers responded to these challenges at first by seeking to limit the penetration of the state and of wage-labor into their homes,
mainly by having women carry on subsistence activities while men moved
beyond subsistence. By contrast, in some areas of Asia and Europe in the
nineteenth century and in an ever-growing portion of the third world today,
capitalist development, cash-based commerce, and wage-earning dominated
(and dominate) the lives of rural and city dwellers, of rich and poor, and of
men and women alike.

Beginning in the late nineteenth century, and increasingly in the twentieth, the women and men who have immigrated to the United States have left
behind the economically developing areas of the other side of the capitalist
world economy, rather than the poorest and most subsistence-oriented areas.
Migration to the United States has always extended migrants' involvement
with capitalism, even when it was intended to protect subsistence families
from capitalism, as in the case of lone men temporarily migrating in order to
earn extra cash for their families. Today's immigrant women enjoy better educations and greater familiarity with wage-earning work, with urban life,
and with industrial workplaces than did the European and Asian women of
the early to mid-nineteenth century. As will be discussed below, substantial
numbers have benefited from solidly middle-class or elite privileges in their
homelands.

Whether the confrontation with capitalism in the homeland introduced
women there to greater autonomy is a complex matter. What many
women in the United States accept as female autonomy—individual wage-
earning outside a family economy and full participation in a "public
world"—was also an index of female proletarianization on the other side. It
seems a troublesome oversimplification to label these changes emancipatory
when women lost resources they valued—notably kin ties and familial self-
sufficiency—in the process.

As the next chapter follows the women of the other side to the United
States, the importance of their starting places will be apparent. Not only did
it matter whether a woman was Irish or Chinese, Italian or Japanese, Cuban
or Kanjobal—with all their attendant culturally distinctive gender assumptions—in her own homeland; it also mattered whether she had lived as an isolated peasant for whom the challenges of wage-earning were brand new, or
had been a domestic servant, factory worker, or market woman already accustomed to an urban and commercial life and a national identity. Where a
woman started from culturally, economically, and politically heavily influenced where in the United States she landed—both as an immigrant worker
and as a woman confronting the United States' new and different gender
assumptions.

THREE

From Minority to Majority

Over the last two hundred years, the ratio of female to male immigrants has varied greatly (see Table 3.1).[1] Though initially women were a small minority of incoming immigrants, their representation increased, along with immigration totals, during the early nineteenth century. After holding steady at about 40 percent until 1890, the proportion of women immigrants dropped to its lowest post-1820 point—30 percent—even as total immigration reached its historical peak. Then women's representation again rose, as total immigration declined. Female majorities characterized the Great Depression, war, and postwar years, when total migrations were very low. Most recently, as immigration has once more increased, male and female immigrants have arrived in roughly equal numbers.

In their origins, culture, and demographic characteristics, women immigrants roughly resembled men of their own backgrounds and thus sometimes differed considerably among themselves. However, because they were (1) accustomed to dividing men's and women's labors into complementary tasks, and (2) facing immigration laws which increasingly institutionalized American assumptions about proper gender relations, immigrant women migrated and lived their new lives according to patterns that were in some respects unique. A careful examination of these two factors will help us understand the transition from female minority to female majority.

IMMIGRANT WOMEN

The lives of individual women contain important hints to women's motives and points of view as migrants, as well as introducing us to female patterns of migration. Ida Lindgren, for example, left Sweden with her husband and children, intending to settle for good in the United States as a farm family. Rosa Popovich's mother came to the United States in 1912 from rural Croatia to join her husband, who had been in the United States for two years, living as a boarder and working for Pittsburgh Steel.[2] Like Rosa, Emma Ciccotosto, whom we also met in Chapter 2, never needed her dowry in her native land: she, her siblings, and her mother followed an emigrant father to Australia.

Also Italian, Michelena Gaetano Profeta came to the United States because her father had arranged a marriage for her there. Because of a jealous stepmother, Michelena had grown up with her grandmother, studying sewing and earning 30 cents a week for her work. Michelena hoped to follow her sister to their maternal aunt in New York, and to work as a dressmaker. Instead,

Table 3.1

Percentage Female among Immigrants to the United States, 1820–1980

	PERCENT FEMALE	TOTAL IMMIGRATION
1820–29	31.0%	128,502
1830–39	37.6%	508,381
1840–49	44.5%	1,497,277
1850–59	41.2%	2,670,513
1860–69	39.8%	2,123,219
1870–79	39.0%	2,742,137
1880–89	38.8%	5,248,568
1890–99	38.4%	3,694,294
1900–09	30.4%	8,202,388
1910–19	34.9%	6,347,380
1920–29	43.8%	4,295,510
1930–39	55.3%	699,375
1940–49	61.2%	856,608
1950–59	53.7%	2,499,268
1960–69	55.6%	3,213,749
1970–79	53.0%	4,336,001

SOURCES: Houstoun et al., "Female Predominance," Table A-1;
Walter F. Willcox, *International Migrations,* vol. 2 (New York:
National Bureau of Economic Research, 1931), Table 9.

her father listened to the promises of a Pittsburgh man taken with Michelena's wavy hair. Michelena objected—she did not remember meeting the man—but then obeyed.[3] Similarly, when Michiko Sato reached nineteen, her parents in Hiroshima arranged a marriage to Saburo Tanaki, who was in the United States with his father. (Saburo's mother ran a small confectionery store that traded with the Satos.) Saburo returned to Japan to marry Michiko; then the young couple left for the United States in 1923. Far harsher was the experience of Lalu Nathoy, who was sold by her kidnapper to a Chinese man exporting indentured women and prostitutes to California. And unlike any of these women, Martha Vásquez de Gómez went back to her native land to marry; she never returned to the United States.

Sometime around 1920, Mrs. Shinoda also traveled to the United States as a bride—but she had always dreamed of doing so. In a grade school essay called "What I Wish For," she announced her desire to emigrate. She told her father she would not marry unless she could go the United States, and she persisted until her father gave in and found her a Japanese husband in California. At twenty-eight, Mrs. Shinoda traveled to the United States as a "picture bride."[4] Equally adventurous was Beatrice Pollock, who wanted to escape her stepmother. Beatrice left Poland at age eighteen, without saying good-bye to the woman she hated. With her father's understanding and blessing, she traveled alone, just before World War I, to Chicago; there her sister had married a kind and prosperous (if boring) small businessman.

Mrs. Bardusky, on the other hand, came to the United States (also from Poland) because she had to help support her orphaned siblings. She lost both parents—proprietors of a butcher shop and grocery store—before she was fourteen. An older married sister took a few of the children so Mrs. Bardusky could first go to Warsaw to support them by working as a cook. At the same time, her oldest brother went to the United States planning to finance her emigration. In 1885 Mrs. Bardusky joined her brother; the two worked together to bring over other brothers and sisters.[5] Norah Joyce, by contrast, had to think mainly of supporting herself. Leaving her Dublin job, she traveled alone but joined an emigrant sister and aunt in Boston, where she again quickly found work.

Hannah Kalijian, an Armenian girl, fled to the United States from Turkey with her mother and siblings. Her father had disappeared while serving in the Ottoman Empire's army in 1915. In 1920 she and her family heard reports of Turks destroying a nearby Armenian town. Fearing deportation, the family escaped across the mountains to Constantinople (where a married sister refused them refuge), then to Cyprus (and temporary shelter with an aunt), and finally to a refugee camp near Beirut. More fortunate than many, Hannah also had an older sister in the United States, who agreed to help. In New York Hannah started school as a thirteen-year-old third-grader.[6] Years later, "Celia" Vann Noup and Isabel Ramírez followed this refugee trail to the United States. Celia and her surviving daughters flew to the United States after being sponsored by a sister-in-law in Washington, D.C., while Isabel Ramírez walked most of the way through Mexico, following taped messages to her kinsmen in Indiantown, Florida.

Immigrant women's personal desires and intentions varied enormously, as did their levels of choice and control over their migration. Still, four patterns of migration can be traced in their stories. One pattern is composed of refugees, among whom women are usually very well represented, if not always the majority. For many of the refugees, marriage or family reunification and the search for wages have intertwined with a threat in the homeland to spark emigration and draw women to the United States. Quests for family wholeness and/or for income have been even more obvious motivations for the other three groups of migrant women. (John Bodnar has argued that this has been generally true for men, too.)[7] Two varieties of family migration can be identified. In one, women like Angela Heck and Ida Lindgren migrated together with their husbands, intending to remain permanently with them as settlers in the United States—often as operators of small businesses (as in the case of Heck) or on the land (as in Lindgren's case). Since the women and the men in these families were traveling together, sex ratios were balanced. By contrast, women like Rosa Popovich and her mother remained on the other side while husbands and fathers emigrated, returned, and emigrated again.

Some of these women also eventually followed—or were sent out from the other side—to marry, to reunite the family group, and to work in family enterprises or family economies. In this second type of family migration, women's representation was initially very low, then rose. (Defined by men's experiences, this migration pattern is sometimes called "sojourning." Their female counterparts have been called the "women who wait.")[8] A fourth migration pattern is represented by Martha Vásquez de Gómez, Norah Joyce, and Mrs. Rosalyn Morris, who emigrated without nuclear families in order to earn wages. Even these independent women often enjoyed considerable help and support from relatives. And for some, the search for cash or adventure was inseparable from the hope for marriage. Whether classified as "labor migrations" or "marriage migrations," women were well represented among such migrations of young wage-earners.

Independent of background or gender, working-aged people predominated among U.S.-bound immigrants, past and present. In the nineteenth century, migrants varied mainly in whether they migrated prior to or soon after marriage. Roughly equal proportions of women immigrants (43%) and men immigrants (46%) were unmarried. Immigrant groups with high proportions of single women (like the Irish) tended also to have high proportions of single men; similarly, groups with high proportions of married women (Chinese, Mediterranean) tended also to have high proportions of married men. The migrations of unmarried men and women were more gender balanced, while heavily male-dominated migrations involved more married persons, of both sexes.[9]

The presence of married women and young children among immigrants indicated family (specifically "nuclear" family) migrations. Between half and two-thirds of women migrated in nuclear family migrations before 1920. The Irish case seems a noteworthy exception: only 17 percent of Irish women in 1910, for example, came with nuclear families. Family migration is even more common today. In the 1970s, two-thirds of adult men immigrants and about three-quarters of adult women immigrants had already married before they came to the United States. And about a quarter of today's immigrants are children under 15.[10]

Women's and men's work had differed on the other side, so it is scarcely surprising that the occupations immigrant men and women brought to the United States diverged strikingly—when the women were considered to have an occupation at all. Only 10 percent of female arrivals gave an occupation in the 1870s; by 1900, the figure was still only 30 percent Moreover, the occupational range of these women was highly circumscribed. Of all immigrant women claiming an occupation, the majority (87 percent in 1896) gave their occupation as domestic servant during these 30 years. Seamstresses and dressmakers, spinners, weavers, and teachers made up the only other sizeable groups of female wage-earners. In fact, domestic service was the most important female occupation—one claimed by female immigrants of all backgrounds—from the 1870s through the 1920s. Single immigrant women, regardless of background, most often called themselves domestics. Thus migrations with many single women, like the Irish, contained the highest proportions both of female wage-earners and of domestic servants.[11]

Things have changed less than one might have expected. Today's female immigrants are still much less likely than men to claim an occupation—34 and 77 percent do so, respectively. Depending on the exact date examined, a quarter to just over a third of women immigrants in the 1970s had occupations, or about the same proportion as among early-twentieth-century immigrants. Like their immigrant predecessors, recently arrived women have worked in a narrow range of occupations, many of them female-dominated. Since the end of World War II, U.S. makers of immigration policy have sought to encourage the immigration of skilled and professional workers to the United States, but they have not always recognized traditionally female skills and professions—notably clerical work—in granting occupational preferences. If the desire for human capital is to drive U.S. immigration policy, then it seems the United States ignores human capital in its distinctively female varieties. Men outnumber women admitted with visas for specified skilled and professional occupations three to one; most women admitted with labor certification are nurses.[12]

Among today's immigrants, over half of immigrant women claiming an occupation have done some variety of white-collar or professional work, while the remainder have worked, in fairly equal numbers, in blue-collar and service industries. The largest single categories of immigrant women workers come from white-collar and service work: nurses (9% of immigrant working women) lead the field, followed by private-household housekeepers (6.8%) and secretaries (6.2%).[13] (The reason foreign-born nurses—many from the West Indies, the Philippines, and Korea—are the most visible group of immigrant professional women is that Congress passed special legislation facilitating their admittance in the 1980s.)[14]

Especially in the past, men more often entered the United States intending to return home again. Still, one cannot simply contrast "settler" women with "sojourner" men, for men's and women's rates of return rose and fell together.[15] Furthermore, the female settler/male sojourner pattern is far from uniform for all groups and periods; for instance, New World and southern and eastern European immigrant women often had higher rates of return than northern European men in the early twentieth century. On average, however, women were more apt to stay. And in combination with men's higher mortality rates, women's lower rates of return created a fairly gender-balanced foreign-born U.S. population (46% female) for the period 1860–1920, despite men's higher entry rates.[16]

Occupational differences are thus important reasons for diverging male and female migration patterns. At the same time, however, certain contrasts between the female immigrants of the past and those of the present contain strong hints about the impact of restrictive laws on immigrant sex ratios. Historians have emphasized how the home-country culture and the demands of the U.S. economy limited women's migration among some groups (like the Italians) while encouraging it among others (like the Irish).[17] Meanwhile, most sociologists now see U.S. immigration law as the cause of women's rising presence among immigrants in the twentieth century. Each of these possibilities deserves fuller exploration.

GENDERED LABOR
AND IMMIGRANT SEX RATIOS

Male and female migration can both be traced to changes in the world economy. While both men and women devoted increasing hours of their time to wage-earning in the nineteenth and twentieth centuries, much work—whether we call it "subsistence production," "reproduction," or housework—remained unpaid, and in cash economies it was very apt to be women's work. Where, how, and for whom women would work—with or without pay, within family groups or outside them—became central issues for prospective male and female migrants.[18]

The lives of individual women immigrants introduced us to four female migration patterns. Two aimed to preserve family economies based on subsistence production without wages; a third migration (characteristic of the developing regions of the other side) was simultaneously a migration of young wage-earners mediated by an international market for their labor and an international "marriage market" migration facilitating family formation under changing circumstances.[19] Of these patterns, the third, along with a fourth—refugee migrations—were most often associated with gender balance among immigrants.

Contemporary U.S. observers attributed women's declining presence among the immigrants of 1860–1900 to the immigrants' changing backgrounds. It seems more likely, however, that the disappearance of free and readily available land in the United States changed the migration strategies of subsistence farmers during this period. Never available to Chinese migrants, because of racial discrimination, by 1890 U.S. land had also become less easy for families like the Lindgrens to obtain. New cash sources, not new land, became the primary means of propping up subsistence-level family farming in the Popovich and Ciccotosto families, as it had been earlier for Chinese families. By the end of the century families sought to maintain subsistence at home by sending their men abroad, rather than attempting to reproduce subsistence in the United States by migrating together as the Lindgrens and Hecks had.

Kin structures on the other side also heavily influenced who migrated to the United States, as the search for cash replaced the search for land. In many parts of southern and eastern Europe and China, kin groups larger than the nuclear family practiced agriculture together; nowhere did women and children depend on a lone husband or father as "breadwinner." The result was that men could easily detach themselves—both economically and culturally—to migrate in search of wages. Chinese kin groups may even have initially held wives "hostage," refusing to allow them to migrate in order to force young husbands to return.[20]

The women who remained behind to raise food guaranteed that men could work for low wages abroad. By working without wages, women of the other side also underwrote the reproduction of the developing world's labor force. Male migrants did not have to earn, and rarely received, a wage sufficient to support the birthing, feeding, or education of a new generation. Not surprisingly, male migrations sometimes became a permanent way of life, particularly when a stagnating home economy failed to make a complete transition to capitalist production.[21] From a different perspective, however, women's labors in agriculture emerge as one the the very factors delaying the total proletarianization of European and Asian farming families into the twentieth century.

Whether male migrations also changed gender relations on the other side is unsettled. The women who waited in Poland in the early twentieth century denied their competence as farmers and repeatedly asserted their need for help and guidance, thus demonstrating to absent husbands their commitment to their leadership.[22] And though a Mexican woman who manages her family farm today during a husband's absence temporarily becomes a "mujer fuerte," she will revert to deferential ways once her husband returns.[23] Studies of women left behind in the Caribbean by male migrations prior to World War II, on the other hand, trace these women's autonomy and subsequent independent migration to the United States to female mutual-help networks developed during that time.[24]

From the nineteenth into the twentieth century, wages lured the largest numbers of women, relative to men, to experiment with migration to the United States. Most of those female jobs were in U.S. cities. In U.S.-bound and other migrations, men outnumbered women headed to farming and mining frontiers, while women outnumbered men headed cityward. Within the United States, too, black and white men dominated migrations westward, while black and white women dominated urban migrations.[25] American cities, not farming districts, had the most balanced immigrant sex ratios.

International migrations of women to the United States had a pronounced urban bias because cities offered women the best chances to work for wages, whether they came alone or in family groups. Immigrant women were more likely than men to arrive in East Coast ports, especially New York. And women more than men gave industrial areas like New England and other parts of the Northeast as their destination.[26] Urban domestic service, textile mills, and garment production drew migrant women as workers.[27] Textile jobs and garment production concentrated in New England and the Mid-Atlantic states, where three-fifths of arriving immigrant women in the 1890s hoped to live.[28] Individual city economies also drew immigrants in differing mixes of male and female, depending on their industrial base. While disproportionate numbers of immigrant men preferred heavy industry and mining centers like Pittsburgh, the upper Midwest, or Buffalo, over half of all arriving dressmakers and seamstresses headed for New York and its garment industry.[29]

Immigrant women in the nineteenth century responded primarily to U.S. labor market demand for unskilled and semiskilled female labor. This varied over time, and it developed along a trajectory somewhat independent of U.S. demand for male labor. Because of their differing options on the other side, women in areas of subsistence production and those already earning wages in developing regions responded differently to the changing U.S. market for female laborers.

As the size of the U.S. female workforce expanded, the number of female immigrants increased to its historical peak, and the proportion of immigrant women with an occupation more than tripled.[30] Still, when compared to demand for unskilled male labor, demand for unskilled women's labor stagnated.[31] Middle-class women employers complained incessantly about a "servant crisis," yet demand for domestics increased only slowly between 1870 and 1920. It lagged well behind the overall growth of the female labor force and well behind the growth in the number of arriving foreign domestic servants. Demand for female industrial workers grew more vigorously during these years. But much of the growth in the female work force after 1870 came from skyrocketing demand for female white-collar workers—jobs not open to the foreign-born.[32] Thus, even as the numbers and proportions of servants arriving in the United States increased, domestic servants formed an ever smaller component of the American female workforce, and immigrant women's portion in the female workforce declined from the nineteenth to the twentieth century.[33] Not surprisingly, so did women's representation among newly arriving immigrants.

Two factors nevertheless kept women's representation high in migrations from the developing parts of the other side. Unable to return to subsistence production in the countryside, the women who had worked in domestic service in Europe experienced the opening of middle-class homes and kitchens in the United States as a widening market for their labor. They compared opportunities in the United States to those in Europe, not to demand for domestic service in the United States in earlier decades. And they found those opportunities exciting: the United States seemed a vastly larger market for their labor than any regional European market could be. As noted earlier, in every case where single women made up a high proportion of immigrants—most notably among the Irish and the Scandinavians, but also among some eastern European and Caribbean migrations—there were also high proportions of domestic servants.[34]

Since young women domestic servants, like their male counterparts, had few opportunities to marry at home—in Germany they might even be prohibited from doing so—migration to the United States promised not only wages but hopes for marriage and family life. Germans already in the United States encouraged their female kin and friends to migrate to a land where they could marry quickly and relatively well, and where they could exercise more choice in acquiring a spouse. "I will see to it that each of you gets a good husband who lets you have pretty dresses," wrote one.[35] Youthful domestic servants leaving for the United States recorded their sense of excitement and adventure as they went in search of jobs, husbands, and adulthood in a new country. "We wanted to see the great, big world!" a Finnish maid exulted.[36]

Immigrant men also demanded female labor—both in family households and in a commercialized sex trade. The existence of an international "white slave trade" horrified (and sometimes also titillated) Americans.[37] Although greatly exaggerated, procuring and deception did occur among women travelers. Among Europeans, females journeying alone or with friends from Jewish eastern Europe seemed most often involved. Networks of recruitment reached outward from Hungary to all the major cities of North and South America.[38] Most controversy about immigrant prostitution, however, focused on the sale or indenture of poor Chinese and Japanese daughters by their parents. Like Lalu Nathoy, Japanese, Chinese, and Korean girls traveled under contract and under male supervision directly to New World brothels. Indeed, some Americans falsely believed that all Chinese women entering the United States came as prostitutes or concubines.[39]

Recent female immigration parallels in some ways the wage-earning migrations of European and Asian women in the nineteenth century. Recent immigrants, too, leave the developing rather than the subsistence-oriented regions of the third world, seeking wages. Scholars have particularly emphasized the draw of the U.S. job market on women immigrants from the Caribbean.[40] Demand for female labor in the United States has increased steadily in the course of the twentieth century, particularly over the past two decades.[41] The widening occupational choices of native-born American women have created vacuums into which women from the other side have moved. Middle-class American women's move into the professions has opened opportunities in traditionally female professions (nursing more than teaching) while also creating demand for child care and service workers at the bottom of the U.S. job hierarchy.

But while U.S. demand for female labor remains important in contemporary migrations, more women today than in the past migrate to the U.S. as part of a nuclear family. The most heavily female migrations to the United States today come from countries with large American military bases,[42] where many men marry the women of the other side. Migrations of "war brides" first attracted attention after World War II, but military brides continue to influence overall immigrant sex ratios today.[43]

Men's demands for marital and sexual services also spark present-day migrations. Advertisements for wives in foreign newspapers suggest that some American men perceive foreign-born, especially Asian, women as desirable and submissive alternatives to feminist or wage-earning American women.[44] Researchers have also uncovered linkages between the sex tourist industries of Southeast Asia and the massage parlors of major American cities.[45]

Changing immigrant sex ratios thus reflect the linked transformations of life and labor in immigrant homelands and in the United States. Work options and the demand for female labor, within and outside families, has critically influenced female migration past and present. The influence of labor needs seems clearest in the nineteenth-century migrations, when immigration policy impinged only modestly on migrants' choices. By the late twentieth century, by contrast, immigration law competes with global divisions of labor as the key to understanding sex ratios among those seeking new homes in the United States.

FEMALE MAJORITIES: THE IMPACT OF IMMIGRATION LAW

Together, recent increases in demand for female labor and the growing representation of refugees among today's immigrants would have sufficed to make today's migration more balanced than those in the late nineteenth century. These were the patterns of female migration that produced relatively balanced sex ratios in some nineteenth-century migrations; under dramatically different U.S. immigration laws, they became the patterns that—with some key modifications—resulted in immigrant female majorities after 1930.

Even in the past, when crisis struck at home—whether famine or pogrom—women migrated in numbers equal to or surpassing those of men. Among nineteenth-century migrations, Irish and eastern European Jewish migrations were the most gender-balanced. Women like Hannah Kalijian outnumbered men escaping the persecution of Armenians just after World War I.[46] Women seem also to have outnumbered men among the German Jews who escaped Nazi Germany to live in the U.S.[47] Women have likewise been well represented among recent refugee migrations from Cuba, from Vietnam and other areas of Southeast Asia, and from the former Soviet Union as well. Refugees seem to share "the mentality of those caught in a sinking ship—to reach safety, women and children first."[48] Studies of today's female majorities, however, almost always attribute them to the enactment of restrictive U.S. immigration laws—specifically, to these laws' provisions for family reunification, which give the immediate relatives of U.S. citizens and resident aliens visa preferences.[49] This attribution requires a closer look.

Provisions for family reunification have always been part of racially restrictive migration laws in the United States. Yet historically, protection of immigrants preceded restriction. Nations around the world first regulated migration in the nineteenth century to guarantee the health and survival of immigrants booking passage with private sail and steamship companies. While the passage to America could be hazardous for anyone, especially during the days of sailing ships, women traveling alone also faced sexual dangers, including the risk of procurement by deception. Government pamphlets and already-emigrated relatives warned young women to avoid sailors and men traveling alone. A German advice book cautioned young women emigrants that, no matter what men might say, sea air was not an effective contraceptive.[50] Both immigrants and American reformers organized protective services for immigrant girls and young women arriving at American ports alone and traveling on to a further destination.[51]

Americans also viewed independent female migration as a moral problem in the nineteenth century; Congress first responded with laws excluding "immoral" women. Prostitutes were the first group of immigrants systematically denied entrance to the United States. Responding to anti-Chinese complaints from the West Coast, the 1875 Page Act required careful interrogation and investigation of Chinese women to guarantee that they had migrated voluntarily, rather than as "slave" (indentured) prostitutes.[52] The same act forbade the importation of any woman for prostitution. Chinese women encountered the most rigorous examinations under these laws, but any woman traveling alone might find herself delayed for investigation.

Beginning in 1882, U.S. law denied entrance to people who might become public charges—e.g. unable to support themselves.[53] While in theory gender-neutral—male paupers could as easily be excluded as female—Americans commonly viewed women as naturally dependent on men.[54] Any unaccompanied woman of any age, marital status, or background might be questioned as a potential public charge because she appeared to lack a male provider. Indeed, Ellis Island officials regularly detained women traveling on pre-paid tickets to join husbands in New York if the men failed to show up in person to claim their "dependents."[55] The longest detentions occurred at Angel Island in California, where Chinese women seeking to enter the United States underwent lengthy questioning.[56]

By the end of the nineteenth century, concerns about the fecundity of immigrant minorities—however exaggerated and inaccurate—increasingly fueled nativist arguments for restricting immigration.[57] In the eyes of alarmed Americans, childbearing by immigrant and minority women threatened to provoke the "suicide" of the Anglo-American race; they feared American institutions could not survive the demographic engulfing of "real" Protestant Americans of Anglo-Saxon or northern European descent.[58] Since restrictionists associated women more than men with fertility, they might logically have demanded limits on female migration (as they did directly in the Page Law, and indirectly in provisions against public charges). Or they might have prohibited male labor migrants from calling for wives left behind. Instead, however, every U.S. law restricting immigration by race included at least some provisions for family reunification. American assumptions about proper gender relationships, about female dependency, and about the domestic obligations of women to men seemed to outweigh Social Darwinist fears of race suicide.

The Chinese Exclusion Act of 1882 and the 1907 Gentlemen's Agreement with Japan contained the earliest legal provisions for family reunification.[59] The Chinese Exclusion Act prohibited the entrance of Chinese laborers, including skilled workers operating small businesses; court cases determined that the occupation of a Chinese woman's husband or father determined her status. Chinese merchants and students, however, could enter the United States, and their wives and children enjoyed the right to follow them. Under the Gentlemen's Agreement, wives of Japanese laborers could also follow them.[60]

The Gentlemen's Agreement resulted in the "picture bride" era of Japanese migration, as women like Mrs. Shinoda married by proxy and became one-half to two-thirds of total Japanese migrations.[61] There was no comparable picture bride era among Chinese merchants, however. From 1882–1890, women made up only a third of restricted Chinese migrations. After that date, of Chinese entering for family reasons (about two-thirds of the total), 90 percent were the children, usually the sons, of merchants—not their wives.[62]

Thus provisions for family reunification could, as part of a restrictive policy, push women's representation upward, but they did not always produce female majorities. This would again be evident in the response to the U.S. Congress's attempt to reduce overall immigration from southern and eastern Europe by requiring literacy of new immigrants in 1917. This measure also provided for reunification of families: illiterates could enter the United States to join a naturalized parent, spouse, or child. Almost ninety percent of illiterates admitted under this provision were female, but they were few in number. For example, the exclusion of 24,000 illiterate women admitted under reunification provisions in 1921 would not have altered the gender balance among new arrivals; the majority were still male.[63]

The restrictive national-origins quotas introduced for southern and eastern European immigrants in 1921, and tightened further in 1924, likewise exempted the spouses and children of citizens and naturalized immigrants. Some wives did take advantage of these provisions, but again their numbers remained quite low. In 1925, the first full year under the most restrictive quota law, only 7200 exempted persons (of a total migration of over 500,000) entered the U.S. for family reasons. Of these, just over half were wives; the rest were children of naturalized citizens.[64]

It is thus very likely that the earliest female majorities of the 1930s and 1940s represented men's loss of interest in migration during depression and war, not the impact of family reunification provisions. In the nineteenth century, the Irish and a few other groups had experienced occasional female majorities when migrations (of men) dropped sharply during depression years. World War I, too, had sent women's representation soaring temporarily as total numbers of male migrants plummeted. Throughout the 1920s and 1930s, furthermore, female majorities characterized only those groups affected by restrictive quotas. Northern and western Europeans with generous quotas saw no significant change in gender balances during this period. And among the unregulated Latin American and Caribbean migrants, women's representation actually declined, as men from Mexico began replacing laborers from the formerly male-dominated southern and eastern European migrations. Like sex ratios among southeast Europeans prior to World War I, sex ratios among unregulated groups in the 1920s correlated closely with total migrations; when male migration dropped off sharply in 1921–22 and again in 1924, the proportion of female immigrants jumped temporarily and sharply upward. As long as New World men remained free to respond to the vigorous U.S. market for their labor, migrations continued unbalanced.

Today, by contrast, provisions for family reunification provide migrants with otherwise sharply restricted opportunities to enter the United States with the chance to do so. Although U.S. immigration policy's family reunification rules make no distinctions on the basis of gender, most who take advantage of reunification preferences are still female: wives significantly outnumber husbands among those claiming visas; mothers significantly outnumber fathers.[65]

One reason so many more women than men enter the United States under family reunification provisions is that women are rarely migrant pioneers. Another is that few women in the United States or the U.S. military choose foreign-born husbands. A third and very important reason is the likelihood that clerical and blue-collar women enter the United States as family reunifiers because they have few opportunities to do so as labor migrants: as noted above, few traditionally female occupations, except nursing, rate an occupational preference under current visa provisos. Far more than in the past, the migration strategies of today's immigrant women are tied to marriage and motherhood. A third world woman has a better chance of entering the United States by marrying an emigrated man or an American citizen or by having a child in the the United States than she does waiting unmarried, or childless, for a visa allowing her to work as an office cleaner, factory operative, or clerical. Not surprisingly, the INS has been unable to prevent the proliferation of "green card marriages" under laws privileging citizens' spouses.[66]

Critics of U.S. immigration law have argued recently for reducing the numbers of visas available for purposes of family reunification. Their goal is to encourage further the entrance of skilled, professional, and entrepreneurial migrants. Critics justify their proposals by comparing the occupational backgrounds of U.S. migrants to those of immigrants entering other countries: proportionately more U.S. migrants lack occupations or have low-skill qualifications.[67] Needless to say, nations which today attract more skilled and professional workers also attract proportionately more men and fewer children than the United States. As was pointed out earlier, three-quarters of the skilled, professional and entrepreneurial migrants entering the United States with occupational visas are male. And, although rarely argued in gendered terms, concern about female majorities indirectly enters discussions about the quality of today's immigrants. Early popular reports on the female-dominated migrations of recent years warned that immigrants were no longer the productive and ambitious contributors who had arrived in earlier migrations; women and children migrants, they seemed to imply, would not serve the nation as well as the male-dominated migrations of the past.[68]

Assumptions about gender, and about proper familial relations between men and women, have thus shaped discussions of immigration policy since the nineteenth century. Legislators may have included provisions for family reunification in laws otherwise intended to limit the creation and re-production of immigrant minorities in the United States because they believed men deserved the benefits of women's company and labor, and be-cause they assumed women needed men to support them. Viewed from this perspective, restrictive laws which made exceptions for family reunification encouraged the domestication of migrant women, solidifying their status as dependents. Restrictive immigration laws disrupted the interaction of home-land and U.S. demands for female labor, while still accommodating male im-migrants' demand for female labor within family and households. In this regard, U.S. immigration law parallels colonial development schemes in third world nations.[69] Domesticity became a requirement for female migra-tion—and one that poses large challenges for the economically independent, if poor, market women and domestic servants of today's Caribbean and Central and South America.

Historical connections among female dependency, domesticity, and im-migration restriction place foreign-born women in a double bind. Still criti-cized falsely today for their tendency to bear too many children, immigrant women have at the same time lost opportunities to make free choices about their own employment, and they find themselves disparaged, however indi-rectly, as low-quality immigrants as a result. The positive mythology of the immigrant as builder of a free and economically expansive United States is off-limits to immigrant women on all of these counts. For the unknown pro-portion of undocumented or illegal immigrants like Martha Vásquez de Gómez among migrant women, this is doubly true.[70]

CONCLUSION

In sum, the nature of men's and women's confrontations with the capitalist world economy in their homelands shaped their migration patterns, and thus their entrance into the U.S., in sharply differing ways. For women of the subsistence-oriented other side, migration was part of a family strategy to preserve subsistence as a way of life. Whether these women remained behind to preserve the household farm or workshop while men sought wages abroad, migrated as parts of family groups to farm in the Midwest, or fol-lowed their husbands and fathers to work at home or for wages in U.S. cities depended mainly on women's and men's perceptions of female work options in the New World. For the wage-earning women of the developing world, past and present, the opportunity to earn wages and establish or support families by doing so was even more important, even though legal require-ments increasingly restricted their choices. For men and women fleeing per-secution at home to seek asylum, the draw of the U.S. labor market has been less important; sex ratios among refugees have always been more balanced than among other migrants.

Overall, far more than native-born women generally, immigrant women had worked on the other side—both with and without wages—and they showed every intention of doing so once in the United States: that is why they came. But by contrast with the men with whom they otherwise shared much, immigrant women in the nineteenth century had to balance family demands for their labor with relatively limited and declining opportunities to earn wages in the United States. This situation would now seem ripe for change, for unlike the overwhelmingly unskilled immigrant women of the past, some immigrant women today are trained to compete for jobs held by native-born white and minority women. But, with a few very important exceptions, their occupations earn them no privileges under U.S. immigration law; most enter the United States as wives or mothers, not as job seekers.

Thus, both in the past and in the present, homeland experiences and migration patterns have combined to bring to the U.S. immigrant women of vastly differing resources and intentions. Differences like these have meant, among other things, that there exist not one but several patterns of female immigrant life and female adjustment in the United States. The next section explores the range of immigrant women's responses to American life—in the workplace and at home, in the kin group and in the community.

PART II.

Foreign and Female:
Continuities in Immigrant Life

FOUR

Lives of Labor

The women of the other side were accustomed to hard work, although not always as wage-earners. Not surprisingly, all the individual women immigrants we have met in the last three chapters worked after they arrived in the United States, too. But not all worked for wages or outside their homes, especially in the nineteenth century. For those enmeshed in the family economies of subsistence agriculture on the other side, agricultural work often continued in the United States. In the nineteenth century, Ida Lindgren farmed with her family on the prairies of Kansas. She found the fireflies of Kansas enchanting, but she also reported to relatives at home about wolves, droughts, and plagues of large grayish grasshoppers. Having already struggled unsuccessfully to wrestle a living from Sweden's stony soil, a discouraged Ida wrote from Kansas, "Don't you think, Mamma, that I could bear a little bit of *success*?" By the late twentieth century, however, work in U.S. agriculture meant waged work and poverty: Isabela Ramírez, who had walked from her scrap of land in the mountains of Guatemala, settled with her family in Florida's Blue Camp, which had been built originally for Mexican migratory laborers in the 1960s. Isabela and her husband and children worked in the fields, harvesting crops for low pay, little stability, and no benefits.

Domestic service, although undergoing far-reaching reorganization from the nineteenth to the twentieth centuries, also provided work opportunities for large numbers of immigrant women wage-earners from the developing parts of the other side. Norah Joyce, from Ireland, found live-in work as a servant in a Boston household, earning seven dollars a week. Although born into a prosperous Japanese family, Michiko Sato worked as a cook when she reached California; her husband became a farm laborer. More recently, Martha Vásquez de Gómez was first rejected as too young by prospective employers in San Antonio, but was then referred to a bilingual Chicano family looking for "a girl." With a long life "in service," Mrs. Rosalyn Morris quickly found day work in private households in New York; she maintained her own home, as she had in Jamaica.

Past and present, a small group of industries have offered employment to the many immigrant women who migrated in family groups and pooled earnings with other members of their families. Beatrice Pollock—who followed her sister to Chicago—immediately found work in a garment shop, sewing pants on a machine; although frustrated in her desires, Michelena Gaetano Profeta had dreamed of doing the same. Today, Asian and Latina women do much the same work, often under similar conditions, in textiles, garments, canning, and other "light" industries.

Work in family businesses has dominated the lives of many married immigrant women and mothers. At home in Croatia, Rosa Popovich's mother had tended vineyards and raised grain and vegetables. As soon as she arrived in Pennsylvania, this Croatian woman transformed her home into a boarding house and began cooking and cleaning for twelve male miners. Mrs. Bardusky, from Poland, worked first in her brother's grocery store, then in her husband's carpentry shop. In Pittsburgh, Michelena Profeta had to learn the fundamentals of housework from her new mother-in-law; besides caring for her children, she kept her husband's barbershop supplied with fresh linens. More recently, the Cambodian school teacher "Celia" Vann Noup became proprietor of a doughnut shop in Santa Monica, California.

For immigrant women past and present, the combination of paid work with heavy domestic responsibilities has been the norm. In both of these respects, the immigrant women of the nineteenth century led lives more like those of America's racial minorities than those of white women of the American middle classes. Over time, however, the work lives of all these women have converged. Increasing proportions of American women have found employment in white-collar and professional work.[1] More education and less child labor, along with continuous wage-earning from maturity through marriage and motherhood to retirement, has transformed the female waged workforce from "working daughters" to "working mothers."[2] As a result the lives of wage-earning women now seem dictated more by their gender in a sex-segregated job market than by their race, ethnicity, or nationality.

THE WORLD OF WORK AND WAGES: THE PAST

For most immigrant women of the past, life in the United States meant an ever more inescapable confrontation with the capitalist world of wage-earning, money, and commerce. Foreign-born women and their daughters constituted over half of the American workforce of female wage-earners before 1900, and slightly less than half of all female wage-earners in 1920. They worked in large numbers because few immigrant men earned a family wage; they worked to support families more often than to pursue an independent existence.[3]

Like immigrant men in the nineteenth century, immigrant women found employment mainly at the bottom of the occupational ladder. They worked at jobs held—in earlier decades—by native-born women, not by men of their own backgrounds. As native-born white women withdrew from farming, domestic service, and factory work to feminize formerly male professions (like teaching) or take new jobs in offices, foreign-born women found their own niche in a female occupational hierarchy. Foreigners joined African American women in agriculture and domestic service, while factory work in women's industries—from which African Americans were generally excluded before World War II—became the most uniquely female and foreign occupational niche in the American job market. As late as 1920, 34 percent of foreign-born females worked in manufacturing and one-quarter in domestic service.[4]

Labor force participation rates among immigrant women varied somewhat with background, but these differences seem small when compared to large differences in the work lives of married and single women, and in the jobs taken by women of differing backgrounds.[5] In the nineteenth century most immigrant servants and factory operatives were young and unmarried, while foreign-born married women of many backgrounds were like African American women in combining intermittent or continuous employment, often at home, with marriage and child-bearing.[6]

While domestic service was a segregated, female occupation, both immigrant women and men toiled in "immigrant industries" like shoes, garments, and textiles. Gender hierarchies, however, were common: men held the more skilled jobs—cutters and pressers in garments; fixers and weavers in textiles—while women more often became operatives and machine tenders.[7] Over time, too, textiles and garments, along with canneries, increasingly feminized as male immigrants clustered disproportionately in industries like steel, chemicals, and construction.

In agriculture, too, both women and men toiled for wages, although often at separate tasks. In Hawaii, sugar and pineapple plantation owners employed Korean, Okinawan, Japanese, and Filipino women as laborers.[8] Like peasant women on the other side, Asian women working in agriculture often continued earning wages after marriage and childbearing. About a quarter of Japanese women became agricultural wage-earners in California, while Sicilian women raised family food on Louisiana sugar plantations where their husbands and fathers worked for wages.[9]

Ethnic and gender segmentation resulted from both immigrant preferences and discriminatory employment practices. Greenhorn women, like men, depended on family and friends to help them find work and to show them the ropes once employed. Such networking meant that an ethnic group might be concentrated in jobs of a certain type simply because the network's earliest members had happened to find jobs in that field. This was especially true for women—employers rarely expressed strong preferences for women workers of a particular background in the way, for example, that steel industry employers deliberately matched men of different backgrounds to jobs they believed "racially" suited to them.[10]

Domestic service was a different story. Single immigrant women of every background had called themselves domestic servants when they entered the United States, but women of only a few backgrounds worked extensively as servants in the United States. In 1920, 87 percent of employed Swedish women were servants—a rate almost matched by Norwegian (86%), Irish (81%), and Slovak (86%) female workers. By contrast, only 8 percent of Italian and 7 percent of Yiddish-speaking Jewish women worked as servants.[11]

The reasons for this disparity are still in dispute. Some scholars argue that immigrant women from Russian Jewish and Italian families avoided domestic service because of their cultural proscriptions against female contacts with outsiders.[12] Others believe instead that Italian, Jewish, and some other women who migrated as parts of families wanted jobs that allowed them to live at home. Still others argue that these groups rejected domestic service because they had more and better opportunities to earn wages in industry, whereas before 1880, Irish, Swedish, and German women seeking work had few options outside of domestic service.[13] But these same women—whether from Ireland or Slovakia—also saw domestic service as a step up from the farm labor they had done at home. Racial discrimination limited options for Japanese and Mexican women, who also worked in large numbers as servants in the West and Southwest.[14] Specific employer priorities also encouraged ethnic segregation. Protestant American housewives worried about Catholic Irish servants corrupting their children, but many hired female Irish immigrants anyway, because they wanted English-speaking servants. Others preferred Germans, Scandinavians, or Finns, who rarely spoke English, but were Protestant, and—having worked in large numbers as domestics prior to departure—may also have brought with them greater familiarity with bourgeois standards of cleanliness.

How immigrant women evaluated domestic service varied with their ethnic background. It certainly had its drawbacks. Domestic servants lived in; they had little control over their own time; they worked irregular and very long hours (enjoying only one half-day free each week) for extremely low cash wages (employers considered room and board the larger part of servants' pay). Relations between mistresses and their servant girls were unpredictable, ranging from harsh, distant, and exploitative to familial and controlling or warmly friendly. Some servants complained about sexual harassment by male members of families they served; more prostitutes had previously worked as domestic servants than at any other job. Still, as mentioned earlier, Swedish and Irish women saw domestic service as a positive occupational choice, since it provided a kind of domestic apprenticeship and thus was an improvement on agricultural work. For independent single women, work in a middle-class home provided necessary housing as well as a wage.[15]

In the industrializing northeast of the United States, Irish, Germans, and French Canadians pioneered immigrant women's employment in shoe and textile mills in the 1840s; after 1880, Polish, Italian, and Syrian women joined them. The same groups entered the burgeoning garment factories of New York, Chicago, and smaller American cities. Textiles, garment shops, and canneries all employed ethnically mixed female workforces—Mexican, Jewish, Italian, and northern European women in California canneries; Polish, German, and south Slavic women in the canneries of Pittsburgh.[16] In Philadelphia, New York, and Chicago garment factories, Jews and Italians mingled with smaller numbers of Irish and German immigrants or daughters of these earlier migrations.

The typical factory operative before 1920 was born either on the other side or shortly after her parents' arrival in the United States. Some Polish and eastern European Jewish young women also migrated independently to factory settings. Most immigrant factory operatives had had some schooling but had left at a young age to work for wages. In the nineteenth century, girls began work between ages ten and twelve; later, child labor and school-leaving laws raised the average age for factory beginners first to fourteen, then to sixteen.

Most immigrant girls worked for about ten years, typically in a variety of short-term, seasonal, and low-paying jobs. Almost all left factory employment upon marriage, or in some cases (Italians, Poles) after the birth of a child. In large cities with a strong demand for female labor in a particular industry, young female workers could build up their skill levels and spend an entire working life in one industry. More commonly, however, young women tried their hand at many trades during their wage-earning years. Seasonal periods of slack production characterized all the major industries employing immigrants, so many women had to change employment regardless of their desires or ambitions: this was an experience they shared with men. But women factory operatives also frequently mentioned sexual harassment as an incentive to seek a new position.[17]

Smaller numbers of older immigrant women worked at the same jobs as younger single women. Laundries, too, often employed significant numbers of older women. A few of these workers were independent women who had never married, but older women in industry typically had children to support; they worked because their husbands were deceased, unemployed, disabled, drunken, or absent. Many took night work in order to combine family and child-rearing responsibilities with wage-earning. The exhaustion caused by their double days of labor attracted considerable attention from reformers and resulted in the abolition of night work for women in many states by World War I.[18]

Female factory workers earned from one-half to two-thirds of the wages paid to men, which meant few could live independent of a family.[19] Their workplaces were arguably safer than in men's industries like mining and steel, but few satisfied American notions of female gentility. In laundries and canneries, girls worked in their shifts; many had to stand all day at their work; in many workplaces, employers made no toilet provisions for women workers at all. The Triangle fire, in which over 140 Russian Jewish and Italian girls died, highlighted the dangers of factory work in women's industries and resulted in the passage of New York State's first factory regulations.[20] But Americans worried almost as much about the moral dangers women faced in factories. Observers decried the "frivolous" dress and manner of factory girls, and their casual flirtations with men; they wrongly assumed that work in the factory led directly to prostitution.[21]

Unlike Asian immigrants or Mexican American and African American wives and mothers who typically worked in domestic service or on the land, married immigrant women from Europe most frequently did industrial work at home for piece rates. In the Southwest, growing numbers of Mexican American women also worked at home in the 1930s and 1940s. In New York, women produced garments and cigars in small tenement workshops until regulation forced them out of residential buildings. Many then became "out-workers" or "homeworkers" for large-scale manufacturers, working again in their own kitchens or front rooms. Homeworkers completed an enormous range of tasks at piece rates: they packed food into jars, stripped feathers, basted pants, made buttonholes, crocheted slippers, and assembled toys. By working at home, married women combined domestic responsibilities with wage-earning. They also transformed their young children into helpers, learners and (on a pitiably limited scale) wage-earners for the family.[22]

American reformers and labor activists worked to prohibit homework, and to protect women from exploitation by greedy employers or idle hus-bands.[23] Immigrant women, however, were often relatively uninterested in the exploitation question; they saw their children as the main beneficiaries of their endless, exhausting labors. Reformers' campaigns to abolish homework progressed slowly, in part because many foreign-born wives saw only im-poverishment in their proposals. Homework survived long after night work and child labor fell to state regulations.

In a very different realm, immigrant prostitution attracted even more neg-ative attention than industrial homework. In New York, only French and native-born women worked as prostitutes in numbers disproportionate to their ethnic groups' weight in the general population. Irish and eastern Eu-ropean Jewish women were the largest groups of foreign-born prostitutes; Germans and Italians rarely prostituted themselves.[24] Given the multiethnic population of New York, and its sizable population of southern and eastern European male sojourners, it is unlikely that all the clients of these prostitutes were men from their own backgrounds. The Jewish prostitutes of New York's Lower East Side red-light district on Allen street, for example, attracted clients from well beyond their immediate Jewish neighborhood. A few pros-titutes, working with a multiethnic male clientele, transformed sex work into successful businesses: Polly Adler, who became a sex worker after being raped by a factory supervisor, eventually became a prosperous madam.[25] A contrasting and more typical example is the Jewish prostitute Maimie, who entered the sex trade as an unhappy rebel from a loveless home; she eventu-ally left prostitution to enter an equally loveless, but respectable marriage.[26] So many Jewish women worked as prostitutes that Jewish Americans orga-nized their own anti–white-slave campaigns.

On the West Coast, ethnic segregation and gender hierarchy character-ized prostitution. Large proportions of female wage-earners of all back-grounds worked as prostitutes during the boom years of Western mining; as many as three-quarters of the Chinese women of San Francisco were sex workers in the late nineteenth century. An occasional Chinese woman opened a brothel herself: in fact, one such madam, Ah Toy, became a favorite character in the novelty literature depicting San Francisco's wild early days.

But male Chinese merchants dominated the brothel business, recruiting and transporting women like Lalu Nathoy to work in low-cost "cribs" providing sexual services to Chinese laborers.[27] Although exposed to extreme exploitation and high death rates, some Chinese prostitutes nevertheless were able to meet and marry husbands in the United States, contriving in this way a potential happy ending.

Although far more respectable than prostitutes, immigrant midwives were perceived as threats, too: as American physicians consolidated their monopoly over health care in the late nineteenth century, they portrayed foreign women health providers as backward and ignorant. The effects of these attacks were all the more serious in that midwives were the only female professionals working in large numbers in immigrant communities before 1920. In Chicago, in fact, almost all practicing midwives were foreign-born women. Some immigrant midwives had received professional training in Europe; others more closely resembled folk healers, having received a pragmatic education as apprentices to older female practitioners, or having merely developed a special charismatic talent for assisting women kin and neighbors during birth.[28] Some folk healers like the Mexican radical Teresa Urrea acquired regional reputations for their expertise.[29] Midwives maintained and continued traditions of Mexican curanderas, Asian herbalists, and other wise women common in European, Asian, and New World folk medicines.[30] In the United States, however, they were increasingly forced to operate outside the law, their practices under legal and public attack from both American doctors and female American health reformers.[31]

Since most immigrant women saw the home rather than the hospital as the proper place for giving birth, they guaranteed immigrant midwives income and influence into the twentieth century. Pregnant immigrant women preferred midwives because they spoke their languages, were usually mature, married women and mothers, and offered familiar home-centered birth, unlike male American doctors and unmarried, childless American women professionals. In New York, however, upwardly mobile Jewish women began to seek birth support from doctors and women's dispensaries by 1920.[32] And today immigrant women sometimes view a hospital birth as one of the advantages migration to the United States makes available.[33]

By the 1920s, broad patterns of immigrant women's wage-earning had begun to change. Domestic service declined steadily in importance as an employer of women of all backgrounds from the nineteenth to the twentieth century, and homework, as already noted, came under increasing attack from reformers. Nonetheless, the numbers of wage-earning wives increased rapidly after World War I. Industrial employment of foreign-born women peaked in the 1930s and then began a gradual decline as immigration to the Northeast slowed, as African American, Mexican, and Puerto Rican women replaced European-born workers, and as both textile and garment production moved first south and then "offshore."

Even before the deindustrialization of the United States, immigrant daughters first from northern European and later from southern and eastern European backgrounds were abandoning factory jobs to work in department stores as sales clerks and in offices as white-collar clericals. Between 1910 and 1920, the number of foreign-born clerks increased by over 200 percent; the numbers of stenographers and typists, by over 100 percent.[34] By 1920, foreign-born female clerical workers already outnumbered immigrant women working in family businesses. Yet many clericals had at first found employment in ethnic businesses; after 1920 more moved into English-speaking offices and stores, which required training in a commercial high school or business college. Daughters of artisans, skilled workers, and widows sought training for office employment with special frequency. The depression of the 1930s, with its relatively low rates of clerical unemployment, in turn convinced other immigrant parents reluctant to forego female earnings that it made sense to keep daughters in high school. A daughter working as a sales "girl" or secretary symbolized status and financial security for many blue-collar parents. But immigrant and second-generation clerical workers also remained firmly ensconced in their working-class networks; immigrant clerical workers often had fathers, brothers, or fiancés with blue collars.[35]

For immigrant women from Asia and Mexico, racial discrimination slowed women's transition to white-collar work. Nisei (second-generation Japanese) women abandoned domestic service more rapidly than African American women, but they worked in larger proportions as domestics than the daughters of European immigrants.[36] For many Japanese American women, furthermore, wartime internment interrupted both education and employment.[37] Mexican American women faced similar difficulties. Over time, however, sales and clerical employment increased even among these immigrant women.[38] Overall, immigrant daughters' entrance into white-collar work lagged about fifty years behind that of native-born white women, while preceding that of African American women by about thirty years. And the direction of change was the same for women of all backgrounds: proportionately more of them than in earlier periods came to work in clerical and professional fields.

THE WORLD OF WORK AND WAGES:
THE PRESENT

Immigrant women today enter the United States with a wider range of skills than their counterparts of earlier decades: they are more likely to have professional training than native-born women (see chapter 7), but they are also more likely than the native-born to have worked at blue-collar tasks or in domestic service prior to migration. Once in the United States, this bifurcation continues to characterize their employment (see Table 4.1). The clustering of foreign-born women at the top and the bottom of the job hierarchy in the United States, furthermore, may be increasing. As some Latinas take blue-

TABLE 4.1
Employment of Immigrant Women in the U.S. in 1970, by Economic Sector

Occupational Distributions

FB=foreign born	Professional	Clerical /Sales	Service	Operative /Labor
Mexican	7.6%	31.3	26.9	18.5
Central and South American	11.5	32.4	20.2	35.8
Other Hispanic	18.7	44.4	22.4	14.4
FB Japanese	15	21	30	33
FB Chinese	26	21	11	42
FB Filipino	43	23	20	13
FB Other	17	30	24	29

SOURCE: Borjas and Tienda, *Hispanics in the U.S.*, Table 8.5;
Morrison G. Wong and Charles Hirschman, "Labor Participation
and Socioeconomic Attainment of Asian-American Women,"
Sociological Perspectives 26 (1983): 423–46.

collar and farm jobs abandoned by native-born Americans, many refugee, Asian, Cuban-born, and West Indian immigrant women compete with native-born American women in clerical and professional employment.[39]

Foreign-born women work for wages in about the same proportions as native-born women. They work for the same reasons as most other women: they, their children, their parents, and their husbands depend upon their earnings. Income pooling within families is alive and well in the late twentieth century.[40] At the same time, immigrant women's rates of labor-force participation vary by national background more now than they did in the past, largely because of differences among married women.[41] Married Cubans (64%), Chinese (54%), and Filipinas (61%) work at rates comparable to those of married native-born Black women, and at higher rates than native-born Puerto Ricans or Chicanas or Mexican immigrant women (45%).[42] Refugee women from Southeast Asia seem to have experienced the greatest initial difficulty in finding work, though their rates of wage-earning, too, are rapidly increasing.[43] By contrast, Soviet Jewish refugees, many of them professional or highly skilled, adapted quickly and relatively easily to wage-earning in the United States.[44]

While immigrant women recently arrived in the United States earn slightly less than native-born women in the same jobs overall, they rapidly attain income parity with their native counterparts—far more rapidly, for example, than do immigrant men. This hold true even for African-descent women from the West Indies.[45] Immigrant women today often earn considerably higher wages than native-born women in professional jobs. Foreign-born clerical workers, by contrast, find that their education or experience on the other side does not allow them to earn wages comparable to their native-born clerical counterparts.[46] Still, high rates of wage-earning among many foreign-born wives keep household incomes among some immigrant groups close to the American average. And, while a somewhat higher proportion of foreign-born than native-born households have at least one member receiving public assistance, immigrant women who head their own households are less likely to receive public assistance and more likely to work for wages than native-born women heads of households.[47]

Agriculture has remained an important employer of immigrants in the twentieth century, largely because of expanding agri-business in the Southeast and Southwest (most notably California and Florida). Special recruitment of male agricultural workers during World War II aimed to bring Mexican and West Indian men to the United States—temporarily. But women eventually joined them. By the 1950s, Mexican migrant families followed a cycle of harvests from the Southwest to the fields of the upper Midwest. Today, men, women, and children from Mexico and Central America—many of them, like Isabela and Francisco Ramírez, without proper documentation—lead itinerant and difficult lives in the Southwest, Florida, and the Southeast. Despite efforts by farmworkers' unions (see chapter 6), labor in the fields remains some of the most physically arduous and poorly paid work in the American economy. Work in the fields generally requires women, men, and children to live in camps, where schooling, housing and domestic life remain notorious for their low quality.[48]

Given the decline of domestic service in the American economy, it may seem surprising that about a quarter of foreign-born women still work in service. However, immigrant women arriving in the United States without proper documentation find that work in private households—for cash pay—is the only work readily available to them. While immigration regulations prohibit other employers from hiring workers without proper visas, the INS declines to check employment in private homes. Unmarried and independent women—like the Irish and Swedish women of the nineteenth century—find live-in positions a solution to their pressing need for both housing and employment.[49]

Unlike the domestic servants of the nineteenth century, however, immigrant domestic live-in servants from the Caribbean and Latin America today may have children, either left behind with female relatives in the homeland or living with relatives in the cities where their mothers work. For such women, work in corporate service jobs—as office cleaners and as employees in hospitals, nursing homes, home health care services, and restaurants—represents a qualitative social if not economic step forward.[50]

Factories in New York, Los Angeles, Miami, and Texas continue to depend heavily on foreign-born women as low-wage operatives. Women seeking work in garments, textiles, and canneries often discover that neither

sweatshops nor poor working conditions have disappeared. Today's cannery workers are women from Mexico and other Latin American countries,[51]
while garment factories attract workers from China, Latin America, and
the Caribbean.[52] Male immigrant entrepreneurs have taken over declining
garment production industries in cities like New York; they prefer to
hire women of their own backgrounds. Immigrant women without proper
documentation have strong incentives to accept appalling working conditions and wages in exchange for an employer's willingness to pay cash and
remain silent.[53]

In parts of New England and the West Coast, immigrant women from
Asia, Europe, the Caribbean, and South America also find employment as assembly workers in high-tech electronic firms—the American counterparts of
factories on the other side. Immigrant women also work in older low-capital
industries where labor represents most of the employers' fixed costs (jewelry,
for example). These industries pay women through elaborate piecework systems, which complicate workers' efforts to compare their productivity to that
of others or to predict wages due at the end of the week. In these industries,
too, employees are of mixed backgrounds, and informal segregation by culture and language group frequently occurs at work.[54]

Even homework survives, and its survival reminds us of a final continuity in immigrant women's working lives. The context, however, has changed.
The nation's labor unions remain firmly opposed to homework. But whereas
once native-born women reformers clamored to prohibit homework, professional and clerical American women now sometimes advocate it as a solution
to their own difficulties in combining wage-earning with domestic responsibilities.[55] As this suggests, native-born white women have joined immigrant
and minority women in seeking ways to balance work for money with labor that carries no financial rewards. No examination of immigrant women,
past or present, is complete without attention to this dimension of their working lives.

LABORS OF LOVE AND THANKLESS CHORES: UNPAID WORK, PAST AND PRESENT

Although immigrant women devoted more time to the pursuit of money than
they had on the other side, labor without financial reward remained a constant in their lives. In the nineteenth century, subsistence production survived in modified form on family farms. In cities it has survived down to the
present in family-operated businesses and in domestic or "house" work. Of
these three, housework alone showed initial signs of becoming a uniquely
female task in the United States—the domain of women "breadgivers" and
their daughters.

Most European and Japanese immigrant women who settled on the land
in the nineteenth century worked without pay on family farms. In censuses,

they—like other rural women—appeared as "not gainfully employed" or "housewives." Because immigrants initially transplanted Old World divisions of labor to the New World fields, however, their lives little resembled those of urban middle-class women, or even American farm women, who had largely withdrawn from field to "house" work. Immigrant women attracted attention—some of it negative—for their haying, plowing, harvesting, cultivating, and care of animals.[56] Women's farm work was demanding, but flexible: Korean Mary Paik Lee worked in the fields, sold produce from a vegetable stand, and did domestic work for the owner of the farm where she and her husband and sons were tenants.[57]

Immigrants gradually adopted American notions of female agricultural work. Norwegian, Swedish, and Danish women initially cared for cattle and processed dairy products into cheese. When these became family commercial ventures, however, men joined women in specific dairy-related tasks. And where Norwegians failed to develop dairying as a commercial specialty, men ultimately took over complete care of family livestock, while women retreated from the fields to American-style domesticity and the keeping of a kitchen garden.[58]

Small family businesses also reproduced household-based work groups familiar from the other side.[59] Chinese, Japanese, Korean, Greek, Lebanese, and Arab immigrants, along with Jewish immigrants from Germany and eastern Europe, often founded small retail businesses catering to ethnic or American consumers. Small "Mom and Pop" operations required the labor of many family members, often in or near the family residence.[60] Studies of immigrant family businesses emphasize their sharply patriarchal nature.[61] Family workers may receive no wages, giving tiny businesses a competitive edge but making it difficult for wives and children to challenge parental or masculine authority or to establish their independence from the family group without leaving it.[62] On the other hand, within family businesses women have been apt to exercise managerial influence as operators of cash registers and keepers of business accounts. Immigrant businesswomen (see chapter 7) have often begun their careers as workers in family enterprises.

Women immigrants specialized in the business of keeping boarders. Korean women on Hawaiian plantations cooked, laundered, and cleaned for bachelor men while their husbands worked for wages.[63] Migrations of male sojourners guaranteed a plentiful supply of boarders for other groups, too: a quarter to a third of immigrant households at any given point in time between the 1850s and the 1920s contained at least one boarder, and a woman with three boarders would generate about a third of a typical family's income in 1900.[64] Still, since women's work for boarders was the same as the work done without pay for family members, few immigrant women saw the keeping of boarders as a business.[65] And American observers insisted that it was the male boarders, not their female keepers, who contributed to immigrant family income.

Production of meals and clean clothes left immigrant women with little time for housework tasks more highly valued by middle-class Americans—

child-rearing and housecleaning.[66] Thus "breadgiver" rather than house-wife or mother best describes immigrant women working without pay. As keepers of kitchen gardens, rural women raised much of the food their families ate.[67] Surprising numbers of immigrant women in urban and indus-trial settings continued to produce at least some of their families' food. High prices in company stores in mining towns encouraged the practice.[68] But even in late nineteenth century New York, Americans complained about immi-grants' pigs roaming the streets, their chickens roosting in tenement kitch-ens, and their goats stabled in tenement basements. Urban women marketed once or more often a day, purchasing only small quantities that would not spoil. Since boarders and wage-earners worked irregular hours, women often served food over a period of several hours in the early evening. Meat, sweets, and bountiful meals symbolized the well-being of America; women's work guaranteed that bounty. Immigrant women treated this task as their most serious challenge.[69]

Like other American women in the nineteenth century, immigrant women laundered once a week. If their water supply was a pump in the back yard or alley, they worked outside. As builders and landlords installed faucets in urban homes in the twentieth century, women laundered and dried clothes inside, where they dripped over the kitchen stove in the winter. In New York's tenements, women preferred the roof for drying clothes, but this required a long climb with wet clothes. More frequently, they hung laundry out a rear window.[70]

Cooking, laundering, and dishwashing required urban women to fuel and care for a stove—usually the coal stove that heated most immigrant homes until the 1920s. In the countryside, women produced much of their own fuel, splitting and stacking wood. In cities, women or their children helpers scavenged fuel from railroad yards or construction sites; they carried purchased coal from the basement to the stove; they removed ashes and other household refuse. They kept the stove—along with any lamps used prior to gas piping—clean, polished, and in working order. And they maintained a fire that allowed cooking, even in the heat of summer.[71]

In the past, immigrant women lacked the time to read aloud to their chil-dren or have long maternal talks with them the way middle-class native-born mothers were supposed to. Their major goal as mothers and childrearers was to keep their children alive through infancy—no minor undertaking. In New York, for example, as many as a quarter of all babies died in their first two years, usually as a result of spoiled food or milk during the summer months. The infant mortality rate did vary among ethnic groups, although the reasons are not always clear. For instance, Jewish babies generally survived at higher rates than Italian babies, a pattern which may have reflected the superior eco-nomic position of Jewish families (and their purchase of modern medical care), superior standards of cleanliness related to Jewish requirements for rit-ual bathing, higher rates of breastfeeding, or better access to pure milk.[72] It is noteworthy that in the United States today, foreign-born women often have healthier babies with higher birth weights and lower infant mortality rates

than do poor African American or other native-born minority women.[73] This
may reflect their superior educational levels, older average age, better health
practices, or more positive attitudes toward pregnancy.[74] Ironically, today's
immigrant mothers quickly abandon breastfeeding for bottle feeding, which
they perceive as more modern even as many American women, along with
the medical profession, have come to see the health advantages of nursing infants in the old-fashioned way.[75]

To native-born observers, as mentioned earlier, immigrant women have
sometimes seemed unconcerned with American middle-class standards of
cleanliness. Immigrant farmsteads were probably no sorrier than American
rural homes generally in the nineteenth century; indeed, observers singled
out German farm houses and yards as exemplary. In cities, however, Americans often claimed that immigrant housewives had "no sense of order to
their housework"—and lived in cluttered and often dirty homes as a result.[76]
But this is not what photographs of immigrant households suggest. Here one
merely finds variable definitions of both order and decoration. Women of
many backgrounds decorated the edges of kitchen shelves with cut paper.
Eastern European Slavs favored embroidered bedding and pillows; eastern
European Jews added the ritual mezuzah outside their door and preferred
carpets and upholstered furniture; Italians decorated walls and dresser tops
with ceramics, pots, calendars, and clocks. The erection of domestic altars
was a female folk art in some groups.[77] Because married immigrant women
spent so much time at home, this was work they did for themselves; these
women saw their homes as beautiful.[78]

They also saw running water, flush toilets (even if outside), coal stoves,
nearby marketplaces, and ready-made cloth or clothing as American luxuries
accessible even to the poor.[79] Similarly, today's immigrant women value the
household tools—especially automatic washing machines—that lighten the
physical burdens of housework. Many feel they achieve upward mobility
simply by purchasing such appliances. German, Italian, and Jewish women
of the past would agree with the Dominican women who argue today that
labor-saving domestic tools (more than improved wage-earning opportunities) convinced them they made the right decision in moving to the United
States. Dominican women do not talk of returning to the homeland with the
enthusiasm of some of their husbands and brothers.[80] At the same time, immigrant women regretfully recognize that poverty can prevent them from
purchasing the "good things" that American domesticity promises.[81]

CONCLUSION

Labor remained the central focus of immigrant women's lives. Few immigrant women stopped work as a result of migration, although most experienced significant changes in the location and conditions of their labor.
Domestic service continued to sustain life outside family economies for
women who had migrated independently to the United States; work in fac-

tories allowed the daughters of family migrations to contribute to family economies in ways sometimes unknown at home. Still, the burden of subsistence production—undergoing a gradual redefinition as housework—increasingly fell to married women and their children helpers, even though women found they had to combine it with work for money. Immigrant women shared with other poor women a common focus on making ends meet; both female wage-earning and housework contributed materially to family well-being among the poor. As laws gradually excluded children from wage-earning, the numbers of immigrant wives working outside the home for wages increased—as they did in all American families—without eliminating their unpaid labor at home.

Although both found themselves listed in censuses as housewives, immigrant women with families labored under conditions that can scarcely be compared to those of their middle-class white counterparts in the nineteenth century. Most earned money. Few could employ a servant to help with household work; even the daughters, sisters, and nieces who might have helped them out served instead as maids and cooks in middle-class households. The tasks that defined middle-class domesticity—particularly the moral and spiritual supervision of a small group of children—fell near the bottom of an immigrant housewife's long list of chores.

As the American economy changed, immigrants' daughters moved into white-collar work and female professions, where they today encounter new generations of recently arrived immigrant women. Both groups now enjoy access to occupations and skills once limited to the native-born Anglo-American elite. Overall, ethnicity, race, and nationality no longer segment the female work force as sharply as they did at the turn of the century. But it would be a mistake to see the transformation of women's occupations as the seamless assimilation of former outsiders, or even as evidence of immigrant women's successful adaptation to American models of appropriate work for women. The working lives of today's women, regardless of background, resemble those of the immigrant and minority women of the past. Most women work throughout their lives, including during their childrearing years. Most juggle unpaid domestic work with money-earning. Most must seek ways to limit the burdens of household work, yet few can adopt the strategy of middle-class women of the nineteenth century: their family incomes will not support hired service workers, let alone full-time domestic servants.

This chapter has emphasized the many similarities between immigrant women and other groups of American women in the past and the present. Changing focus, however, and attending to family ties and kinship (in the next chapter), and to collective action among the female and foreign-born (in chapter 6) will bring ethnic and racial differences more sharply into focus again. Race, language, nationality, ethnicity, and religion created important divisions among women who otherwise lived in quite similar economic, family, and community relations. Their contacts largely limited to others of "their own kind," many immigrant women literally could not see what their experiences as workers, daughters, mothers, or community activists gave them in common with women of backgrounds unlike their own. However important the shared and central experiences of laboring—at home and for wages—these alone could not always create common ground upon which immigrant and other American women might learn to work together.

FIVE

All Her Kin

While family responsibilities shaped immigrant women's labor in strongly patterned and homogenizing ways, immigrant women did not view their family ties in exclusively economic terms. From their perspective, family ties more than labor reflected their native cultures, and thus their differences from Americans. Kin patterns also reflected their differences from each other. Immigrants like Lalu Nathoy and Mrs. Shinoda emerged from the patrilineages of Asia, while Mrs. Rosalyn Morris grew up in a matrifocal world of women relatives. While sharing the consanguineous (bilateral) kinship structure of other Europeans, an Italian woman like Maria Zambello counted kin ties "to the fifth degree"—which meant to a village half-full of distant cousins.

To American observers, however, poor immigrant families appeared notable for their disorganization and their harshly patriarchal relations.[1] In reaching these conclusions, they limited their focus to nuclear families. Immigrants, by contrast, portrayed their family life far more positively by emphasizing the close affection and unbreachable solidarity among a much wider group of relatives, including those anthropologists call "ritual kin."[2] Immigrants from the Caribbean, Asia, and Europe defined this wider group of relatives in differing ways, but their shared emphasis on the wider kin group is an important key to understanding both immigrant women's life in patriarchal families and their strong sense that family is more important to them than to many Americans. Immigrants as different as Beatrice Pollock, Isabel Ramírez, and "Celia" Vann Noup resembled native-born African American women and Chicanas in seeing kinship as a valuable resource, not the origin of their oppression as women.[3]

KINSHIP, CHAIN MIGRATION, AND IMMIGRANT SETTLEMENT IN THE UNITED STATES

Almost everywhere on the other side, men and women had defined kinship more broadly than most Americans do at present. Patrilineage, marriage, inheritance, and mothering all constructed and maintained kin groups on the other side. Even where men performed most rituals associated with Confucian patrilineages, Chinese women cultivated cross-generational "uterine families" (see chapter 2 above). Arranging marriages, Sicilian women sought congenial daughters-in-law. In lands as diverse as Jamaica, Poland, and Laos, mothers turned to their own mothers, sisters, or female cousins for help caring for their children, creating women-centered, and sometimes matrifocal, kin networks. "Patriarchal" inadequately describes any of these family systems: no woman on the other side completely escaped men's power, yet no woman completely acquiesced to it either.

Most of the immigrant women we met in earlier chapters sought help from kin when they migrated to the United States. For men, too, kinship became the single most important link in the construction of migration "chains" from specific locations around the peripheries of the other side to specific locations within the United States.[4] By the early twentieth century, half to two-thirds of newly arriving immigrants could give the address of a relative awaiting them, or traveled with a ticket prepaid by kin in the United States.

Even when they remained at home, the women of the other side forged many links in migration chains. Portuguese women nagged or cajoled men to migrate and then became intermediaries between the emigrated men and daughters, sons, nieces, nephews, and cousins needing advice and help in order to follow.[5] Either because women became communication nodes in worldwide information networks, or because kin ties through women had a more emotional or affective dimension, Sicilian immigrants in New York favored women's rather than men's relatives when they offered help to new migrants.[6]

Today, of course, visa preferences for close relatives of American citizens guarantee that kinship remains important in creating chain migrations—but only as Americans define kinship. Family reunification provisions fail to recognize the informal marriages of many women in the Caribbean, for example; they do not privilege grandparents or the many half- or adoptive siblings, "fostered" children, ritual kin, and stepparents of this region. They prefer a citizen's wife's mother over an (Asian) husband's patrilineal nephew. Immigrants in turn view U.S. policy as irrational and overly legalistic; they seek to manipulate its provisions in ways that more nearly meet their own sense of which kin should remain together or migrate sequentially.[7]

IMMIGRANT HOUSEHOLDS AND KIN NETWORKS

Chains of migrating kin in turn encouraged immigrants to live in households violating American norms of privacy and propriety. Americans saw boarders in immigrant households as strangers "disorganizing" their host families. They blamed boarders for overcrowding, and they worried that unmarried boarders preyed sexually on immigrants' daughters.[8]

For immigrant women, by contrast, keeping a boarder was a way to help kin or friends while earning money at home. Although most boarders were men, immigrant women breadgivers especially welcomed female kin as boarders because they—like daughters—helped with the housework, though they paid lower boarding fees on the lower wages they earned. Like the breadgiver's daughters, female boarders and *gruene Kusine* ("green", or recently arrived, cousins) might either complain about their exploitation or take satisfaction in helping an overburdened woman they loved.[9]

Immigrant men sometimes expressed ambivalence about male boarders. Jokes about "star boarders" abound in the folklore of Hungarian immigrants.[10] But fictional accounts of Jewish, Italian, and Polish life include tales of illicit sexual relationships only between boarders and the adult women who served them their meals. Thus when immigrants worried (and they worried less than Americans did), they focused their fears on boarders' seduction of wives and mothers, not their exploitation of young immigrant girls.

Immigrant households also opened their doors to whole families of recently arrived kin and friends. Italians in New York City sublet front or back rooms of three-room apartments to families of new arrivals, often siblings. The two families, observers puzzled, "lived entirely separately." This was true, in the sense that they did not pool income—but they did share space. The wives in both families used a common kitchen, where boarders might sleep at night. And they shared chores: one of the wives would work for wages outside the home, while the other cared for children at home.[11] Immigrant children of many backgrounds later remembered endless streams of newly arrived cousins, aunts, and uncles who took over their beds and crowded their families around common meals. Not all memories were positive. Kate Simon reported sexual abuse at the hands of both male and female relatives with whom she shared bed and bedroom.[12]

Because young working-age adults dominated migrations, immigrant women could not simply duplicate the kin networks they knew on the other side. During migration, Latin American and European women, accustomed to close cross-generational ties—especially those to their own mothers—wove new kin networks that more nearly resembled peer groups than lineages.[13] Asian women, however, more often depended on female friends to replace the mothers most never saw again.[14] In this case, migration set a seal of finality on a separation already troubling to young women in Asian kinship systems. It was true that by migrating to the United States, young women escaped harsh mothers-in-law and felt "freed from the elders," but they also found themselves farther away than ever from mothers and sisters they loved.[15] Asian picture brides could not call over sisters or cousins after 1921, heightening both their feelings of loneliness and their dependence on friends. Italian women immigrants, by contrast, bound their female relatives closer in the New World, where frequent moves threatened to disrupt carefully balanced exchanges among neighbors. Laotian women do the same today.[16]

Women's kin networks supported cooperation across gender and generational lines. Even more than in the homeland, maintaining contact among kin—sometimes called "kinship work"—became immigrant women's responsibility.[17] Women kept in touch with relatives through regular visiting and by investing considerable female labor in family rituals, including meals, parties, and gatherings organized around the milestones of birth, religious maturity, marriage, and death. Jewish women had long enjoyed responsibilities for religiously defined domestic rituals. But even Japanese women, from a Confucian world where it was normally men who owed service to their ancestors, managed everyday kinship obligations in the United States.[18]

Family rituals in the United States varied with cultural origin and religion. Many immigrants discovered the American custom of birthdays, and layered American-style birthday celebrations onto Old World rituals related to name days or saints' days. For Christians, baptisms brought together large kin groups for both church services and family parties. Even more, funerals and weddings—most notably Irish wakes and Polish weddings—came to symbolize distinctively ethnic kinship solidarities in the eyes of American observers. American observers at first found the displays of emotion and the costs of such rituals excessive, distasteful, and even harmful. More recently, Americans concerned about declining family values instead see ethnic funerals and weddings as expressions of a praiseworthy commitment to a group larger than the individual or the nuclear family.[19]

Few immigrant women commented on this work, finding it natural. Still, considerable female labor and skill—especially in the kitchen, but also in conversations, condolences, and emotional performance—underwrote kinship celebrations. In this way, women in the immigrant working classes created a "female world of cards and holidays" that functioned somewhat as the female world of "love and ritual" did for middle-class women. Within their world, women enjoyed sociability beyond the nuclear family, while demonstrating their power and expertise to a sizeable social group. Unlike the middle-class female world, however, immigrant women generated celebrations that drew men and children into their world, to emphasize what all celebrated together across the generations and the sexes.[20] Kinship empowered women—but not to challenge kinship's dictates or to pursue female separatism or autonomy.

Studies of today's Latina immigrants point to the continued centrality of family, friendship, and kin networks.[21] For other groups, too, these networks remain essential, their loss deeply traumatic. Fear of social isolation remains a troubling theme in the lives of Asian immigrant women.[22] Asian refugee women may suffer particularly from the violence of their earlier lives and the many family members it has cost them.[23] Women from the Caribbean, too, sometimes describe their early days in the United States (when their mothers or children remained behind) as isolated and lonely. Hence the efforts of Caribbean women to recreate matrifocal kin networks may require years, as these traditionally emphasize cross-generational ties. Thus among today's immigrants, too, women are responsible for kinship work. But as in earlier times, they realize their own visions of kin networks in the United States.

MOTHERS AND FATHERS; HUSBANDS
AND WIVES; SONS AND DAUGHTERS

Even within their nuclear families, immigrants fell far short of Americans' critical standard. Middle-class Americans expected fathers to be breadwinners, the sole support of families. They expected mothers to devote time to children. They expected parents to protect the innocence of their children but to allow growing sons and daughters considerable control over their leisure and courtship.

Few immigrant fathers in the nineteenth century earned a family wage sufficient to support dependents. The least skilled immigrant men, like immigrant women, suffered seasonal unemployment, and those in construction left home for months in search of work. Unlike middle-class American breadwinners who allotted a household allowance to their wives, immigrant women typically controlled the family purse, collected family earnings, supervised expenditures, and gave men allowances.[24]

Because few immigrant men were the only breadwinners for their families, they may not have defined their masculinity exclusively in those terms. During the Great Depression of the 1930s, at least some blue-collar immigrant men endured poverty and unemployment without the intense crises in self-esteem common among American businessmen of the era.[25] In today's immigrant families, too, unemployed women are as likely to suffer from stress and depression as unemployed men—and both worry more about diminished incomes than unfulfilled gender roles.[26]

The heady notion of American "freedom," along with differences in Old and New World marriage customs, encouraged some immigrant men to abandon their family obligations. Yiddish newspapers carried numerous advertisements placed by wives in Europe and the United States, searching for husbands who had disappeared. (Jewish divorce custom, which required no civil proceedings, may have facilitated male desertion.)[27] Immigrant men of peasant backgrounds, learning that common-law and civil marriages were legal in the U.S., sometimes concluded that Old World religious prohibitions against bigamy or cohabitation by the unmarried had no force in the United States, where "people could do as they wanted" sexually.

Yet the statistics on divorce, desertion, and female-headed households varied enormously among immigrant groups. Irish men deserted their families in the highest proportions, while Jewish men more frequently divorced their wives.[28] Irish women headed households (the products of both death and desertion) about as often as did African American women. With their own local traditions of common-law marriage, Mexican American women also frequently became female heads of household.[29] Among Italians and Germans, by contrast, women rarely headed households. Today, divorce continues to vary considerably with ethnicity: Mexican and Cuban immigrants have much lower divorce rates than either Puerto Rican or African American native-born minorities.[30] Mexicans and Central and South Americans, like

African American women, are more likely to head households than the white female population generally.[31] Single mothers from the Caribbean frequently head their own households in the United States.[32]

In the past, widows outnumbered unmarried or deserted mothers as female heads of immigrant households. And when they lived alone, elderly widowed women suffered disproportionately from poverty. For both these reasons, widows numbered prominently among older female wage-earners, boardinghouse keepers, and labor activists.[33] Immigrant women with grown children depended heavily on them for assistance and companionship in old age. Aging women immigrants remained very much part of family and kin circles.[34] Among Cuban and Chinese immigrants today, daughters' desires to house aging mothers, however, conflict with the need to earn money for their support. Immigrant households with working wives now more often institutionalize aged mothers.[35]

Even when alive and at home, immigrant fathers' long working hours and their adherence to traditions of leisure-time gender segregation made them shadowy figures to their children. But it was immigrant women whom American observers repeatedly charged with neglecting their children.[36] Paradoxically, Americans also found immigrant childrearing practices overly strict.[37] Some observers even now measure immigrant women's mothering skills by how often they play with their children.[38] And even today, immigrants charge social service agencies with misunderstanding their childrearing aims and methods, which foster sibling solidarity more than individualism.

Charges of neglect may have followed, in part, simply from the many children immigrant women bore. Actually, immigrant women in the early twentieth century generally had fewer children than their counterparts on the other side.[39] Still, at least in the urban Northeast, immigrant fertility did outstrip that of white native-born women, fueling nativist fears of demographic conquest by the foreign-born. Ironically, even as native-born Americans worried about race suicide, immigrant women—most notably Jewish women from eastern Europe—were already limiting their fertility.[40] We do not know whether immigrant couples used abstinence or withdrawal as birth control; we do know that abortion was a widely used birth control measure of last resort for women of all backgrounds.[41] Oral histories suggest that birth control worked only when immigrant husbands shared women's desire to limit births.[42] Some immigrant women firmly believed that middle-class Americans had a secret for preventing pregnancy, and they begged nurses like Margaret Sanger to share the secret.[43] The fertility of women living in cities, regardless of background, declined most dramatically.[44] It also declined as immigrant women's education levels and earnings increased.[45] And for both yesterday's and today's immigrants, fertility declines correlate with length of time in the United States.[46]

Today, as before, immigrant women bear fewer children than their sisters on the other side, and, as a group, they now bear no more children than native-born women.[47] Still, ethnic differences remain strong. Most research on the fertility of today's immigrant women focuses on Mexicans because they—along with other Catholic immigrants—are believed to control their fertility reluctantly, for doctrinal reasons.[48] This is a questionable assumption. Mexican immigrant women do have higher fertility rates than other immigrant women and than American women generally. Refugees from Southeast Asia, however, who are mostly non-Catholic, also lack familiarity with Western birth control practices and also have large families.[49] Meanwhile, studies show that Mexican, Cuban, and other Latina women hold a wide range of attitudes toward both birth control and abortion: religion does not explain their high fertility.[50] It is worth noting that among Mexicans, women with above-average education, as well as those earning wages outside the home, have lower rates of fertility than uneducated and unemployed women.[51]

Daughters of immigrant women had about as many children as their mothers in the nineteenth century, but bore fewer in the twentieth.[52] The lower fertility of the second generation was the consequence of later marriage age: parents seemed reluctant to let daughters marry early once they became industrial wage-earners; the Great Depression also interfered in the marriage plans of many second-generation daughters of southern and eastern European migrants. Culture mattered, too: in the second generation, Irish women married latest and Mexican women earliest.[53] Contrasts between fertility in the first and second generations are weaker in recent migrations. Among Mexican Americans, however, fertility does decline with time and the rise of new generations, much as it did among earlier high-fertility immigrants.[54]

Americans today seem as concerned with childbearing outside of marriage as with overall fertility rates. Childbearing outside of marriage was not unknown in the past, either, and seems to have been particularly common among German and Scandinavian servant girls, who generally surrendered children to kin in order to return to domestic service.[55] Pregnant girls in more recently arrived Mexican immigrant families come under strong parental pressure to marry, even at a relatively young age.[56] Recent studies show, however, that it is the most assimilated, English-speaking daughters of Mexican immigrant communities who are most likely to become sexually active as young girls.[57]

Once immigrant mothers bore and guaranteed the survival of their infants, they turned as many childrearing tasks as possible over to older daughters—called "little mothers." As mentioned above, the practice encouraged sibling solidarity, but fueled Americans' complaints about child neglect.[58] Older daughters minded younger siblings on the stoop or sidewalk, or in barnyard, backyard, alley, street, or backlot play spaces.[59] Little mothers represented a New World version of a much older solution. In Hawaii, immigrant mothers of Asian and Portuguese backgrounds seemed unhappy to depend on daughters; they lamented the absence of older women.[60] Filipina mothers today claim they limit their fertility because they have no older women relatives to raise children while they earn wages.[61]

While criticizing mothers for neglecting children, American social welfare workers also sometimes complained that Jewish (and other immigrant) mothers "over-loved" their children—dressing them too warmly, stuffing them with inappropriate foods, hugging and caressing them too often or too closely.[62] Jewish sons seemed most aware of discrepancies between their mothers and American ideals of a constantly watchful but "cooler" motherly presence: many have written of the guilty dependency their mothers' love produced in them.[63] Daughters of immigrants reacted with less ambivalence to their mothering. Even when they pointed to their mothers' failings, or note ways they expect to differ from them, daughters have viewed their immigrant mothers as important role models.[64] Many also felt that their mothers had spoiled their brothers.[65] (Their mothers may well have shared this perception: it is likely that the many mothers who pampered sons nevertheless resented them for remaining "forever boys and burdens," in the words of a study of Irish families.)[66]

Sons and daughters saw mothers as powerful and anything but neglectful. Children described immigrant mothers as collectors of wages, as organizers of expenditures and everyday life, as engagers of their help in domestic chores and industrial production, as dispensers of discipline and punishment, and as women who rewarded children with food, affection, small gifts, and personal services.[67] Immigrant mothers spent little "quality time" with their children, yet fostered emotionally close ties to them.

For many immigrant mothers, hard work and the sacrifice of their own needs—for food, for rest, for money—were important mechanisms for communicating love.[68] And separated from other kin by migration, many immigrant mothers saw children as their best long-term protection against social isolation. Today, too, Mexican and Central American mothers emphasize the sacrifices they make for children but anticipate rewards for their sacrifices: they see children as more dependable emotional and financial supports than their husbands.[69] Both Chinese and Irish mothers expect their children will support them financially in old age.[70] Fear of isolation in later life persists among Asian immigrant women today, although it is not limited to them.[71]

POWER IN IMMIGRANT FAMILIES

The common images of chaotic immigrant households, overseen by fertile, slovenly women and overrun by children and kinfolk, offended native middle-class sensibilities on many fronts. But nowhere did American and immigrant notions of proper family behavior clash more visibly than in the realm of parent-child power relations. Though only vaguely aware of immigrant family economies, American observers nevertheless saw immigrant families as little dictatorships ruled by primitive and violent men untouched by American notions of gender equality or chivalry.[72] They saw immigrant children turn over their wages and submit to physical discipline. They saw Italian and other Latin daughters forbidden to move freely outside their homes; they even saw some children accept spouses chosen for them. Social welfare workers at the turn of the century thus successfully focused American attention on power within immigrant families. Feminist theorists of patriarchy have helped hold our attention there.

American critics described immigrant family power relationships accurately enough in a broad sense, but missed the complexities and the fluid character of generational and gender struggles. Immigrant parents from the more subsistence-oriented areas of the other side certainly required sons and daughters to surrender pay envelopes unopened; unlike both Americans and immigrants from industrializing areas, they did not view wages as individual property. Immigrant fathers and mothers also quickly discovered that children could rebel against family claims to their wages, lives, and loyalties. Sons and daughters struggled to control their own earnings, or at least some portion of them. Sons usually succeeded at an earlier age and in larger numbers; by paying their mothers half their wages they became, in effect, boarders.[73]

Conflict over daughters' wages became the most common source of generational conflict in immigrant families, pitting daughters against mothers as often as against fathers. Some mothers demanded every cent of daughters' earnings; others tolerated daughters' holding back small sums for clothes or entertainment; still others collected wages but gave allowances in recognition of girls' loyalty and support.

While some mothers firmly insisted that children subordinate individual desires to collective needs, others had recognized the lure of the marketplace long before arriving in the United States.[74] German and Jewish parents, with their longer experience of wage-earning, allowed daughters freedom to explore life outside the family.[75] Portuguese and Italian daughters may have gained little autonomy through wage-earning, but Mexican daughters gained control over their pay envelopes, and with it the power to control their recreation and leisure, consumer decisions, and courtship. Daughters controlling their own wages gained in self-esteem, too.[76]

Whether linked to wage-earning or not, daughters' desires to control their own courtships became another source of conflict in Latin and Asian families. Here, too, daughters often wrested power from their mothers as well as from their fathers; they challenged not patriarchy but traditions of family oligarchy.[77] Mexican and Italian parents seemed particularly concerned about supervising daughters' courtships to prevent premarital sexual contacts or possible pregnancy.[78] Thus conflicts grew after 1920 as dating outside the family or community circle became the preferred form of courtship among Americans. Among contemporary migrants, Cubans and Dominicans show similar concerns about preserving their daughters' sexual innocence and virginity during courtship. But even West Indian parents, with their more flexible attitudes toward sexuality outside marriage, feel perturbed at the sense that they lose control over their daughters' social lives in the United States.[79]

Even today, arranged marriages characterize some groups of Asian immigrants,[80] as they did Italians, Jews, and Japanese in the past. In all of these cases, immigrant sons and daughters have struggled to claim for themselves what they perceive as the freedom and individualism of American courtship customs. Daughters with little control over their own movement had limited options for participating in commercial entertainments, where American courtship increasingly occurred. Aware that parents no longer possessed social networks broad enough to make sensible decisions, yet forbidden from experimenting with American-style dating in dance halls and amusement parks, daughters from Latin and Asian backgrounds wondered whether they would ever find a mate.[81] Brothers and sisters depended heavily on each other and on ethnic and religious community activities to provide them with a pool of potential spouses acceptable to, yet not directly selected by, their parents.[82] Immigrant parents fought with sons, too, but over different issues: parents' complaints about rebellious sons focused more on criminal activity than on male sexuality or independent courtship.[83]

Young women from the developing economies of northern Europe had begun experimenting with new courtship rituals prior to migration; they easily extended their control over marriage in the United States. Having migrated independent of parents, and frequently working as domestic servants, they could chat with delivery men in their kitchens, dance at commercial and ethnic halls, and promenade on rural main streets or urban avenues on Sunday afternoons. Young Jewish women from eastern Europe, along with the home-living daughters of Irish and German immigrants, also enjoyed the expanding commercial cultural entertainments of American cities as places to examine and experiment with male partners unknown to their parents. For Jewish daughters, summer camps became an important place to meet prospective mates.[84] Being "treated" by young men may have created morally questionable areas on the boundaries of courtship, marriage, and prostitution in parents' eyes, but immigrant daughters experienced it instead as freedom from supervised courtships.[85]

Still, surprisingly few immigrant girls with parents in the United States fled parental control to the rooming-house neighborhoods that were developing in U.S. cities between 1880 and 1920.[86] Even daughters who could afford to live independently remained at home. When domestic servants had families nearby, furthermore, they saw separation from parents and siblings as a loss rather than as one of the fringe benefits of service work.[87] When immigrant girls did leave home, they did so to escape extremely controlling fathers rather than in response to the common everyday conflicts with mothers.[88]

Much more than romantic love guided the most independent single immigrant women in choosing husbands. German women seemed less interested in the physical appearance of potential husbands than in their religious beliefs, place of birth, and work and drinking habits. One wrote home in great detail about her wedding gifts but said no more than a word or two about the man she had just married.[89]

Some immigrant women said they did not wish to marry—"I won't have things as good as I have them now," as a Swedish domestic servant wrote to a friend—and a small but significant number of Irish women did remain single in the United States.[90] When immigrant women married, as most did, they tended to choose husbands of their own culture and religious faith. For Poles and Italians, endogamy (marriage within the group) might mean marrying a boy from the home village or home region. For Jews from eastern Europe, endogamy meant finding a Jewish husband whose religious faith or dialect of Yiddish most nearly approximated one's own.[91] For most Chinese girls, marriage to a Korean or a Japanese was unthinkable. West Indian women and men expressed their reluctance to marry native-born African Americans: the men found American women resentful of their "authoritarian" manners, while the women found American black men upset by the children they may have borne in previous relationships.[92]

Some immigrants had little choice but to marry outside their groups, however. Prohibited from marrying whites, but with few women among them, male migrants from India working in California chose the daughters of Mexican immigrants or native-born Chicanas as their wives.[93] Heavily male-dominated migrations from China placed sharp pressure on Western antimiscegenation laws. Chinese men in Hawaii married native Hawaiian women. Marriages between Filipinos or racially mixed Puerto Ricans further challenged racial boundaries in U.S. marriage laws.[94] Today, by contrast, women from China, Japan, and Korea are more likely than men to intermarry.[95]

By the 1930s and 1940s, immigrant sons and daughters increasingly (25 to 30 percent) married outside their nationality group as they freed themselves from parental influence. Most married other second-generation immigrants of similar religion: Irish American married Polish American; Lutheran German married Lutheran Finn or Norwegian. West Indians increasingly married native-born African Americans; Jews of varying backgrounds and religious convictions formed a marital melting pot of their own.[96] By the third generation, the majority of European immigrants' descendants married outside the ethnic group (see chapter 8).

Thus while daughters clearly seized marital initiative from their parents during migration and adjustment to life in the United States, they nevertheless gave weight to old criteria along with new ones of romantic love when choosing a spouse. Marital relationships within immigrant families shed a similarly contradictory light on power and subordination within immigrant families. There can be little doubt, for example, that most immigrant wives, even if they worked only at home, faced what is today called "a double day."[97] That "double day" explains why married immigrant women in the past avoided wage-earning outside the home. Nevertheless, heavily overburdened immigrant women often viewed their marriages more positively than their daughters and granddaughters.[98]

Married women wage-earners among the foreign-born also gained in decision-making power and received more help with their domestic work than wives working without wages. Even American social workers sometimes begrudgingly concluded "they work together, these immigrant husbands and wives," after finding a husband washing dishes or windows.⁹⁹ In the past, men may have done domestic work only when no daughters or other female kin were available. More recently, however, immigrant men of many backgrounds have increased their work in the household, especially when they become unemployed.¹⁰⁰ Wives' wage-earning sparks family conflict, as members of the families renegotiate their rights and obligations, but it also fosters real domestic change.¹⁰¹

One Mexicana, for example, describes her husband as macho in Mexico, but a considerate "delicate butterfly" in the United States, where she, like her husband, works for wages.¹⁰² Dominican women report more consultation and shared decision-making about purchases when they pool incomes with their husbands.¹⁰³ Vietnamese men, too, take over child care and domestic tasks when their wives work for wages outside the home. For Chinese women, managing family finances itself represents a new arena of power and influence.¹⁰⁴ Only studies of some Korean, Japanese, and Cuban families report little significant change in men's involvement in domestic tasks, perhaps because these men very often work long hours in family businesses.¹⁰⁵

Domestic change has occurred more readily in immigrant than in middle-class American families, where many studies find little significant alteration in family decision-making or the allotment of domestic chores in response to women's wage-earning. American women depend more on their children and on paid help to replace their labor. Immigrant parents cannot afford paid help; they may also prefer fathers as child-minders to day care, which exposes young children to English speakers and to American cultural values. Perhaps, too, immigrant men and women view change at home as just one in a long series of adjustments required by life in a new country, not as a chapter in the battle of the sexes or a crisis in their marital relationship.

While Americans in the nineteenth century attributed the subordination of immigrant women and children mainly to religious and racial backwardness, feminist theorists more often trace men's power in families to their control of women's sexuality. Until recently, for example, scholars have argued that Latin men of many backgrounds established their manliness through fathering many children, enjoying sex with many partners, and confining their wives and daughters to the home, rather than through "masculine" breadwinning.

Because students of immigrant women have paid less attention to sexuality than to other dimensions of family life, the place of sexuality in defining power within immigrant families can only begin to be addressed. In many groups, sexuality seems to have been a taboo topic, as it was also among native-born middle-class Americans. Immigrant daughters of many backgrounds learned nothing about sexuality from their mothers. They experienced the onset of menstruation as shocking; Jewish girls remember it as the occasion for a sharp motherly slap in the face—symbolizing the shame of the two women's shared sexuality. Other women claimed to have been ignorant of sexual intercourse and pregnancy prior to marriage. That taboo on communicating about sexuality often provoked guilty feelings about sex in later life.

In other ways, however, immigrants' sexual assumptions departed sharply from those of Americans. Few southern or eastern Europeans and few Latin Americans believed women to be naturally passionless—as many Victorian Americans did. On the contrary, Jewish and other eastern Europeans saw women as the descendants of Eve, whose sexual curiosity had caused man's fall.[106] And Latins sought to control female sexuality precisely because they assumed women's desires matched or exceeded men's.[107] It is important to note that today many scholars deny the existence, or at least the uniqueness, of Latin machismo, seeing in it a value-laden misunderstanding of Latin gender relations.[108]

Such preconceptions tell us little about actual sexual relations, however. We know from interviews with Italian and Jewish immigrant women that Jewish women enjoyed greater opportunities for sexual experimentation prior to marriage, perhaps because Jews of both sexes were more familiar with birth control. Jewish women and their husbands also cooperated to limit the size of their families; they seemed to view sex as a means of companionship within marriage more than of procreation alone. By contrast, many of the immigrant women Margaret Sanger visited as a nurse regarded sex as a service men demanded of wives, regardless of the costs for them or family living standards.[109] Whether expressed sexually or in other ways, companionship between husbands and wives was at best a new ideal, developing among immigrants and Americans generally as women gradually withdrew from circles of female kin and sex-segregated socializing; it was far more influential in twentieth-century than in nineteenth-century marriages.[110]

With the exception of Caribbean peoples, most peoples from the other side have frowned on extramarital sexuality; from their perspective, that kind of sexuality made no contribution to kinship networks. Many immigrants seem to have regarded homosexuality with horror, too, either for religious reasons or because such sexuality likewise creates no new kin. But very little is actually known about sexual orientation among the foreign-born. Among Latin immigrants today, homophobia isolates lesbians and gay men from their kin groups, while their cultural difference from native-born Americans does not always allow homosexual immigrants easy integration into a gay or lesbian counterculture. Still, they are more likely to "come out" in the United States than in their homelands.[111]

Feminist theorists have also argued that men's control over women rests on their recourse to physical violence: families are not "safe havens" but institutions subordinating women to men. Certainly, immigrant families provide evidence of this. Patterns of family violence among the foreign-born differ only slightly from those of the native-born, suggesting striking cross-cultural parallels in male domination modes. Similarly, foreigners seem not to have differed much from native-born Americans in their expressed attitudes toward physical violence: in particular, both native-born and immigrant rural and working-class people, men and women alike, supported a husband's right to discipline a wife physically and a parent's responsibility to discipline children harshly.[112] Mothers, as childrearers, punished children physically and—in extreme cases—violently.[113] Husbands were more likely to attack their wives than the reverse. Mexican and Asian immigrant women today sometimes claim that women beaten by their husbands deserve their punishment—yet no beaten woman accepts her own punishment as just.[114] Unlike their mothers, furthermore, the daughters of immigrants rarely accepted a father's or mother's right to physically discipline other family members.[115]

The *kinds* of conflicts leading to family violence did vary with ethnicity. Alcohol abuse by both sexes was at the root of most physical conflict in Irish families.[116] Among Italians, enraged men attacked wives and daughters when they feared they had lost control of women's sexuality. Overall, in fact, female sexuality was the most common source of conflict and violence within immigrant families, especially as daughters assumed greater responsibility for their courtships. The most common cause for an immigrant daughter's jailing or institutionalization was parental disapproval of her sexual activity.[117] Immigrant fathers who murder their rebellious daughters provide grist for tabloids even today.[118]

Regardless of triggering event or ethnicity, violent immigrant families all shared a common trait—considerable social isolation.[119] Immigrant families were not more violent or disorganized than other Americans, but when violence had occurred on the other side, people expected relatives to intervene. Without a sufficiently dense network of kin or friends, women and children in the United States lacked the social resources that could stay the hands of angry kinsmen or mothers.

Overall, did foreign-born women more often experience kinship as a burden than native-born American women did? Some historians of immigrant women have applauded daughters' escape from family oligarchy as important steps toward their emancipation as women. They measure immigrant women's progress against the norm of the native-born American middle classes' family lives. Other scholars have instead called attention to the resources and support women lost when migration rearranged or obliterated the kin networks they had depended upon; these scholars measure immigrant women's plight against the norms of subsistence societies on the other side. Daughters appear as historical winners; mothers as historical losers. But since most immigrant women were both daughters and mothers, it seems likely that neither interpretation satisfactorily describes their own views of changing family dynamics.

CONCLUSION

Immigrant women's family and kin ties exhibited strong variation by cultural background and by generation. Whatever their form, family and kin groups were at the center of immigrant women's experience of migration and ad-justment to life in the United States. Not surprisingly, many immigrants and their descendants believe that the breadth and depth of their family inter-connections differentiate them from other Americans, who seem to be less in-volved with and less committed to kin. Americans, too, saw family ties as important measures of the difference between foreigners and Americans.

It is impossible to measure whether kinship became more or less impor-tant to women as they migrated from the other side to the United States. Scholars have argued both possibilities, and assessed each differently. What-ever their behavior, however, immigration may have made immigrants' com-mitment to the ideals of family solidarity both more consciously felt and more forcefully expressed. In response to American glorification of individualism and to the rebellions of the second generation, immigrant parents of both sexes harped incessantly on family solidarities and family loyalties as moral, lineal, and ethnic desiderata.[120]

Nor can the symbolic importance of kinship and family ties be divorced from immigrants' position in relation to the men and women of America's racial minorities, particularly African Americans. In the nineteenth century, white native-born middle-class Americans dismissed the men and women of both groups as inadequate fathers and mothers, often focusing on precisely the same alleged failings.[121] The "talented tenth" of African American com-munities shared with articulate immigrant parents a deep commitment to de-fending and publicizing their strong and respectable family values, often in contradistinction to an American upper class they excoriated for its loveless marriages, governesses, boarding-school educations, and materialism. By elaborating ethnic ideologies of kin and family commitments, African Amer-ican and immigrant minorities sought social, economic and geographical mo-bility and acceptance.[122]

Middle-class African Americans, and feminist scholars among them, con-tinue their campaign to gain recognition and respect for African American families. By contrast, the descendants of immigrants—both European and Asian—have won their battles. American newspapers and popular culture now evoke affectionately humorous images of close and expansive ethnic kin groups, while respectful reportage tells of the tightly knit families of suc-cessful Asian students. Romanticized depictions of immigrant mothers abound in such portraits, but bear little resemblance to the hard-working lives described here. These approving portrayals of family-centered ethnic women appear in a world dominated by negative images of prolific, and black, welfare mothers. By elaborating on the very real emotional and in-strumental importance of kinship for their immigrant parents and grand-parents, and for themselves, the descendants of immigrants have claimed for themselves the title of model minorities, presumably in contrast to native-born African Americans.

Family, kin, and labor dominated the lives of immigrant women past and present, reinforcing both claims on women, but sometimes also pulling women in conflicting directions. Family and kin ties generated communities defined by shared ethnicity and religion, but wage-earning and the other challenges of American life instead pulled immigrant women beyond relations with their own kind into cooperative and conflictual relations with people of other backgrounds. The next chapter examines immigrant women's successes and failures in working together with others—both male and female, and both within their ethnic communities and outside of them.

SIX

Working Together

Nowhere on the other side were nuclear families or kin networks—whatever their importance—the only basis for collective action and cooperation. Instead, a family's status rested on the breadth, depth, and extent of its social connections. The men and women of the other side needed circles of assistance and mutual aid beyond the family economy and kin network, and they routinely built communities through personal ties to neighbors, kin, and co-workers. Americans, by contrast, often pursued mutual aid via voluntary associations—individuals joining together in formal organizations to pursue shared interests. Unlike communities, voluntary associations had formal membership (often with requirements), leadership positions (often elected), and clearly understood (often written) goals.

Voluntary association was known on the other side, too, but it was practiced unevenly—more by men than by women; more by wage-earners than by subsistence producers; and more by middle-class than by poorer people. Voluntarism marked some elements of religious practice among Protestants and Jews; it characterized as well the confraternalism of Catholics. Secular fraternalism, developing in the face of political centralization in countries as diverse as China and Italy, spread especially rapidly among the men of the other side in the nineteenth century. Individual wage-earners also experimented with voluntary association in organizing strikes and labor unions.

As we might expect, the social contacts and interests of most immigrant women extended beyond the boundaries of their front doors and kin circles—reaching out to their neighbors, ethnic communities, and churches or synagogues. But of the individual immigrant women introduced earlier, only Beatrice Pollock attempted to solve problems by working with people much beyond her ethnic community. (Pollock, the young woman who migrated to live with a sister and work in a garment shop in Chicago, became a labor activist.) As this suggests, immigrants' desires for connection and the practical problems they faced in the United States did not immediately push them outward toward greater contact with native-born Americans and thus toward what Milton Gordon has termed "structural assimilation."[1] Generational status and gender ideology deeply influenced the path of immigrant community-building, as it had family economies and kinship networks.

In the United States, immigrant women moved gradually toward voluntarism in building community life. Immigrant wives and mothers more often learned the lessons of voluntary association from men of their own backgrounds and from home-country traditions of fraternalism, while their daughters, the second generation, more often learned it from their immigrant peers and American sisters. In both cases, a clear division of labor by gender developed in immigrant efforts to build community through voluntary association. Gender divisions within ethnic communities guaranteed that the lives of immigrant women paralleled those of native-born American women in striking ways. Parallels, however, did not mean common ground: the two groups rarely worked together in the first generation.

OPPORTUNITIES FOR CONTACT

Work and residence heavily influenced immigrant men and women's opportunities to meet, socialize, and solve problems collectively. While immigrants' settlement preferences often segregated married women among their own kind, wage-earning more frequently pushed men and unmarried women into ethnically mixed workplaces. Domestic servants grew to know intimately the habits, customs, and language of their native-born employers. Female industrial workers, by contrast, more commonly met other immigrant women. Today, many foreign-born women still work segregated from native-born workers if they are employed in agriculture, industries, and family businesses; sizeable minorities of service, professional, and clerical women, however, have extensive work contacts with native-born Americans—white and minority, women and men.

Immigrant communities in the United States often developed on shared territory.[2] In the nineteenth century, immigrants went disproportionately to the Midwest, Far West, and Northeast, where they created neighborhoods identified as "Little Italy," "Chinatown," "Klein Deutschland," "el Barrio," and "the [Jewish] Ghetto."[3] Comparable rural clusters appeared in farming areas, where community-building could result either in opportunities for foreign-born and native-born to meet and socialize or in insular communities of Swedes, Norwegians, or Germans. Even a generation or more later, some rural townships were American communities with a decidedly ethnic flavor.[4]

Clustered in the urban North and Far West, labor migrants from Europe and Asia demographically dominated American cities in the nineteenth century. Segregation of European immigrants by ethnic group and class, while visible and persistent, was voluntary, and it never approached the levels seen in Jewish ghettoes in Europe or in African American ghettoes in the twentieth century.[5] The poorest immigrants shared their slum neighborhoods with immigrants of other backgrounds and with co-ethnics working in small businesses and the professions.

Urban immigrants in the nineteenth century encountered few middle-class natives. Only public schools and the welfare services provided, initially, by settlement houses brought immigrants and natives together. White, middle-class women dominated both institutions. In the nineteenth century, immigrants had few opportunities to meet the native-born minorities, who still lived heavily segregated in the South and Southwest, typically in rural communities and in agricultural employment.

Today, immigrants from Asia, Latin America, and the Caribbean also tend to settle near their "own kind." Vietnamese and other southeast Asian refugees, consciously and systematically scattered throughout the U.S. by sponsorship programs, rapidly reasserted their own social needs by moving in large numbers to California and Texas.[6] While some Koreans and other well-educated immigrants spread themselves widely through a city,[7] the emergence of Asian suburbs in California and wealthy Cuban enclaves in Miami speak of immigrants' continued preference for life among people of their own background. As in the past, however, segregation of the foreign-born is more visible than all-encompassing. In cities, immigrants of several backgrounds share territory with each other and with native-born Mexican American, Asian American, Puerto Rican, and African American minorities.[8] Like the immigrants of the past, too, today's immigrants encounter disproportionate numbers of native-born American women—white and black—as social workers, health care employees, and school teachers.

IMMIGRANT MOTHERS
AND THEIR NEIGHBORHOODS

Neighborhoods had special importance as social arenas for married immigrant women. Few immigrants of any background or sex recognized firm lines separating family from community or household from neighborhood. In cities, immigrants left their doors open or unlatched, encouraging frequent and casual visiting. Family life spilled out of the apartment, down the corridor, onto the sidewalk, and into the street.

Middle-class Americans reacted with dismay to this easy blending of private and public: American standards demanded the separation of the home, women, and children from the public world. Immigrants in turn saw Americans as coldly indifferent to human needs beyond the material concerns of the nuclear family. Jewish eastern Europeans criticized peers aspiring to American standards as "all-rightniks." One man dismissed his all-rightnik children as "machines."[9] Immigrants contrasted American ideals of the private individual to that of the sociable, humane "mensch."[10]

One became a mensch only in a community. Immigrant men valued their street-corner camaraderie and their local places of entertainment, sociability, or worship,[11] just as children of both sexes often ganged together to protect their turf from children of the next street or neighborhood.[12] Even groups known for their conservative attitudes toward female mobility, most notably Mexicans and Italians, raised no objections to women moving through neighborhoods. Only Chinese merchant wives lived secluded lives, and only their wealth—and the employment of an indentured servant—made this seclusion possible.[13]

A poor mother could not function as breadgiver without neighborhood social resources. The permeable line between home and neighborhood explains why many immigrant women remembered impoverished lives in overcrowded, poor housing as richly satisfying: sociability counterbalanced at least some of the difficulties of poverty. One immigrant described herself as "a people's person" who "blooms through sustaining others."[14]

Distance complicated socializing in rural areas: men, more than women, traveled to town or to neighboring farms. American neighbors seemed far off to some women immigrants. In *Giants in the Earth,* a novel reflecting widespread and very somber agrarian realities, the Norwegian woman Beret's sense of isolation on a prairie homestead brings her to the point of madness, even though other families live within sight. But such situations were far from universal. Unlike Beret, the Swedish Ann Oleson enjoyed much company; in her Iowa village, women met to do church work.[15] German women homesteaders had social lives like their native-born neighbors, but suffered more homesickness. Fear of social isolation was one factor that discouraged individual immigrant women from homesteading.[16]

Both rural and urban women sought neighborly solutions for everyday problems. The poor did the most significant charity and welfare work in the nineteenth-century city, and most who gave or needed help were women.[17] They handled predictable crises like childbirth, illness, and death; they shared cash when unemployment threatened rent, food, or clothing payments. Immigrants, like poor African American women, seemed firmly convinced that "what goes round, comes round": they gave in some measure because they expected help in return, sometimes across ethnic lines.

Neighborliness could provide immigrant women with a loud public voice, too. When subtler means failed, women made their complaints known through mob action. Immigrant Jewish women in New York mounted the best-known protest when they rioted against high prices in kosher butcher shops.[18] Italian and Polish housewives organized similar campaigns.[19] Rent increases also spurred immigrant housewives and neighbors to action.[20] In 1906, a mob of angry Jewish women attacked New York public schools, where—they had heard—"children's throats were being cut."[21] Like immigrant families, then, immigrant neighborhoods were often places of violent yet intimate conflict.

Women's neighborhood protests may in some ways have reflected a female consciousness originating in breadgiving.[22] In other respects, they resembled peasant riots in Europe and Asia or the spontaneous protests of unskilled male gang laborers.[23] In any case, women's mob action generated no formal organizations and no women leaders. When male Jewish socialists attempted to build a long-term campaign on the issues raised by rioting housewives, the women themselves withdrew. Over time, women's collective action, like men's, increasingly originated in the workplace, not the neighborhood. And it was more and more apt to be based on voluntary association rather than informal neighborly solidarity or the kin network.

KINSHIP AND VOLUNTARISM

Ethnic communities originated simultaneously in ties of kinship, neighbor-liness, and voluntarism.[24] While men initially dominated the latter, women's community activism bridged all three. In fact, by viewing men and women together, one sees that "informal" ties of community and "formal" voluntarism were not conflicting foundations for cooperation. Neither were they exclusively male or female strategies. While sharp, the gender divisions in community-building were also complex. Kinship influenced immigrant men as community builders, while immigrant women also organized voluntary associations.

Chinese bachelor society in the nineteenth century provides an excellent example of kinship's continued importance for men. Men had always performed more kinship work in China than in many Western societies. In the United States, family and regional companies of Chinese immigrants organized men of particular kin networks and lineages or with the same home towns. Successful Chinese merchants founded these societies, along with secret societies called tongs, and used both to dominate community life. Large numbers of male sojourners—"men without women"—joined these companies.[25] (Under different circumstances, Jewish and Italian family or cousin clubs showed the influence of kinship on European immigrants' voluntarism.)[26]

Among southern and eastern Europeans, too, it was middle-class immigrant businessmen who founded the earliest community institutions.[27] Like Chinese merchants, these were men with families, running saloons, boarding-houses, banks, employment agencies, and grocery stores as family businesses. Unlike their Chinese counterparts, however, male sojourners from Europe rarely joined middle-class-led voluntary associations until they had married or called over wives and children.[28] For European men, the women's presence—and their kinship work—seemed a precondition for male participation in community institutions.

Regardless of background, immigrant men in the United States—like migrants to industrializing cities everywhere in the nineteenth and twentieth centuries—organized a very similar range of institutions, notably secular fraternals (including their radical variants) and religious institutions. Fraternals provided insurance and self-help (savings clubs, education) for male wage-earners. Their radical counterparts expanded to function as unions.[29] Religious institutions—ethnic churches, temples, and synagogues—reproduced elements of familiar homeland religious practice.[30] Over time, all of these groups expanded to provide family sociability and entertainment—dances, sports, singing, theatrical events, banquets, and picnics. They also experimented with providing welfare services to immigrant communities—notably hospitals, employment bureaus, and charity. Some in turn assumed responsibility for the reproduction of the ethnic group itself by organizing schools or social clubs to teach home-country language, history, and social customs to their children. With many immigrant institutions offering similar services, community among immigrants became multiple and shifting rather than unified and monolithic.[31]

Fraternalism by its very definition excluded women.[32] In contrast, religious institutions always provided for female participation. The relative openness of religious institutions to women may help explain why these organizations successfully challenged and defeated secular and/or radical fraternals for dominance of some immigrant communities. Certainly this occurred among Italians, Germans, and eastern European Jews, where the waning of anticlericalism, free-thinking and socialism left religious faith to define ethnicity.[33] In any case, immigrant women did not long accept their exclusion. Instead, they sought to replace fraternalism with an inclusive voluntarism, in community organizations organized by women.

WOMEN IN RELIGIOUS AND SECULAR COMMUNITY ORGANIZATIONS

Like native-born whites and blacks, immigrant women often found their first entry into voluntary activism through religious faith. In Jewish and Protestant immigrant communities, married women pioneered female activism. Among Catholics, by contrast, unmarried women defined activism within religious sisterhoods.

On the other side, Judaism had assigned prayer and study in shul and synagogue to men, while women carried out domestic rituals. In the United States, a new division of labor by gender emerged. Beginning in the 1830s and 1840s, men and women organized male and female Hebrew benevolent societies within synagogues to provide self-help and charity. Men's benevolent societies governed synagogues, but women's benevolent societies financed and supported them: women's earliest efforts aimed to pay off building costs. They then remained synagogue fundraisers, often through the preparation and sale of meals or festivals offering entertainment for the whole community. Organized separately as women, immigrants in Jewish female societies nevertheless drew all members of the religious community into their activities.[34]

As the second generation came of age, female benevolent societies reorganized as synagogue sisterhoods. The change in name and organization reflected an understanding of women's community life that seemed more American, since it focused on women's special responsibilities for the welfare of the entire community.[35] At the same time, second-generation Jewish women began organizing women's clubs independent of synagogues, although still to further women's religious education; these federated in 1893 as the National Council of Jewish Women (NCJW).[36] Sisterhoods, too, federated in the early twentieth century. The NCJW helped connect Jewish female welfare institutions to comparable American women's groups.[37] In the twentieth century, by contrast, the newly formed Hadassah extended

Jewish women's efforts into Zionist activism.[38] Because Jewish women's organizations shared a common focus on the ethnic community and its needs, theirs was no linear history of progress toward individualism or cross-cultural sisterhood.[39]

Protestant women's religious activism paralleled Jewish women's. Among Norwegians, for example, women had already begun organizing sewing circles in the old country to support foreign missions. In a typical U.S. Norwegian community, the pastor's wife would found a "Ladies Aid" that further expanded women's fundraising tasks. In Europe, state taxes had supported churches; in the United States, women would.[40] More precisely, the Ladies Aid would finance and pay for construction of a church, while men's groups arranged to pay the salary of the minister, whom the men also chose.[41] Lutheran fundraisers—suppers, bazaars, and community entertainments—closely resembled synagogue fundraisers, as well as fundraisers in Protestant American churches, black and white alike. Like synagogue sisterhoods, Ladies Aids attained a degree of autonomy from home congregations when they federated at the state and national levels. Within federations, women developed unpaid careers as church volunteers, acquiring considerable organizational expertise and financial know-how.[42]

The Syrian Ladies Aid of Boston, like others, did not create a separate female world within a church or ethnic community. Although faced with initial male opposition to its existence, its separate headquarters, and its welfare work, Syrian men quickly began to participate in the events sponsored by the Ladies Aid. Women encouraged them to join and to attend meetings, but excluded men from holding major offices. Thus Syrian women, too, organized separately to encourage cooperation between men and women.[43]

Among immigrant Catholics (the vast majority of all American Catholics in the nineteenth century), religious orders of celibate sisters, rather than married lay women, first became community activists.[44] In Europe, most sisterhoods had sought wealthy women whose dowries financed lives of cloistered contemplation. In the United States, Catholic parish priests requested practical help from European and French-Canadian sisterhoods.[45] Parishes offered sisterhoods financial support in exchange for their services in parochial schools.[46] This opened sisterhoods to poorer women, who saw a life of service as upward mobility. Sisterhoods also demanded devotion to the poor, however. Nuns' labors created Catholic welfare programs so extensive that they challenged the government welfare programs originally pioneered by native-born women.[47]

Irish sisterhoods grew enormously during the mass migrations of the nineteenth century, as ambitious girls with no prospects for marriage or self-support "took the veil." New and old sisterhoods sent women all over the world. Austrian, Belgian, Dutch, French, and German orders all sent women to begin work in the United States. Immigrant women also formed their own orders.[48] Within them, capable young novices could aspire to become mother superiors through competent social service, administration, and fundraising.

Like the first generation of college-educated American women, they chose celibacy, education, and the helping professions over "the family claim." Like the American welfare reformers, too, Catholic sisterhoods especially supported the education and organization of girls and women. Their welfare services—nurseries, orphanages, hospitals—often focused on the special problems of immigrant women, girls, and children.[49]

Catholic women of the second generation more closely resembled their Jewish and Protestant sisters in organizing Catholic laywomen's organizations. Called sodalities, these voluntary associations quickly assumed responsibility for parish fundraising. Others cared for altars or cultivated particular (and distinctively female) religious devotions.[50]

Immigrant women's challenge to secular fraternalism followed some of the same paths, as women acquired responsibility for welfare work within ethnic communities and for reproduction of the ethnic group. Within ten to twenty years of a fraternal's foundation, immigrant men would abandon exclusionary practices to welcome women as auxiliary members. It is true that their move may have been simply an effort to bolster declining memberships. In organizing female auxiliaries, at any rate, male leaders often recruited women from their own families as members.[51]

Auxiliaries organized family-oriented leisure-time community activities, some of which functioned as fundraisers. Female auxiliaries organized schools to teach language, folk arts, folk customs, or homeland history. Women helped transform fraternals from groups that supported male sociability and breadwinning into organizations dedicated to the creation and reproduction of ethnicity. In opening their fraternals to women, men offered women the opportunity to institutionalize their kinship work and extend it to the entire community. A Finnish IWW (Industrial Workers of the World) hall made this dimension of the female auxiliary explicit: children called all the women of the group "auntie."[52]

Women eagerly took up the task of community service autonomously, too, creating a female public sphere of women's voluntary associations.[53] Many women's groups focused on the maintenance of the ethnic community and strengthening ties to the homeland.[54] Sometimes, women's activism financed homeland nationalist movements: both Methodist Korean women and Polish women in the Women's National Alliance raised funds for advocates of independence and to advance social and political change on the other side, a kind of "patriotic feminism."[55] Other women worked to solve problems nearer at hand. German women in Chicago organized and operated their own home for the elderly. They followed a distinctly American model in doing so; in Germany the government and state-financed churches provided such services.[56] Autonomous female action led some immigrant women to differentiate their interests from those of men, and to develop a community perspective American women today would recognize as feminist. In New York City in the 1870s and 1880s, for example, a German women's socialist group at first functioned as a support organization for male socialists.[57] But while men continued to emphasize women's responsibilities for creating "one big socialist family" through their community work and remained ambivalent to female wage-earning, German women came to see the organizing of women workers and the pursuit of suffrage as equally important tasks for socialists.[58]

Male fraternalism also provided a model for women helping themselves toward economic independence. Organizations of single working women often focused on mutual aid. Like many male fraternals, the Lithuanian Woman's Alliance provided health insurance for its members.[59] Korean, Japanese, and Afro-Caribbean women banded together to create rotating credit associations which underwrote small female businesses or other female initiatives.[60] Other "female fraternals" engaged in a game of catch-up, offering women services denied them by men's organizations. For example, German Jewish women quickly organized a Young Women's Hebrew Association to duplicate for women the programs of the Young Men's Hebrew Association.[61]

Immigrant women's community activism aimed both to support women and to guarantee the survival of ethnic communities and ethnic loyalties. For immigrant women, the ethnic community probably remained a private space, shared with men, while the public world began in English-speaking and multiethnic arenas outside their communities—in workplaces and in institutions dominated by Americans or immigrants of other backgrounds.[62] Women who arrived in the United States as married adults rarely crossed that boundary into the English-speaking public world. But single immigrants, and immigrant daughters born in the U.S., could rarely avoid doing so. For Americans accustomed to defining women's entrance into the public sphere as emancipation or individualism, immigrant daughters' steps toward structural assimilation appear as first steps toward their liberation as women. However, their mothers' activism was an equally new and significant experiment in the assumption of responsibility and—within limits—of power closer to home.

BEYOND THE ETHNIC COMMUNITY

American workplaces drew grown men and children of both sexes beyond families, kin networks, neighborhoods, and community organizations into a multiethnic world. Not surprisingly, immigrant daughters explored mutual-help possibilities outside their communities more readily than their mothers. They learned to cooperate with fellow workers, many of them other immigrant women. They helped convince activist brethren and American women alike that "girl workers" could organize. These immigrant women built cross-gender alliances with multiethnic but male-dominated workers' organizations and cross-class alliances with American women reformers interested in labor's problems.

Immigrant women participated in some of the largest and most militant strikes in U.S. history, in the garment and textile industries.[63] While Irish, British, and German women helped create permanent labor organizations in these industries, Jewish and Italian women joined them later. Even the supposedly passive and submissive Mexican women of the Southwest had carved out a notable record of labor activism in canneries and garment factories by the middle of the twentieth century.[64] And even domestic servants sometimes organized to improve job options and hours of work.[65]

The example of family members and work colleagues encouraged immigrant girls to experiment with workplace voluntarism. Like their mothers in their neighborhoods, wage-earning daughters created female networks of friendship at work, a powerful source of solidarity in times of labor conflict.[66] Just as Irish, Jewish, and German men gained a reputation for labor activism in the nineteenth century, Irish and Jewish women also quickly moved into activism and labor leadership. And as Italian men increasingly joined unions in the twentieth century, so did Italian women.[67]

Family identities may have undermined some women's identification with wage-earning, weakening their commitment to challenge workplace problems,[68] but family economies supported young women workers who actually struck. Immigrant women gained a reputation as particularly determined strikers because family income pooling supported their persistence.[69] For some single immigrant women, too, the financial difficulties of surviving on female wages provoked labor action: independent female foreigners stood out among labor activists. Older, widowed women—especially Irish women in the collar industry—also figured prominently in labor conflicts.[70]

The generally exclusionary craft unions of the American Federation of Labor expressed hostility and indifference to immigrant women's problems and initiatives, even though immigrant men and their sons led the organizations. Male labor leaders often regarded female and foreign-born workers as unorganizable. The AF of L's general hostility to unskilled wage-workers and its support for a male family wage prevented many trade unionists from supporting female unionism.[71]

But conflict among women workers could prove equally troublesome. "Old immigrants" feared "new" in meat packing and garment production; these "new" female immigrants in turn looked askance when Afro-Caribbean, Puerto Rican, and African American women joined them on the job.[72] Ethnic locals of men and women unionists became almost as common as ethnic parishes. In predominantly female ethnic locals, furthermore, men monopolized leadership positions well into the twentieth century.[73]

Unskilled, ethnic, and female strikers sometimes turned to the IWW for assistance and leadership in the years prior to World War I. Most were not revolutionary syndicalists, but all could recognize an organization that valued solidarity across gender, ethnic, and racial lines. Mass strikes in Lawrence, Massachusetts, Paterson, New Jersey, and Little Falls, New York, drew on communal protest traditions of the Old World and on urban female neighborhood networks.[74] Women participated both as strikers and as "neighborhood women" who attacked strikebreakers closer to home. Strikers protested wage or hour cuts; neighborhood women sought instead to humiliate opponents in community eyes. They might remove the pants from a policeman before dumping him unceremoniously in the river, strip clothes off scabs, dirty them, cut their hair, or loudly harass their families.[75]

Native-born and middle-class American women reformers in the social welfare movement became aware of the special problems of young female wage-earners in industrial neighborhoods. Recognizing the hostility of male leaders to young women wage-earners, well-educated American reformers saw work with girl strikers as a way to support and to uplift "downtrodden sisters," while at the same time encouraging reform of industrial workplaces and cities. The Women's Trade Union League, founded in 1903 and surviving until 1950, facilitated a cross-class alliance of immigrant workers and middle-class reformers.[76]

The WTUL enjoyed impressive successes. Women's membership in the ILGWU in New York multiplied several times over; the proportion of organized women in New York reached a level unmatched today. Similarly, many women labor leaders in the early to mid-twentieth century got their start as immigrant activists in the WTUL. Labor activist Rose Schneiderman, for example, carried early WTUL experiments with worker education into the ILGWU.

Still, ethnic and class tensions shook the WTUL. Jewish and Irish immigrant girls believed in class struggle, organization, and action in the workplace. Middle-class allies instead hoped to introduce young workers to American gentility and the advantages of American democracy. As citizens, suffragists, and members of the native-born elite, they believed protective legislation could solve workers' problems. Some allies' open, and probably racist, dislike of Jewish immigrant women also marred the early years of New York's WTUL.[77]

The WTUL nonetheless succeeded as "a united front of women"[78] where the American suffrage movement failed. The U.S. women's suffrage movement peaked during the mass migrations of the early twentieth century. Abroad, educated women knew of the movement; several Norwegian feminists even migrated to the United States hoping to participate.[79] Immigrant men, however, varied widely in their attitudes toward the suffrage movement: Irish, Germans, and Italians seemed generally hostile, while Jews, Scandinavians, and Finns more often supported women's rights.[80]

Some immigrant WTUL activists joined the suffrage movement, but in organizations of their own—wage-earners' suffrage leagues organized on an English model and introduced by Harriet Stanton Blatch. These leagues argued that suffrage would help end female poverty, ignoring the arguments of middle-class suffragists who stressed that women's votes would counterbalance the votes of ignorant foreign-born and minority men.[81]

Immigrant supporters of women's rights seemed more interested in challenging the prejudices of men of their own backgrounds than in changing U.S. law.[82] Feminist ideas developing in revolutionary struggles in Mexico or Russia, or from the enfranchisement of Finnish women in 1906, worked a greater influence in immigrant communities than did the U.S. suffrage movement.[83] For those without citizenship, the vote seemed less relevant than female emancipation (as anarchist Emma Goldman defined it), women's rights in the labor movement,[84] or workers' power in industry (the goal of Irish activist "Mother" Mary Harris Jones). Immigrant women had their own feminist issues: they showed considerable interest in Margaret Sanger's early agitation for birth control, for example, but their concerns about sexuality and poverty did not build easy bridges to the suffrage movement.

Even after the passage of the Nineteenth Amendment, immigrant women played in politics a "part somewhat, but not much, more important than that played by snakes in the zoology of Ireland."[85] This was true, also, of American women generally; no women's voting bloc emerged in the 1920s, and American women generally failed to make much progress in mainstream politics as a result. But second-generation women like Shirley Chisholm and Belle Moskowitz did attain modest success as Democratic Party activists during and after the 1920s.[86]

Only in radical politics did immigrant women leave more of a mark. Jewish women shared with Jewish men a particular prominence as radicals.[87] Anarchism, with its emancipatory promises, also strongly attracted the foreign-born.[88] Within the Socialist Party, support for women's suffrage after 1907 forged a coalition of foreign-born German and American women.[89] By the 1930s, both foreign-born and second-generation women were also well represented in the leadership of the Communist Party.[90] West Indian women preferred radical activism, too, supporting Marcus Garvey, not the Republican Party.

The female reformers of the social welfare movement, many of whom were suffragists, had little better luck working with immigrant women. Many of the earliest social services and welfare organizations developed by female social reformers aimed to provide services to immigrant women and their children. But most of these "social housekeepers" were earnest Protestants. They were never able to abandon a missionary approach to welfare work. Pitifully small numbers of adult immigrant women used settlement services; Jewish and Catholic women preferred services offered within their own communities.[91]

Immigrant women did sometimes turn to social reformers in search of allies for their own causes, however. Donaldina Cameron's mission to rescue Chinese women from prostitution, for example, aimed to introduce immigrant women to "higher" American standards of morality and domesticity, by teaching prostitutes domestic service or garment making.[92] Chinese women used missions for their own ends—to escape an abusive husband, or one they did not love; to marry men met while working as a prostitute; to escape indenture.[93]

In similar fashion, immigrant women, children, and neighbors appealed to settlement workers or the Gerry Society (Children's Aid Society) when a violent husband, son, brother, father, or mother violated community norms of discipline or fair treatment. They did this even though they knew of, and resented, Gerry Society agents who "stole" children from parents who failed to meet American standards.[94] In searching for allies, immigrants discovered that American welfare activists gladly intervened on behalf of children but hesitated when faced with wife-beating.[95] Just as American suffragists were often frustrated in their search for foreign-born collaborators, immigrant women tended to find in native-born welfare activists exasperatingly selective sources of support.

HOW DIFFERENT TODAY?

Today, too, immigrant women's community lives remain invisible. Immigrant women entering the U.S. today may bring with them religious faiths—from Islam to Buddhism—little known or understood by Americans. Catholic practitioners of *vodou* and other forms of Afro-Caribbean religious syncretism such as Santería have attracted more—and more negative—attention.[96] Many vodou practitioners in Haitian communities in New York are women who specialize in domestic rituals while leaving to men the larger, louder, and more controversial ceremonies. The Haitian Mama Lola, for example, combines faith healing with general advice-giving through spirit possession. But she hides her altars and her spirit birthday celebrations from skeptical Brooklyn neighbors.[97]

Immigrant women from Portugal, Mexico, and other parts of Latin America often become labor activists in the same industries—garments, canning, textiles—where immigrant women earned a reputation for militancy in the early twentieth century.[98] Like immigrant daughters ninety years ago, today's married women workers "bring the family to work" by introducing family-style celebrations of birthdays, engagements, and retirements into the workplace. Their friendship networks also facilitate labor solidarity.[99] The fact that few Chinese men work in unionized jobs while many Mexican and Mexican American men do may explain the striking difference in activism in these two groups, but so may homeland traditions of labor radicalism. Collaborating with their male co-workers, female farmworkers from Mexico demonstrated considerable energy and skill in the organizing drives of the 1960s. Some UFW women participated as wives and daughters rather than wage-earners; they organized a nationwide boycott of grapes, lettuce, and Gallo wine. This boycott became a successful cross-class "united front" of poor women and middle-class housewives.[100]

The expansion of the welfare state in the twentieth century has also changed the lives of immigrant women as community activists. Whether from Mexico or Vietnam, immigrant women manage their family's contacts with government bureaucracies—the INS, the school, the health clinic.[101] This is a far from easy task. Undocumented women, of course, avoid contacts with public services for fear of discovery, but even women with secure legal status often hesitate to visit clinics or to apply for welfare or counseling.[102] In refugee resettlement programs, government offices, schools, clinics, and welfare agencies, foreign-born women still find themselves enmeshed in deeply hierarchical helping relationships with native-born women.[103]

The most recent wave of immigrants began arriving in the United States just as native-born minorities demanded governmental support for their community-based initiatives. Asian and Spanish-speaking immigrants' community groups could now claim government services and funding as racial minorities. When they did, they found themselves working alongside native-born and sometimes middle-class activists of Mexican, Puerto Rican, Chinese, Japanese, and African descent. Tensions easily developed between immigrant women concerned primarily with change in the homeland, minority (often female) professionals employed by welfare agencies, and ethnic activists, both male and female, who defined ethnicity in ways recently arrived immigrants did not understand.[104]

Immigrant women professionals also now work directly for government agencies to fund and provide services—employment, schools, care for the aged, children's recreation—pioneered as much by ethnic fraternal and women's organizations as by native-born reformers. While such immigrant professionals struggle hard to remain advocates for the communities, they also become bound by bureaucratic rules which have little to do with their clients' needs.[105] In New York's Chinatown, resentful immigrants deride the efforts of these "Chuppies"—Chinese Yuppies.[106]

Today's immigrant women, along with working-class and minority women, generally avoid American feminism.[107] Issues of abortion rights, sexual orientation, and sexual emancipation have not sparked alliances between foreign-born and native-born women. Immigrant women have been concerned instead with unwieldy immigration bureaucracies, low wages in industry and service jobs, poor schools, discrimination, street violence, and crime—not issues central to American feminists of recent decades.[108]

Immigrant women instead resemble African American women in organizing their own feminist organizations. They do so, typically, when they experience difficulties working with men of their own backgrounds. Although primarily a movement of Mexican Americans, the history of women in *el movimiento* (the Chicano movement) illustrates a number of contemporary versions of gender conflicts in ethnic voluntarism. Chicanas resembled their counterparts in the civil rights, student left, and black nationalist movements in gradually recognizing and then objecting to the sexual discrimination they experienced among male comrades. Reluctant to threaten ethnic solidarity, they initially announced that Mexican women "did not want to be liberated."[109] When Chicanas did begin organizing autonomously, male comrades accused them of selling out to white, middle-class feminists. Over time, Chicana activists developed a critique of both Anglo feminism and of Chicano sexism.[110] Like the immigrant feminists of the past, they focused on changing the position and status of women within their own communities. These female activists, too, used women's organizations to improve their options for joining men in a common struggle for community empowerment.

CONCLUSION

Both in the past and in the present, generation and class, more than ethnic background, have determined the kinds of cooperation immigrant women sought with men and with women outside their own communities. In the past, immigrant women turned mainly to the men of their own groups and to other immigrant women as allies; they worked cautiously with middle-class and native-born women, and they had almost no contacts with the racial minorities of this country. Immigrant men and women lived, not in unified or homogenous communities, but rather among competing networks of ethnic solidarity, based on kinship, neighborhood, and voluntary associations of many kinds. To the extent that we understand the community lives of today's immigrants, many of these patterns seem to hold true for the present, too. One difference stands out, however: immigrant community activists now work together with middle-class African Americans, Chicanas, and Puerto Ricans in government-funded welfare programs for minority communities.

We have almost no evidence that earlier immigrant women consciously imitated American women's collective action, though the similarities between the two groups are striking. Still, no matter how similar the social lives of Irish, Jewish, Norwegian, American white, or American black women, each remained by and large isolated within parallel community lives. Informal community activism almost never linked women across ethnic lines. But voluntarism sometimes did: immigrant daughters, as labor activists, created a multiethnic working-class sisterhood; they experimented with cross-class sisterliness as well.

Collective action among immigrant women encouraged a kind of female agency that African American women have called "lifting as we climb."[111] Women did not become community activists in order to create a separate female world, nor did men perceive their activism as creating one. Immigrant women moved beyond the family and kin group to preserve or to strengthen the families and communities they had built alongside of and in conflict with men.

As in the case of native-born women, however, class dynamics shaped their efforts at cooperation. Historians have long known that the voluntarism of immigrant daughters defined what is commonly labelled working-class activism—the female labor movement—in the United States. Voluntarism within ethnic communities can also be viewed as a class-specific phenomenon; as we will see in the next chapter, immigrant women demonstrated their middle-class status when they built volunteer careers in an ethnic women's public sphere. In American eyes, of course, they became social housekeepers, not egalitarian feminists.

Native-born elite social housekeepers—the female pioneers of welfare services—dedicated themselves to cleaning up the "houses" of working-class, immigrant, and minority communities. There, they found themselves in sharp conflict with capable women—from nuns to the NCJW—determined to offer services in their own way, to their "own kind." For immigrant social housekeepers, class status, female activism, and mutual aid were one.[112] They used their "brooms" simultaneously to sweep away native-born competitors, to guarantee their own status, and to promote ethnic group survival. Today's alliances of immigrant and native-born (often minority) welfare profession-als build on a different model. But whether this present-day united front of women will be as successful as yesterday's cross-class, multiethnic WTUL re-mains to be seen.

PART III.

Changing: Class and Culture in the Twentieth Century

SEVEN

Middle-Class Immigrants

Not all immigrants left lives of poverty and hardship on the other side; not all started at the bottom of the U.S. economy or remained there, struggling in poverty all their lives. Michiko Sato was the daughter of prosperous Hiroshima sugar merchants, yet she began her life in the United States working as a cook. On the other hand, Michelena Gaetano Profeta, a seamstress from a humble Sicilian family, eventually enjoyed considerable economic prosperity in the United States—by the 1920s her family owned a car and a big house, and she enjoyed restaurant meals and "shows" with her barber husband before the Great Depression broke the family's luck. And "Honey" Barredo, who, as we saw in chapter 2, left the Philippines for the United States in order to pursue a career in dance, eventually became prima ballerina with the Atlanta ballet.

Women's class status raises tricky theoretical questions, which become more complex when women are also foreign-born. Who, after all, is middle-class? For women, class status may be determined as much by family status or husband's earnings as by individual accomplishment. Class hierarchies, furthermore, are regional and national, not international. Elite status in politically or economically weak countries does not guarantee middle-class status in the United States. (Dependency theorists have been known to call third world elites the lumpenbourgeoisie of the world economy.)[1]

In this chapter, above-average education, a family income significantly higher than that of their fellow immigrants, professional status, or a long-term career loosely define immigrants as middle-class. Measured in any of these ways, the representation of middle-class immigrants of both sexes has increased remarkably in the twentieth century. In the past, immigrants may have sought upward mobility by migrating, but few had been middle-class in the judgment of their peers on the other side. Women professionals were only a tiny percentage of nineteenth-century immigrants, but they alone make up more than a quarter of today's adult female immigrants. Both refugees and students often originate in elite third-world families, and they, too, are well represented among twentieth-century immigrants. Not all remain middle-class in the United States, however: downward mobility is a surprisingly common experience, especially for women. Still, like American women generally, immigrant women more often pursue careers today than in the past; their occupational choices, furthermore, have changed strikingly since 1920.

MIDDLE-CLASS IMMIGRANT WOMEN

While heavily outnumbered by settlers and labor migrants, middle-class refugees did come to the United States in the past. The German Forty-Eighters, fleeing the aftermath of the failed liberal revolutions of 1848, provide one nineteenth-century example of middle-class exiles.[2] Normally excluded from politics on the other side, women in Forty-Eighter families nevertheless knew of and were influenced by the political activism of the men of their families. Mathilde Giesele Anneke (who actually did fight alongside her military husband in the revolution of 1848) became a strong supporter of women's rights and women's education in the United States. Her feminism reflected the Forty-Eighters' concern with human emancipation from the monarchic government and church tyranny. Working in German-speaking communities in Milwaukee and on the East Coast, Anneke enjoyed success as a writer and publicist. She eventually separated from her husband, published *Die Deutsche Frauenzeitung,* and founded the Milwaukee Töchter Institut, an academy for German girls.[3]

In the twentieth century, middle-class Jews fleeing persecution in Nazi Germany also sought refuge in the United States.[4] Refugee German women of Jewish background (Hannah Arendt;[5] Charlotte Malachowski Buehler;[6] and Tilly Edinger, Frieda Fromm-Reichmann, and Catherine Brieger Stern[7]) formed the largest and most highly educated group of notable immigrant women in U.S. history. They were joined by women psychoanalysts like Karen Horney, who, although not Jewish or even necessarily anti-Nazi, found their entire profession attacked by Hitler as "Jewish."[8] Although middle-class German Jewish women were actually less likely than other German women to earn wages, those who did work pursued highly specialized professional careers. Having received a female education, furthermore, many German Jewish women had learned English prior to migration.[9]

Still, like other refugees, including the Cubans of the 1960s and the Southeast Asians of the 1970s and 1980s, most German Jewish women experienced periods of downward mobility upon arrival in the United States. Some could not work in their profession. Charlotte Buehler, for instance, could not survive as a researcher in the United States; she found work instead in clinical psychology. Because many Jewish women scholars had scholar husbands and collaborative marriages, antinepotism restrictions at U.S. universities posed great hardships. Nobel Prize winner Maria Goeppert-Mayer accepted a professorship without pay to evade such rules.[10]

For the much larger group of German Jewish women who had not worked outside the home, downward mobility meant seeking a job and earning wages for the first time. It also meant learning to manage a household without servants.[11] German Jewish refugee women in the 1930s considered it essential to avoid upsetting husbands or children already threatened by change and economic insecurity. As wage-earning wives, they struggled to continue familiar household routines and to do most domestic work themselves, to maintain at least the appearances of traditional bourgeois family life under difficult circumstances. They served multicourse, if simple, meals; they insisted on proper table service. "She has to cook dinner," one refugee man noted, "for most European men do not know how to cook. . . . "[12] Some women found such challenges creative—others found them draining.

Although well educated, a surprising number of German Jewish women in the 1930s first worked in that traditionally foreign and female job—domestic service.[13] Today, too, middle-class women from the Caribbean and South America discover these are the only jobs open to them. It is not unusual for migration to transform an elite woman of the third world "from mistress to servant,"[14] or for former teachers to work as nannies. Even women with transferable professions find themselves clustered in less prestigious jobs: while native-born doctors work in private practices, foreign-born physicians now fill the ranks of hospital employees, especially in urban public hospitals.[15] Nurses from Samoa disproportionately find jobs in geriatric care.[16]

Downward mobility can foster a strong commitment to female wage-earning, even among groups—like Cuban refugees—who discouraged female wage-earning prior to migration. Cuban women initially saw wage-earning in factories and offices as simply a way to regain a lost standard of living or to ensure education for the next generation. So motivated, they worked for pay in far larger proportions than other immigrant women or native-born Spanish-speaking women.[17] By pooling wages, Cuban refugee families could indeed educate their children for middle-class professions.[18] Over time, however, women developed more intrinsic motivations for working. They acknowledged that they enjoyed their work, and benefited from it. They no longer saw wage-earning as a necessary evil or stopgap. Not surprisingly, their daughters saw careers as normal foundations for autonomous and satisfying lives as middle-class American women.

For much larger groups of women and men immigrants of humble background, especially in the past, migration to the United States opened possibilities for upward mobility into middle-class comfort. Although women had often worked hard to ensure family economic success, fiction and family myth typically portray women as recipients, not achievers, of upward mobility. Middle-class comfort for women, furthermore, meant domesticity as American women had defined it: recall Maria Zambello's portrait of the good and "up-to-date" manners of her daughters. Immigrant writers and American observers, however, often poked fun at immigrant women's efforts to transform themselves into American ladies:

> Mrs. Cohen, a fat, middle-class woman, lay on a sofa. She glittered like an ice-cream parlor. . . . Her bleached yellow head blazed with diamond combs. . . . She looked like some vulgar, pretentious prostitute, but was only the typical wife of a Jewish nouveau riche. "Ach, what a headache! How I have to suffer with these headaches! . . . I should not eat at restaurants. My cook's food is better for me; I am of a very nervous nature."[19]

Becoming a lady required women to learn the rules of American domesticity. This was not an easy task for women trained to view life as a hard struggle and to work incessantly for the needs of others. Women who had worked as domestic servants had occasion to observe the domestic culture of American women and to imitate it if they chose, but many urban wives and mothers never saw the inside of an American home.[20] Upwardly mobile, ambitious immigrant women probably turned to social settlements and their elite female workers for the advice, examples, and domestic lessons the settlements were eager to deliver.[21]

Upward mobility also meant acquiring new habits of consumption, leisure activities, community activism, and (by the 1920s) self-beautification. For many immigrant women, models for each probably came initially from the homeland—yet these could differ from American expectations of middle-class women. Chinese merchant wives with their bound feet symbolized adherence to Old World modes of prosperity. At the same time, however, some Chinese merchants preferred women educated in Donaldina Cameron's missions precisely because they had been introduced to American domestic ideals there.[22]

Most portraits of upwardly mobile women are of Jewish immigrants. The popularity of stereotypes of female Jewish "allrightniks" (see chapter 6 above), "dolls," and—more recently—"princesses" reveals deep American ambivalence toward foreign-born or ethnic women who acquire the material perquisites and leisure of American middle-class life. All three stereotypes focus on Jewish women's alleged obsessive and exaggerated concern with possessions, status, and personal physical appearance.[23] At their most sympathetic, observers might note how meaningless a vigorous woman could find the enforced leisure of American bourgeois life. More often, Americans merely disparaged the enormous energy immigrant women could devote to emulating American customs. Social workers mocked immigrant women who decorated their homes with plush furniture, "Spanish runners," lace curtains, or flocked wallpaper; the more objective conceded that immigrant women's "bric-a-brac" were "not a whit more hideous than their more expensive counterparts." Other Americans (along with conservative immigrant parents) worried over the morality of immigrant girls adopting large picture hats, silk dresses, or fur pieces.[24] In both cases, the purchase of middle-class comforts seemed to reflect an inappropriate absorption with the self, at once uppity and insecure.

If Americans first developed negative images of upwardly mobile women, it was more often immigrant writers—many of them sons of immigrant mothers—who transformed them into biting and widely popular stereotypes. Feminist scholars trace the tenacity of jokes about Jewish women as devouring wives and mothers and as selfish shoppers to Jewish men—not to condescending Americans.[25]

Contemporary women from the third world experience other difficulties adjusting to middle-class expectations. Today, education and professional careers increasingly mark middle-class status around the world. But middle-class Americans' assumptions about female sexuality can place conflicting demands on upwardly mobile immigrant women. In prerevolutionary Cuba, for example, upper-class men displayed their status by appearing in public with attractive mistresses. In the United States, they can neither afford this display nor find cultural support for it. Cuban wives say they are happy to put mistresses out of their lives, yet they also feel new pressure to care for their appearance and to remain slim so husbands will have an attractive woman to affirm their economic success.[26]

Both immigrant men and immigrant women find the paths to middle-class prosperity complex ones. More or less bourgeois origins on the other side may make initial adjustment to the United States—with its expectation that immigrants start in humble positions—a difficult process of dealing with temporarily lost status. At the same time, those who move up into the middle class often find that a middle-class lifestyle is harder to acquire than material possessions. And foreign-born women who too visibly claim leisure and America's material abundance as their own find themselves criticized as selfish by Americans and by men of their own ethnicity.

BRAIN DRAINS: MIGRATORY CAREERS

The pursuit of education, training, and career advancement has always motivated migration, but this is especially true for twentieth-century migrants. Some scholars even regard "brain drain" migrations of students and careerists as a special type of migration. Still, today's brain drain from third world nations arouses heated controversy, for some believe it inhibits economic development on the other side.[27]

The professional opportunities drawing educated immigrants to the United States changed significantly from the nineteenth to the twentieth century, as the country changed from an agricultural and isolationist backwater into an expanding and industrializing world power. In the nineteenth century, the United States demanded brawn more than brain, and a native-born, white, and Anglo-American Protestant elite monopolized the limited market for brain work. But culturally, this American elite possessed little self-confidence, looking to Europe in such matters. Thus it was in the performing and other arts that cultivated immigrant men and women first clustered.

With their traveling troupes and concert tours, the performing arts encouraged migratory careers. Local tours of performers gradually extended into transatlantic journeys, bringing whole families of immigrant actors and actresses to the United States. Caroline Chapman was typical. Born illegitimately into an English theatrical family, she traveled with them to the United States, where they operated the first showboat on the Ohio and Mississippi Rivers. Later, individuals like ballerina Maria Bonfanti came to the United States as adult "stars" instead.[28]

Immigrants from England and Ireland figured prominently on the English-speaking American stage in the nineteenth century.[29] Americans praised the English Julia Marlowe as the greatest romantic actress of the century.[30] Fanny Kemble became almost as well known for her writings on her temporary American life and unhappy marriage as for her acting.[31] Troupes of non-English-speaking actresses and actors also played in every major immigrant settlement, in Yiddish, German, or Italian theaters.[32] Members of both groups developed truly transatlantic careers. The Canadian Julia Arthur, for example, first made a name for herself as an actress touring the United States. After study in Germany and England, she worked for a number of years in a San Francisco company before venturing to London to begin her years performing Shakespeare. She then toured the United States again with an English company and afterwards began her own American company. Polish-born Berta Gersten began her career in the Yiddish theaters of the Lower East Side of New York before touring the major cities of North and South America and Europe, including her birthplace.

By the late nineteenth century, instrumentalists and opera singers had joined migratory actresses. Less dependent on English-language facility, more female performers now came from the southern and eastern European homelands which were sending the new immigrants of the period. New musical stars included singers (like Italians Luisa Tetrazzini[33] and Adelina Patti, Mexican Lydia Mendoza,[34] Polish Marcella Sembrich, German Lotte Lehman,[35] Romanian Alma Gluck,[36] and Scottish Mary Garden), stage actresses like Sarah Bernhardt,[37] and instrumentalists like Italian violinist Camilla Urso and Venezuelan pianist Teresa Carreño. Wealthy American cities became ever more important stops on the concert tours of peripatetic male and female performers.

The cultural institutions of the United States remain an important draw for talented women and men around the world to this day. But international artists who perform in Hollywood or at the Metropolitan Opera today are overshadowed by the far greater numbers of foreign-born women who in the twentieth century view migration to the United States as an important stage in the pursuit of technical or scientific careers. Health care workers are the largest group of female professionals migrating to the United States, but engineers, computer technologists, and scientists also find many employers for their skills in the United States.

Many begin their migrations as students. The earliest foreign students in the United States, including Charlotte Manye Maxexe—the first African woman to graduate from a U.S. university—returned to their homelands.[38] Today, however, residence in the United States as a foreign student is one of the best predictors of eventual settlement in the United States.[39]

Among students, unlike other present-day migrant groups, women remain a minority. In 1980, 211,000 men and 94,000 foreign-born women were studying at American universities; ten years later, the 149,000 foreign-born female students in the United States made up a larger group, but constituted only 37 percent of foreign students in the country.[40] Study in the United States apparently produces few changes in men's gender attitudes, but women students—exceptional in having convinced families to support their study abroad in the first place—often adapt quickly to an environment that encourages experiments with female independence and accomplishment.[41] Sometimes, however, women students have special problems because their notions of female sexual propriety conflict sharply with American ones.[42]

Like men, women foreign students enroll disproportionately in technical and scientific programs of study. But marriage, more often than their professions, brings them to the United States later in life. Only one in five of the foreign-born women listed in *Who's Who of American Women* entered the United States to work. About half instead had either arrived in the United States as children (migrating with their parents) or had settled in the United States within a year of marriage to an American man. An early foreign student— Persia Crawford Campbell, an Australian-born economist and consumer advocate—illustrates a common pattern. Campbell came to the U.S. to study at Bryn Mawr. After a number of years in her homeland, she returned to the United States with a Harvard fellowship. She then remained in the United States after marrying an American.[43]

IMMIGRANT WOMEN AND THEIR CAREERS

Even those women who come to the United States for other reasons have found that careers for themselves and their daughters require increasing levels of education. In the past, foreigners seemed to lag behind native-born Americans in their commitment to education, especially female education. Today, however, both the educational expectations and the educational achievements of the foreign-born exceed those of the native-born. And gender distinctions may now be sharper among native- than foreign-born.

In the nineteenth century, education and literacy varied enormously among immigrants arriving in the United States. Women and men from subsistence economies rarely had more than a few years of schooling, but women and men from developing economies about duplicated the limited education of nineteenth-century Americans. Both men and women immigrants to the United States had literacy rates superior to those who remained behind,[44] but while almost all Scandinavian women could read and write, only about a third of Italian women could. Today, by contrast, immigrant women (12.5%) are more likely to have completed advanced degrees than native-born women (7.5%).[45]

Not surprisingly, immigrant parents of the past differed in their attitudes toward compulsory U.S. schooling, as well as in their financial ability to support students. Jewish immigrants both desired the education of their children and were most able to support its pursuit. Educational accomplishments remained more modest among the children of poorer immigrants, whether Irish, Italian, or Mexican.[46] Still, compulsory elementary education in the United States guaranteed that ethnic, class, and gender differences emerged mainly in the amount of schooling offered youngsters of high school and college age.

Middle-class and business families of all ethnic backgrounds expected their children to graduate from high school prepared for white-collar jobs leading to business or professional careers.[47] In poorer families, parents instead might choose to educate only one child—and that one child was frequently male. Girls more often went to work to support the education of their brothers than the other way around. As we learn from Mary Antin's tales of her own schooling and from scholarly studies of high school and college attendance, Jewish women clearly demonstrated the lust for learning they shared with men, often attending night school when poverty forced them to find jobs.[48] Yet even Jewish parents, with their generally strong support of education for both sexes, more often sacrificed the education of girls than that of boys when resources were scarce. Italian and German parents regularly argued that educating girls wasted family resources, as girls did not need education to marry and to do domestic work.[49] Birth order also mattered. In the highly supportive family of Sofia Kleegman, for example, two elder daughters migrated to the United States to pay for the emigration of family members. They then supported two younger sisters through medical school.[50]

Daughters of immigrants gradually attained educational parity with native-born Americans in the twentieth century, while still lagging slightly behind their brothers.[51] The discrepancy between male and female education remained quite pronounced in some groups. As late as the 1960s, for example, immigrant Italian parents regularly advised daughters to prepare themselves for clerical employment; their rates of college attendance lagged behind those of other women and of Italian American men as well.[52]

Perhaps because so many more of today's immigrants are themselves well educated and of middle-class origins, foreign-born Americans now seem more strongly committed to education and professional careers than either the immigrants of the past or their native-born American counterparts. Immigrant mothers have significantly higher expectations for the education of their sons and daughters than native-born mothers. Their daughters share these high expectations and surpass native-born Americans in their educational achievements.[53] Much public attention has focused on these new "model minorities" and on the educational accomplishments of Asian immigrant children.[54] But strong commitments to academic success can also be found among Jews from the Soviet Union, among West Indians, and among immigrants from Mexico and Central America.[55]

Mexican immigrant children, for example, are more often native speakers of Spanish than their native-born Mexican American (or Chicano) peers. Yet children born in Mexico stay in school longer and in greater proportions than native-born or later-generation Mexican Americans who have spoken English since childhood.[56] Immigrants and children like these commit themselves to education in part because they assume their investment will be rewarded.[57] Native-born minorities do not always share their optimism. Chicano youths may attack an ambitious peer as a "wannabee"—defining ambition and academic accomplishment as an Anglo or white trait.[58]

Today's immigrants exhibit no strong biases against female education. Some young women of Latin or Asian descent may have to abandon cultural habits of deference and holding silent to achieve as students,[59] but most studies of immigrant children's educational patterns find emphatic familial support for female as well as male accomplishment.[60] In fact, immigrant daughters are far more likely to pursue studies in scientific and technical fields than young American women generally.[61] Whatever their other attitudes toward gender, immigrants from the third world do not believe that females lack an aptitude for math and science.

Given their limited education, the immigrant women of the past seemed poorly positioned to pursue careers. Yet despite their educational disadvantages, foreign-born women made up roughly ten percent of the women in *Notable American Women* and *Notable American Women: The Modern Period* (the latter includes women living after 1950)—or close to their representation in the female population as a whole. The far larger group of second-generation daughters did not match the accomplishments of their foreign-born mothers.

Few of these high-achieving immigrant women had careers like those of the proverbial Horatio Alger heroes: few rose from rags on the other side to American riches. Instead, over two-thirds of notable immigrant women in the nineteenth and twentieth centuries had academic, professional, prosperous, or otherwise solidly middle-class parents. Unlike the average immigrant woman who worked as a domestic servant, notable immigrant women grew up in homes—both on the other side and in the United States—that employed servants. Even labor activists like Fannia Cohn sometimes had prosperous— if also politically radical—parents.

Just as immigrant women generally clustered in a few kinds of jobs in the wider economy, the careerists among them clustered in distinctive niches, too. Far more than native-born women, nineteenth-century immigrant women achieved their successes in the performing or other arts and as ethnoreligious community welfare activists. In the earlier part of the twentieth century they clustered disproportionately in business and in the labor movement. Today's notable immigrant women concentrate heavily in technical and scientific professions.

Compared to American women, surprisingly few foreign-born women built careers as feminists or women's rights activists. But there were some prominent exceptions to this generalization: English-born Anna Howard Shaw,[62] the Pole Ernestine Rose,[63] the Hungarian Rosika Schwimmer,[64] and the Scotswoman Frances Wright.[65] The need to speak English seems to have been a formidable obstacle for some: the Norwegian feminist Aasta Hansteen, who had come to the United States to experience what she believed were unique opportunities for women, returned home in frustration because of language difficulties.[66]

The concentration of foreign-born women in the performing and other arts reflects both brain drain migrations and the peculiarities of the performing arts as a professional niche defined by race and ethnicity. Immigrant women shared careers in arts and entertainment with native-born African-American women, especially in the nineteenth century. While only slightly more than one in ten of all notable women worked as actresses, singers, musicians, and entertainers, roughly forty percent of notable nineteenth-century immigrant women, and about the same proportion of the African American women listed in *Notable Black Women*, worked in these fields.[67]

If African Americans created jazz as an American art form, and African American women shaped distinctly female traditions within it,[68] immigrants arguably created forms of popular culture within which foreign-born women also carved out distinctive specialties as performers.[69] English actresses Louisa Lane Drew, Laura Keene, and Matilda Vining Wood directed their own theaters, introducing new plays and creative art forms to an American public. The first successful ballerina in the U.S. was the French-woman Madame Placide (Suzanne Douvillier). The Guggenheim Museum and its collection of modern or nonobjective art trace their origins to an immigrant woman's education (and manipulation) of a wealthy New York family; the film archive of the Museum of Modern Art has its origins with the energetic collecting efforts of British migrant Iris Barry. Distinctively American cultural forms, from riverboats, vaudeville, and honky-tonk to Hollywood, drew on the talents of immigrant women (and their daughters) like Sophie Tucker, Theda Bara, "Molly" Berg, "Texas" Guinan, Marie Dressler, and Carmen Miranda.[70]

Less positively, foreign-born women's concentration in the performing and other arts also reflected American views of foreigners as exotic, sexualized, and potentially immoral—an image shared with the women of the racial minorities. Women performers of all backgrounds in the nineteenth century attracted moral censure from Protestant Americans; performing was held to be too public an activity for women, whose sphere was more properly a domestic one. And many immigrant female performers' behavior—their divorces and remarriages, sexual liaisons, and personal idiosyncracies—went well beyond American norms of proper female modesty. Even present-day authors see pioneering immigrant female performers more as adventuresses than cultural innovators. Among them, the infamous Irish-born Lola Montez, who entertained the gold rush miners in California, is probably the best known. Madame Blavatsky, the founder of Theosophy and a famous nineteenth-century occultist, also both scandalized and entertained Americans with her many liaisons and her plans for Theosophist activities on three continents.[71]

Another sizeable group of immigrant women made careers for themselves as ethnic and religious activists, especially in the nineteenth century. Founders of nationwide female ethnic and religious organizations, like the National Council of Jewish Women's Hannah Solomon, Hadassah's Henrietta Szold, and Rebekah Bettelheim Kohut, the Jewish community activist par excellence, represent this path to achievement.[72] Also qualifying as career women activists are the founders of large Catholic sisterhoods[73] (Rose Philippine Duchesne of the Order of the Sacred Heart,[74] Mother Marie Joseph Butler of the Marymount Schools and Colleges, the German Mother Benedicta Riepp and the "American saint," Italian Mother Francis Xavier Cabrini),[75] and the spiritual leader of the Amana Society, the German Barbara Heinemann. These were women who created professional jobs within their own communities, by offering the kind of services American women welfare activists offered from without.

Immigrant community activists—male and female—came from middle-class backgrounds, typically from the same families. Activism within their own communities may have been the only form of leadership open to middle-class immigrant women, for their languages, foreignness, and especially their religion (whether Catholic or Jewish) hindered them from participating in the public world of native-born, Protestant middle-class women. Not surprisingly, their careers sought to guarantee the survival of ethnic institutions and ethnic identity.

By the twentieth century, new areas of immigrant female career specialization appeared, first in business and in the American labor movement, and most recently in technical and scientific employment. Some businesswomen like Jennie Grossinger got their start in family enterprises. Although working in a small family business, Grossinger seemed specially attuned to innovative business techniques, most notably advertising; students of the hotel industry usually attribute the success of the Grossinger family resort to her creative ideas.[76] Ida Cohen Rosenthal, too, grew up working in a family clothing business; after marriage she collaborated with her husband in yet another clothing shop. Rosenthal designed the modern brassiere, transforming her family business into Maidenform Bras. Of her role in the enterprise, Rosenthal said "Quality we give them. Delivery we give them. I add personality."

Standing sharply apart from the world of family enterprise were entrepreneurs Hattie Carnegie in the fashion arena and Helena Rubinstein, the founder of a huge international beauty concern. Beginning in Australia with 12 pots of a face cream developed by her mother, the Polish Jewish Rubinstein initially developed her business in London and Paris. Marriage to an American (from whom she later separated, because—she argued—of her business involvement) brought her to New York. From there she further expanded her business in the years after World War I, pioneering the sale of cosmetics to the new women of the 1920s.[77] Although these independent women prospered by selling to other women, the Irish entrepreneur Nellie Cashman was able to do her business among men, running boarding houses and restaurants for miners on frontiers from Arizona to Alaska.[78]

The life of Anna Trow Lohmann reminds us that immigrants have also specialized in illicit business. Most students of immigration history know immigrants made money evading antialcohol and antiprostitution laws.[79] They know that today's immigrants play an important role in organizing an illicit drug trade.[80] But few know of the English-born Lohman (Madame Restell), known as "the wickedest woman in New York" and pursued by the police for providing abortions as well as other services to women with reproductive complaints.[81]

Twentieth-century immigrant women and their daughters also built careers in the labor movement that developed in industrial workplaces dominated by foreign-born women. In the 1870s and 1880s, the Knights of Labor had encouraged the organization of housewives as well as women wage-earners, and for a time employed the Irish-born Leonora Barry to organize females. Unlike Barry, the later Irish labor agitator Mary "Mother" Jones worked primarily with men, in the United Mine Workers; she disapproved of female wage-earning. Blending labor radicalism with conventional views about gender roles, Jones continues to puzzle her many biographers, one of whom described her as a "kind of secular nun."[82] Other immigrant women also gained attention for their support of leftist and labor causes generally— most notably the much-studied Emma Goldman,[83] along with the lesser-known Anna Sullivan,[84] Rose Pastor Stokes,[85] Clara Lemlich,[86] Rosa Lemberg, Luisa Morena,[87] Elizabeth Morgan,[88] Theresa Malkiel,[89] and the second-generation Elizabeth Gurley Flynn[90] and Margaret Dreier Robins.[91] Unlike "Mother" Jones, all combined labor radicalism with a strong interest in female emancipation; this group gained notoriety for their unconventional relationships with men.

Most women labor activists emerged from the garment industry and its major unions, the International Ladies Garment Workers Union and the Amalgamated Clothing Workers of America. There, they pioneered in workers' education, the organization of women, and industrial unionism.[92] Given the large female workforce in garments and the sizeable female membership in the ILGWU and the ACWA, the list of women leaders seems a short one. A handful of eastern European Jewish women (Rose Pesotta,[93] Pauline Newman,[94] Fannia Cohn,[95] Rose Schneiderman,[96] and Dorothy Bellanca)[97] and one Italian woman (Angela Bambace)[98] rose to positions of authority over considerable male opposition. Today, Mexican immigrant women and their daughters, like Hope Mendoza Schechter, stand out as labor activists.[99]

The professions of immigrant women in the nineteenth and early twentieth centuries more resembled the professions and achievements of men of their own backgrounds than they did those of native-born women. Jewish women shared with Jewish men their concentration in business, labor, and the learned professions.[100] Irish women shared with Irish men their activism in labor and labor politics.

In combining community activism or careers in business, the arts, or labor reform, with marriage and family commitments, foreign-born women duplicated the professional patterns of African-American women.[101] However, it would be erroneous to attribute their similarities to imitation. The tendency of women of both immigrant and racial minorities to combine careers with marriage and family life reflected similar gender dynamics within ethnic communities, as well as the special circumstances of particular professions. Actresses, of course, often grew up in family troupes; they married other actors, formed new family professional groups of their own,[102] or married men involved in the business end of theater.[103] Businesswomen and scholarly women, too, built collaborative marriages where husbands and wives worked on common projects, whether selling Maidenform bras or—as in the case of Sidonie Gruenberg—writing childrearing books for parents.

The much smaller group of immigrant women who followed prevailing white patterns of professional accomplishment—that is, by remaining unmarried in order to pursue careers—often had close contacts with native-born women who may have served as role models. Mary Anderson,[104] Elisabeth Christman, and Rose Schneiderman—labor activists all—probably learned these patterns of professional achievement through their work with the Women's Trade Union League. Emma Lundberg, a social welfare worker, followed the example of her close associate, Katharine Lenroot (chief of the Children's Bureau). She, like some of the WTUL labor activists of foreign birth, formed life-long female friendships—sometimes called "Boston marriages." Women of Canadian and British background—for example, the Canadian botanist Alice Eastwood, the Australian Alice Henry,[105] and the English-raised archaeologist and museum curator Gisela Richter—more often pursued achievement through celibacy.

Not every unmarried immigrant woman had adopted specifically American models of celibate caréerism. Neither Rose Pesotta nor Emma Goldman married, but this reflected their anarchist convictions, not their Americanization. Neither did the most numerous of unmarried immigrant women with careers—Catholic sisters—respond to the American single-careerist model, even though their lives somewhat resembled those of college-educated American women.

Today, almost two-thirds of the foreign-born women listed in *Who's Who of American Women* work in technical or entrepreneurial fields. While only ten percent (about the average for all notable American women) work in the arts, almost a fifth have excelled in business, one in seven are physicians, and an equal proportion are university professors.[106] Although they may not know it, foreign-born women physicians follow an especially long tradition: the first American woman physician was the English-born Elizabeth Blackwell,[107] while the first female Nobel Prize winner in medicine was the Russian immigrant Gerty Radnitz Cori.[108]

Far fewer immigrant women today than in the past achieve prominence by working within their own communities.[109] Most immigrant businesswomen, for example, work for large corporations with no special ties to particular ethnic communities. Of course some women, like men, use connections to their homelands to build or lead international enterprises—whether a Puerto Rican bank, a Spanish steamship company, or a Jewish welfare foundation, to name just a few employers of professional immigrant women. These female professionals, furthermore, are more likely to belong to professional associations and special organizations for women in their professions than they are to belong to ethnic associations of any sort.

Finally, both past and present, immigrant women authors have achieved special recognition as interpreters of the immigrant experience for American readers. Mary Antin's writings reassured Americans that immigrants at the turn of the century did in fact desire to become American.[110] Women scholars have rediscovered the writings of Anzia Yezierska, an author whose battles for independence speak to feminist sensibilities.[111] The study of literary traditions built by immigrant women is a growing scholarly specialty.[112] Literary critics and autobiographers alike identify writing as both an act of rebellion and a means to survival for foreign-born women. The autobiographical and fictional writings of Paule Marshall,[113] Maxine Hong Kingston,[114] and Jamaica Kincaid[115] have introduced more Americans to contemporary migrations than any scholarly study has. All point to the sense of freedom tempered with strong ambivalence that characterize women's confrontation with American life.

CONCLUSION

Whether on the other side or in the United States, middle-class women have enjoyed advantages over working-class or farm-born sister migrants in pursuing education, ambition, and accomplishment. These advantages, furthermore, are far more marked today than in the past. The relative ease with which many technically trained middle-class women foreigners now find work in the United States points to the increasingly international nature of class formation in an integrating world economy. Moving to the United States can itself give women a sense of upward mobility. Because foreign-born women compare their lives to those on the other side, and not to the middle or upper classes of the United States, they view their lives more positively, and with greater hope, than do many native-born minority women.

Still, even middle-class and very well educated immigrant women have often encountered troubling obstacles upon migration to the United States. Many moved downward in terms of money, jobs and class after arrival. They also more easily acquired recognition as leaders and innovators within their segmented ethnic communities than outside them. In a sense immigrant notables, male and female, formed the upper crust of immigrant communities; if they ventured outside, they were no more than marginal members of the American middle classes. Their experiences remind us that theoreticians have not grappled adequately with the location and mutability of class status in a multiethnic society like the United States.

Recently, all American women have come to replicate the patterns of foreign-born and African American working women in combining lifelong work and careers with marriage and childrearing. If immigrant women did not always have more family support for their career choices, then at least they—like African American women in the past—felt less inclined to reject family claims and marriage in their pursuit of achievement. But there were differences, too. In the past, at least, African American females obtained more education on average than foreign-born women or their daughters—yet that education did not translate into professional recognition comparable to that of elite white women or substantially different from the career patterns of their less educated foreign-born peers.[116] Immigrant women's concentration in community service and the performing arts, furthermore, disappeared in the twentieth century, while both remain important niches for African American female accomplishment down to the present.

Elite immigrant parents and husbands often supported women's ambitions, suggesting that the elites of the other side—past and present—tolerated more, not less, gender equality than the Anglo-American middle classes of the nineteenth century. For an immigrant women of modest origins, however, pursuit of a life's work or a career might require severance of family ties. In her study of Jewish women's autobiographies, Sally Ann Drucker notes that Yezierska, Antin, Cohen, and Elizabeth Stern all depended on non-Jewish mentors and on romantic unions with gentile men to help them break away from families that considered them selfish for their ambitions.[117]

Immigrant women performers and artists demonstrate even more clearly how sexual and familial experimentation, rather than conformity to family dictates or ethnic traditions, might accompany female ambition and accomplishment. Rebels in the heterosexual arena, relatively few of these foreign-born free spirits took the American path to achievement through celibacy, unmarried sisterhood, or Boston marriage. Perhaps this explains the extraordinary popularity Emma Goldman enjoyed among the most recent wave of young feminists, who named daughters, feminist bookstores, magazines, and their housepets after her. Decidedly and proudly an outsider among female American notables, Goldman offered a trenchant critique of female achievement, American-style. She pointedly rejected what she perceived as American feminists' and social housekeepers' Puritanism. And she claimed passion—including free love—as central to both women's emancipation and the emancipation of the poor.

The lives of middle-class immigrant women thus present us with a paradox. They both enjoyed greater familial and marital support for their ambitions and more often experimented with new sexual, marital, and familial ties with men than native-born white women. Their lives seem simultaneously more enclosed in ethnic communities and freer from cultural constraints, especially in the nineteenth century. In very different arenas, this paradox repeats itself in the complex story of how immigrant women's descendants changed to "become American." In that story, too, women appear as both the most assiduous conservers of old ways and the most eager of cultural innovators.

EIGHT

Preservation and Innovation

When two societies come together, they provoke the mutual antagonisms and adjustments termed cultural change.[1] For the last four hundred years, an expanding world capitalist economy has brought large numbers of people together, primarily through political centralization and migration. In so doing, this economy may be said to have encouraged cultural innovation and diversification, as well as the creation of new ethnic and racial groups.[2] In another sense, however, capitalism has undermined cultural diversity, for it has not brought people together on terms of economic or social equality. Cultural differences have been assessed as "better" and "worse," or "inferior" and "superior." Under these conditions, the less powerful may grow to mistrust their own cultural values and seek to acquire those of the more powerful.

The study of immigrant cultural change likewise has a long history. Researchers have shifted away from examining immigrants' inability to adapt, instead demonstrating their easy and relatively complete assimilation and adaptation. Most recently, scholars of "the new ethnicity" have discovered first the persistence, and then the construction of ethnic identity among immigrants' descendants.[3]

More specifically, scholars have drastically changed their views of immigrant women's cultural changes over the last decade. Ninety years ago, sociologists described immigrant women as resisting change; they considered women's reluctance a side effect of their passivity, isolation, and subordination: "She cannot keep up with [her husband and children]," wrote one.[4] Present-day women's historians instead describe how immigrant women actively, if selectively, broke ties with parental traditions to pursue individual, American, or modern lives.[5] They argue that young immigrant women had specifically female reasons to distance themselves from homeland patriarchy and family interdependence. Because of their subordination, women had the least to lose through change.[6]

In sharp contrast to these positive views of cultural change among immigrant women in the United States, studies of a related area—colonized minorities in the third world—emphasize women's losses. They show how contact with capitalism and colonialism domesticated women by institutionalizing middle-class and Western concepts of gender. Viewed from this perspective, women's refusal to change culturally is a positive act of resistance, and one that defends female autonomy.[7]

With the exception of immigrants coming to the United States as young children, foreign-born women rarely could "become American" in their own lifetimes; cultural change continued into the lives of their children and grandchildren. And so did the adjustment of the United States to immigrant women and their descendants. This chapter draws on the limited materials describing immigrant women's cultural contacts with Americans to identify some particularly female dimensions of cultural change. Its main focus is on the descendants of the immigrants of the late nineteenth and early twentieth centuries.

AMERICAN IMAGES, IMMIGRANT IMAGES

Foreign- and native-born do not come together without preconceptions of each other. For the people of the other side, important sources of information about the United States were letters and word-of-mouth reports from returned immigrants. Today, popular culture and the American media also broadcast selective images of the United States. "I expected all Americans to be blond and blue-eyed, like Robert Redford," one immigrant reported.[8] For Americans, nineteenth-century missionaries and evolutionary anthropologists introduced key images of foreigners. Today, as citizens of a world power, Americans instead depend on televised news reports for images of the other side.

Alongside reports about land prices, high wages, plentiful food, and cheap clothing, nineteenth-century immigrant letter writers reported that the United States was a land "where women ruled." Cuban exile José Martí singled out for special negative comment the "exaggeratedly emancipated behavior of the women."[9] European peasants reported that American women did not work in fields and hired domestic servants to do their housework.[10] German men especially castigated the laziness of American women, who seemed to them a privileged leisure class.[11] An Irish church newspaper, for its part, dismissed Hull House activists as "tactless, hysterically emotional, childless female slummers."[12] Immigrant women reacted more positively to the American cult of true womanhood; a group of Slovenian peasant women waiting for a drink of water on Ellis Island cheered, "Hurray for America, where ladies come first!"[13] Irish women, with their own cultural traditions of sex segregation and celibacy, and Jewish women, with their culture's enthusiasm for human rights and education, saw in America's well-educated, independent, and reform-minded women the best expression of American democracy and personal freedom.[14]

Today's media images of American women as sexy yet career-oriented professionals and as married jugglers of children and briefcases can be equally confusing. "Americans seem to me to be very sex conscious," a West Indian woman observed already in the 1930s.[15] Latin parents today express fears that American women lack sexual modesty.[16] For many immigrants, then, American women have become ambivalent symbols of American individualism. Can family life survive female freedom? Native-born Americans themselves worry over the issue. Indeed, people around the world often believe that Americans have no real family ties.[17] Their criticisms focus as much on stereotypical lazy African American welfare mothers as on selfish white career women. "Get [these young mothers] a job," Mrs. Rosalyn Morris (whom we met in chapter 3) told an interviewer, "and put their children in a day care center."[18]

Americans past and present have focused on the material poverty and moral backwardness of peoples from the other side. Through the lens of Social Darwinism, they saw foreigners at worst as racially inferior ("unassimilable") and at best as benighted children waiting to be raised through contacts with white Westerners.[19] But because they have viewed men as breadwinners, Americans imagined the women of the other side more with pity than with fear or scorn. Americans in the nineteenth century generally believed that the status of women—measured by domesticity and bourgeois gentility (sexual modesty, manners, etc.)—reflected a society's evolution toward Anglo-American and Protestant standards. Europeans and Americans cited women's poor treatment at the hands of foreign men as justifications for imperial expansion and intervention in the lives of the poor. They saw European and Asian peasant women as unappreciated beasts of burden awaiting salvation from heathen male oppression. Missionaries repeatedly publicized the poor treatment of women in other religious traditions—the binding of Chinese women's feet, lecherous priests preying on cloistered nuns, the Jewish man's daily prayer thanking God he is not female.[20]

Today, Americans view the oppression of women in the third world as often in feminist as in religious terms, but parallels to the past are striking. Americans still too often describe third world women only in terms of their maltreatment at the hands of particularly backward and violent men and particularly patriarchal cultural traditions; the early feminist discussion of female circumcision in Middle Eastern and African countries provides only one example.[21] Criticism of patriarchy in other cultures remains an important prop for American ethnocentrism, casting foreign women as victims in need of the help of empowered or superior American women.

Mergers of Protestant morality with theories of social evolution also encouraged Victorian Americans to develop eroticized notions of foreign women (as they did also of the women of the United States' colonized minorities). Americans saw African American women as more sexually passionate and dangerous (because primitive) than passionless American ladies.[22] Accounts of Korean, Japanese, Chinese, and Jewish prostitutes produced similar images of foreign-born "exotics."[23] The popularity of dark (especially Jewish, Latin, and Asian) "vamps" in early films popularized eroticized images of female immigrants[24] which persist to the present.[25]

Immigrants and Americans came together with considerable ambivalence. Immigrants expected to change, but in ways they chose. Few immigrants imagined, could welcome, or could in fact succeed in making all of the changes Americans desired of them. Immigrants saw the United States as a land of significant opportunity, yet also as a country inhabited by a cold, individualistic people of odd and questionable morals. Significantly, immigrant men singled out American family life, American individualism, and American women for harsh criticism.

Given their own assumptions that theirs was the richest and freest country in the world, Americans expected immigrants would be eager to shed distinctive cultural traits. When they contemplated cultural change among women, they thought of it as *saving* women—often from the men of their own families and communities. Thus immigrant women's adjustment to life in the United States became, to some unmeasurable degree, a symbolic conflict for women's moral, familial, and sexual loyalties. Americans eagerly sought evidence of a group's Americanization in women's changing behavior, and believed that when reformers or schools "went after the women" they gained the children, too. Conversely, immigrant men, parents, and female ethnic leaders interpreted even minor changes in female behavior, especially among growing daughters, as signs of moral decay and ethnic suicide.[26] Immigrant women walked this symbolic minefield with great difficulty, but also, as we shall see, with considerable success.

MEASURING CHANGE

Cultural change is difficult to measure. Unable to explore the state of mental constructs among masses of ordinary people directly, scholars must depend on behavioral indicators. But the relationship between culture and behavior is complex; behavior may reflect cultural ideals or depart significantly from them.

Measured by their behavior, women immigrants and their descendants changed quickly.[27] They acquired jobs not much different from those of American women; their fertility fell to the American average; and, with few exceptions, the education of the third generation equaled or surpassed that of American women as a whole. Today, average family incomes of third-generation Catholic and Jewish Americans surpass those of longtime Americans.

Other measures point in the same direction. For women born on the other side and traveling to the United States as adults, learning English was a key marker of cultural change—and the most formidable challenge of American life. Illiterate, monolingual, and less educated people—regardless of gender—master a new language with difficulty after the age of about twelve or thirteen. In the United States, moreover, married immigrant women had fewer opportunities to learn English than their husbands, sons, and daughters. Not surprisingly, many immigrant children remembered with embarrassment mothers who spoke English haltingly if at all; social workers agreed that adult women lagged behind other family members in mastering English. "We speak no other language at home but that of our parents," one proud woman reminded an impatient son.[28] The children of immigrants were bilingual, speaking their mother tongue at home and English elsewhere. Generation, not gender, mattered: siblings of both sexes spoke English among themselves; parents addressed children in the mother tongue; the children responded in English.[29]

In most immigrant groups—including heavily segregated Asians—few immigrant sons or daughters passed on the mother tongues to their own children, the third generation. Only in the Southwest (where a native-born population of Spanish speakers preserved their language in rural villages and urban barrios, and where new immigrants arrived continuously from Mexico) did slight majorities of third generation sons and daughters learn Spanish at home.[30] By the third generation, linguistic change was far advanced in all immigrant groups.

American law automatically granted immigrants' American-born children citizenship, guaranteeing their civic Americanization. Gender assumptions among both immigrants and Americans deeply shaped naturalization rates for foreign-born parents, however. From 1855 until the passage of the Cable Act in 1923, married immigrant women changed citizenship with their husband's naturalization. After 1923, women, like men, had to demonstrate English competence and a knowledge of American history to naturalize.[31]

After the passage of the Cable Act, immigrant women's rate of naturalization (58 percent) lagged somewhat behind men's (62 percent).[32] Considerable numbers of immigrants, male and female, saw few benefits to citizenship. Immigrants of African descent had even fewer incentives to naturalize, since they might not obtain the franchise anyway. (Only 28 percent of West Indian men and only 22 percent of West Indian women had naturalized by 1930.)[33] By contrast, immigrant widows often struggled to become citizens eligible for mothers' pensions.[34]

Because cultural change and structural assimilation proceeded at differing rates, the second generation faced particularly complex choices. They interacted with more Americans than their parents did, but remained heavily influenced by parental values and power. Some second-generation girls tried to become what writer Maxine Hong Kingston called "American normal." Others remained firmly within the ethnic worlds of their families and communities. The largest group blended old and new in idiosyncratic ways that made sense in their particular lives. Immigrant children called this "walking on the edge," or living "between worlds." Others have labeled the product of this cultural coalescence "hyphenated" identities, whether Mexican, Italian or Norwegian American.[35]

Domestic servants most easily emulated American ways, having been exposed to them in such intimacy.[36] Women from the developing as opposed to the more subsistence-oriented parts of the other side also seemed to claim American identities more quickly. "You should hear us speaking English" one German servant wrote home only three months after arriving, "we just rattle off what we hear."[37] Even if her assessment seems overly optimistic, scholars by the 1950s assumed that culture change among the descendants of nineteenth-century immigrants had in fact been complete and successful. Culturally, European immigrants' descendants had become hyphenated Americans, while the descendants of Asian immigrants had created a new "Asian American" racial minority.

Recent studies of the second and third generations note a seeming paradox among Euro-Americans, however. They document behavioral convergence and increased intermarriage, but at the same time note the persistence of ethnic identity among children, grandchildren, and even great-grandchildren of immigrants. Although declining proportions of Americans of the third and subsequent generations claim an ethnic identity (and most must choose among ethnically mixed ancestors to do so), about two-thirds of descendants of post 1820-immigrants still claim hyphenated identities rather than calling themselves white or merely American.[38]

Scholars now debate why ethnic identities have survived. Some view them as essentially meaningless, symbolic, or romantic—a harmless way to add spice and color to individual identity, without any real constraints or responsibilities.[39] Others see them as a way to express a racial identity.[40] Still others believe that the persistence of ethnic identity signals a continued sense of alienation among the descendants of immigrants.[41]

Measures of cultural change do not show women lagging significantly behind men. Yet women, more often than men, view their ethnic backgrounds as very important to them. They are more curious about ethnicity than men; they more often discuss their backgrounds; and they more often sense a relationship to others of their background. Women also attribute greater importance to family ties. Richard Alba has concluded that increasing intermarriage will in the future "[yank] ethnicity's roots out of the family."[42] In the present context, however, we need to know why women more than men currently see ethnicity rooted there.

DOMESTICATING IMMIGRANT WOMEN

Why did the second and third generation not abandon the hyphen as they changed culturally? The dynamics of cultural change hold some clues. The marketplace, popular culture, American schools and settlements, immigrant newspapers, and community organizations all carried the same message to the immigrant women of the past—that they should pursue exclusively domestic lives. As immigrant women and their daughters committed themselves to what they took to be American or middle-class domesticity, however, they also developed their own rationale for doing so. Their domesticity reflected neither Americanizers' worst jeremiads or ethnic preservationists' most persuasive pleas. Instead, it underwrote hyphenated female identities.

American institutions serving immigrant communities—settlement houses and schools—especially emphasized the importance of domesticity for the female and foreign-born. Jane Addams called on reformers to rebuild "the wrecked foundations of domesticity" in immigrant communities.[43] For many settlement workers, educating girls meant educating them to conform to American domesticity. Training in a privatized American domesticity in turn undermined radical and communal protest traditions rooted in women's communities and kin networks.[44]

Public schools in the United States committed themselves to the broad resocialization of immigrant children in the nineteenth century.[45] For many, going to school was the first time they really "went to America."[46] Assumptions about gender deeply shaped public school curricula and pedagogy. Schools segregated students by sex. Unmarried women of older American (or, by the twentieth century, Irish) descent dominated teachers' ranks. Despite harsh discipline, large classes, and rote learning, many immigrant daughters nevertheless admired their teachers as ladylike models of American womanhood.[47]

Public schools sought to teach girls and boys patriotism, cleanliness, and orderliness alongside arithmetic, writing, and vocational skills. Vocational training for girls meant domestic science or sewing and textile work.[48] Domestic science teachers emphasized the importance of American diet and cooking; they encouraged girls to go home and teach their mothers about the benefits of oatmeal breakfasts and creamed vegetables.[49] Textbooks taught American household standards—which meant fresh air, a rational and fixed schedule of baby care and housework, and the rejection of "extravagance." Early training in home economics introduced second-generation girls to a lifelong habit of turning to experts for advice about home and family life.[50] (Their mothers found them crazy for mothering "by the book.")

Beginning with Jane Addams's famous Hull House, social settlement houses in immigrant communities also attempted to bring together native- and foreign-born in joint endeavors.[51] Settlement houses experimented with programs for girls, adolescents, and mothers to encourage orderliness, physical development (sports), service to others, and courtesy.[52] Most settlements had a Woman's Department with courses in sewing, food preparation, home nursing, and neighborhood charity work. Settlement houses also set up model flats to teach girls housekeeping.

Frustrated in their efforts to attract older women to such programs, Addams and associates developed the positive notion of "immigrant gifts" to encourage the practice and preservation of domestic crafts like weaving, embroidery, and lacework.[53] Their focus on immigrant gifts revealed how far Addams had moved beyond dominant Social Darwinist ideas; clearly Addams felt more sympathy for cultural diversity than the later Americanization movement would. Still, there was a patronizing element in the concern of Addams and other social welfare workers, who worried that immigrant mothers—enticed by the mass-produced wonders of the American marketplace—would otherwise abandon arts and crafts as inferior. They did not completely trust immigrant women to make their own cultural choices but sought to determine themselves what would be preserved or rejected of Old World traditions.[54]

Young immigrant women wage-earners could on occasion seize cultural initiative within the clubs and associations sponsored by settlements and female reformers. As had their American predecessors in the Lowell mills, they defended the dignity of respectable labor for women, criticized working-class matrimony, and sometimes even pointed to the single life as an ideal.[55] And although boys outnumbered girls in settlement programs, neighborhood girls who went received strong impressions of American women and values there. Hilda Satt Polacheck's autobiographical *I Came a Stranger* is the only known description of the settlement from an immigrant girl's perspective—one who apparently drew considerable strength from the experience.[56] Polacheck's contacts with the women of Hull House allowed her to write comfortably about her American life as an adult woman, mother, and reformer, rather than simply ending her story with her childhood, as so many other immigrant autobiographers did.[57] Chinese helpers in Donaldina Cameron's mission to Chinese prostitutes also sometimes adopted the reformers as models for becoming American.[58]

Even the Americanization movement—which was most concerned with issues of political participation and citizenship in the years just before and after World War I—carried an insistently domestic message to immigrant women. While men might learn the political mythology of George Washington in Americanization classes, women learned English from texts focusing on child care, marketing, clothing, and the home.[59] Americanizers wanted to reach isolated immigrant women not so much as citizens but as mothers who needed help to raise American children.

Most adult immigrants could evade Americanizers. But this does not mean that they remained unaware of American life. Immigrants' first important contacts with American ideas and values often occurred within their own communities and in their workplaces. Community activists, ethnic institutions, and the labor movement all sought to transmit American values to immigrants, telling women how to become working-class, Catholic, Polish American, or Jewish American women. All agreed that women's responsibilities were to be domestic ones.

Foreign-language newspapers played an especially important mediating role. Women figured prominently among advice-seekers in the "Bintl Briv," printed in the Yiddish press.[60] In addition, between 1840 and 1940, over fifty newspapers for non-English-speaking women appeared in the United States, while even more foreign-language newspapers carried women's pages or supplements. Typical was *Die Deutsche Hausfrau: Monatschrift für die Deutschen Frauen Amerikas,* which provided a German view of American domesticity and advice on both keeping house *in* the United States, and keeping it in an American way.[61] Later, newspapers like Los Angeles' *La Opinion* would add beauty advice to their tips on housewifery for Mexican American women.[62]

Newspapers published by women's organizations—the Polish *Glos Polek* (of the Polish Women's Alliance of America) or *The American Jewess* (published by the National Council of Jewish Women), for example—more often recognized women's activities in the ethnic public sphere.[63] But like the organizations that sponsored them, they emphasized the domestic origins of women's communal responsibilities. In particular, they saw the socialization of children to ethnic consciousness and the maintenance of ethnic institutions as an alternative to materialistic, secular, or Protestant American institutions as pressing tasks for ethnic American women. For these periodicals, women's voluntarism was not a form of Americanization, but a mechanism for the preservation of the ethnic group.

The foreign-language labor press offered a slightly wider range of advice and information to immigrant women. It acknowledged the activism and militancy of young unmarried women workers, while also emphasizing the importance of domesticity for adult women.[64] German socialists, for example, noted the expansion of women's wage-earning in modern industrialized societies, but argued that the socialist future would allow working-class women to enjoy the domestic privileges and leisure time reserved for the bourgeois wife under capitalism.[65] Some multiethnic labor organizations pioneered in publishing for women, as did the Italian Branch of the Ladies Waist & Dress Makers' Unions in New York with its newspaper *L'Operaia*. Writing for young women workers, some newspapers (like young women workers' organizations) criticized bourgeois womanhood by asserting the respectability of wage work and by defending the morality and respectability of female wage-earners. But only *Toveritar*, a Finnish socialist newspaper, and the women's page of the *Jewish Daily Forward* seemed supportive of female autonomy beyond its potential service to ethnic survival or working-class struggle.[66] Only they emphasized how women might benefit from their own freedom.

Whether in parochial school, church, or synagogue, ethnic programs aimed at women emphasized the importance of marriage, motherhood, and housekeeping "the American way." For example, the Clara de Hirsch school, organized by German Jewish women for independent Russian Jewish girls, provided a curriculum of sewing and domestic service (complete with a three-month practicum in an American—that is, in all likelihood, a German Jewish—family). The school encouraged female self-esteem, but within the confines of nineteenth-century bourgeois womanhood. These included premarital wage-earning, a carefully scheduled domestic day, piety, charity work, and an obligatory savings program. The staff of the de Hirsch school promoted bourgeois womanhood *as* American womanhood.[67]

Within their communities, immigrant women also learned about and experimented with American values in the marketplace, and as consumers of popular culture. Immigrant entrepreneurs in both places became important interpreters of American womanhood for immigrant women and their daughters. Although women on the other side had frequently managed the small amounts of cash circulating through family hands, their use of money increased enormously with the move to the U.S.[68] Monthly rents, weekly insurance payments, daily carfare, or food marketing—all demanded financial skills from women who on the other side might have made only one or two cash transactions in the course of a year. Learning to handle money was a big step toward competent American domesticity.

Immigrant mothers and housewives quickly became avid consumers of American products. Ethnic entrepreneurs eagerly provided them both with goods they needed as breadgivers and with goods to confirm their progress toward longed-for prosperity. If wage-earning in a capitalist economy brought new hardships along with opportunities, consuming in a capitalist economy seemed to promise pure pleasure.[69] Every study of immigrant women notes the rapidity with which women (particularly young women) learned of and adopted American standards of dress: often they exchanged homeland clothes for store-bought American ones the very day they arrived.[70] Older women might resist changing their appearance, language, or clothes, but they happily provided more plentiful and more varied meals for themselves and their families. They equipped comfortable kitchens and parlors, and they left the coffee pot always on the stove so they could offer hospitality to visitors. Whether viewed as Americanization in the marketplace; as evidence of immigrant women's longings for individualism, material comfort, and creativity; or as evidence of the way American goods could be used to support traditional family and community relationships, "buying like an American" reinforced domestic definitions of womanhood by making consumption part of housewifery.[71]

Women's daily ventures into the marketplace roused only occasional male comment. Immigrant radicals most often objected. They saw American materialism and the pleasures of consumption as the most tempting and therefore despicable of capitalism's corruptions: the unflattering portrait of Mrs. Cohen in chapter 7 came from the pen of a Jewish radical. Radical German men also sometimes joined native-born reformers in seeing women with overflowing shopping baskets and eyes eager for American goods as violators of common sense and female modesty.[72]

The relationship of American popular culture and female domesticity during the years of peak migration 1880–1920 is a controversial one, in part because so much of popular American culture was in fact the invention of immigrant innovators, not of long-time Americans purveying their own images of domestic womanhood. Early commercial entertainments like German beer gardens created settings for family leisure in public, while in the twentieth century, movies, dance halls, and amusement parks—all heavily marked by immigrant creativity—focused instead on the excitements of youth and courtship.[73] In all these places, immigrants' daughters learned to spend money on themselves, to care about their appearance, and to enjoy their leisure—usually in the company of young men. Movies established new standards of physical beauty and introduced immigrants to one version (as shocking to many native-born social workers as to immigrant parents) of American sexuality.[74]

In creating a leisure-time world of autonomy and choice for some immigrant daughters, popular culture reinforced independent wage-earning to create a working-class ethnic equivalent to the middle-class new women of the Progressive Era.[75] Popular culture showed immigrant girls new ways to be young and unmarried; it described a modern and American form of courtship—dating—which emphasized individual expression and choice. It even taught them how to kiss—"at least two minutes," insisted a Spanish newspaper in describing kissing as an art, not a science.[76] Popular culture offered a new road to domesticity, and a new version of domesticity, but not a critique of it. The commonest outcome for popular culture's female immigrant consumers was that of many early movies about single working women—marriage, motherhood, and domesticity.

Although the domestic message they carried to immigrant women differed little in its behavioral essentials, native-born and foreign-born interpreters of American culture nevertheless hoped women's domesticity would support fundamentally different ends. Women's ethnic organizations and their press argued that women's domesticity supported community activism and guaranteed the survival of the ethnic community. Public school teachers and settlement workers instead saw domesticity as the first step toward women's successful Americanization.

The daughters of immigrants thus committed themselves almost universally to marriage, motherhood, and American-style domesticity as they became adults. In so doing, they departed from the patterns their mothers had pioneered together with African American women. The daughters of the peak pre–World War I migrations pioneered in creating domesticity as a female right rather than a class privilege. By the 1950s, ethnic workingmen's wives had embraced what Betty Friedan would later castigate as "the feminine mystique."[77]

What women did is scarcely in question—but how to interpret their turn toward American domesticity is another matter. Daughters of immigrant women had pragmatic reasons for wanting lives different than those of their mothers. High rates of infant mortality alone could have encouraged immigrant daughters to listen carefully to American reformers; they did not want to share their mothers' devastating losses.[78] Daughters could see the physical price of their mother's hard-laboring lives, and the leisure that American domesticity seemed to promise. But they also saw their mothers as powerful, and thus as good role models. The second generation wanted something from the domesticity of both worlds they knew.[79] In seeking to emulate only what they found appealing in their mothers' lives, they created an ethnic American domesticity with some of their own mothers' skills and habits. By doing so, they also enjoyed a sense of continuity in the midst of ongoing cultural change. The psychological dimensions of domesticity—not the programs of immigrant or native-born activists—ultimately explain both immigrant daughters' satisfactions with domesticity and the next female generation's continued embrace of the ethnic hyphen.

THE STING OF CHANGE AND THE DOMESTICATION OF ETHNICITY

Cultural change is a stressful and time-consuming process. Humans differ enormously in their capacity to change; only the partially socialized young learn new languages and new ways of life quickly, and then largely because their personalities and their definitions of self are not yet fully established.[80] For adults, cultural and linguistic change call into question many of the assumptions that allow humans to make sense of the world and to construct their identities. In short, one cannot change languages and cultures without changing one's very being.[81] However exciting or freely chosen, culture change also feels disorienting and personally threatening. Anthropologists have called these psychological effects the "sting" of change or "culture shock."[82] This sting is particularly sharp for refugees, whose migration experiences are deeply traumatic.[83]

Scholars have long seen immigrant communities as important mechanisms for cushioning immigrants from the worst shocks while they begin to change their values and behavior.[84] They have helped women and men lead productive lives even while yearning for home or grappling with linguistic and social change. Studies of contemporary immigrants report that family, friendship, and neighborliness are the most important guarantors of immigrant health, happiness, and well-being. Among today's immigrants, women with female kin or with close friends (women differ among themselves in how they rate their relative importance) more often avoid illness, depression, and mental illness than those who feel isolated from other women.[85]

Immigrant women have often expressed the stress of cultural change through illness. Women raised to be deferent or self-sacrificing may know no other way to focus attention on their own needs.[86] Stress-related illnesses, in turn, cannot easily be described or diagnosed by modern American doctors, especially when immigrant women's concepts of wellness and illness differ significantly from those of modern or American medicine.[87] Stress has been shown to affect reproductive health[88] and drug use.[89] Undocumented (illegal) immigrants experience especially high levels of stress.[90] In immigrant women, reaction to stress also takes the form of depression.[91]

Many immigrant women prefer to turn to folk healers specializing in herbal, humoral, and spiritual cures rather than to English-speaking doctors.[92] Familiar foods, often endowed with healing qualities, also cure illnesses related to the stress of culture change.[93] Laotian women, for example, consciously turn to sticky rice to ease emotional trauma.[94] Whether women of their own background help as healers, as sympathetic listeners, or as food preparers, their labors ease the sting of change while selectively reproducing old habits.

It is not surprising that health beliefs,[95] folk curing practices,[96] and ritual food habits[97] are among the elements of culture most often passed along through immigrant daughters to subsequent generations. Healing, food, and family celebrations of recurring life crises provide a sense of continuity that can ease the stress of cultural change.[98] Domestic rituals and habits have thus defined a domestic ethnicity that survived the passing of segregated neighborhoods and immigrant community institutions, shaping identities and loyalties into the third generation.[99] Today, immigrants' grandchildren still claim ethnic identities, even though few participate in ethnic institutions.[100]

Because of women's responsibilities for child socialization and reproduction, Laotian men and women both believe that women are "the strongest part of the family."[101] Immigrant women and their daughters in many groups used their strength to domesticate ethnicity, embedding a changing culture in everyday life and human memory. Responsible for family festivals, family stories[102] and tales, and the socialization of children, women's domestic work created the only material basis ethnic identification had for many immigrants after the first generation. As men and women left ethnic communities and their institutions, ethnicity lost material and pragmatic dimensions for men, while living on more among women.

Immigrants did not hold any more tenaciously to old gender ideologies than they did to old baptismal or burial customs, though there are interesting variations among rates of change. Studies of Latin and Caribbean immigrant groups find more change in gender ideology among women than men,[103] while studies of Chinese and southeast Asian immigrants suggest that men more easily adopt American attitudes toward gender roles than women.[104]

Increasing intermarriage has meant, however, that immigrants' grandchildren can choose an ethnic identity. For women that choice still has practical implications: which food will they prepare; which kin network will claim their labors? Some women adopt the ethnicity of their husbands upon marriage, assuming responsibility for learning and passing on elements of their husbands' mother's or grandmother's domestic skills.[105] Faced with a conscious choice, a small group of women seek to return to their cultural roots with the help of "how-to" books on Jewish orthodoxy[106] or of ethnic cookbooks and festival books.[107] Why do women bother with this "folklorism?"[108] The only plausible explanation seems psychological.

Americans are said to lack a sense of history because the past limits an individual's freedom in forging her own self or destiny. If our history makes us what we are, then we must reject history to make ourselves. But for third-generation women of many backgrounds, historical connection is still a means to individual identity and self-understanding. A young Chinese American woman put it this way: "Our grandmothers are our historical links."[109] An Italian American woman would have agreed: "I am my grandparents' granddaughter, so to speak. I am the reverse immigration."[110] Both women claim American individualism and ethnicity simultaneously, yet observers in the early 1970s often argued that a woman's embrace of ethnicity prevented her from claiming individualism for herself.[111] They conflated ethnic self-identification and family dependency. So did some young women of the third generation, like the Italian American who said, "I didn't want to live out my family's thoughts of women. I'm independent of my family, and I am very happy for becoming a *real* [emphasis mine] person. . . . "[112] For this young woman, as for many Americans, "real" individualism means one with no ethnic or familial "bonds."

The domestication of immigrant women thus resulted neither in a simple Americanization nor in the creation of permanently segmented ethnic communities with their own languages, institutions, and cultural values. Immigrant daughters clearly did not follow in the footsteps of their unmarried school teachers and settlement house instructors. (Indeed, middle-class reformers had not intended them to.) Neither did they traverse the sort of evolutionary domestic path to American womanhood that reformers envisioned for them. They did not and still do not cook, or eat, or keep house as Americanizers might have wanted. But neither do they cook, eat, or keep house as their grandmothers or their ethnic leaders hoped they would. Instead of guaranteeing the survival of ethnic community institutions or an authentic Old World culture, women, especially of the working class, transformed ethnicity into a central domestic, familial, and individual psychological phenomenon. In doing so, they left little room for either unhyphenated feminists or middle-class ethnic leaders to represent them. As one working-class ethnic woman told a female interviewer in the 1970s: "Nobody speaks for me."[113]

PLUS ÇA CHANGE? CULTURAL CHANGE AMONG TODAY'S IMMIGRANTS

Today, immigrant women still remain primary transmitters—and thus transformers—of homeland culture,[114] while learning English remains the single most difficult challenge for adult immigrants.[115] But in sharp contrast to the past, immigrant women's acculturation is now more often measured by their abandonment of domesticity for wage-earning than by their embrace of American domesticity. Whereas once immigrant women fell short of American standards of womanhood by failing to focus exclusively enough on their children or husband's well-being, they now fall short if they appear to do so. As the lives of American women have changed, so too has the way Americans define the "backwardness" of women from the other side.

Still, welfare and educational programs aimed at immigrant women have often continued to train them for domesticity. Refugees, for example, receive crash courses in American life from the voluntary agencies that organize reception camps. In the recent past, refugee English classes tended to focus on teaching women about marketing and domesticity.[116] Almost every refugee camp offered classes for homemakers on providing low-cost meals, decorating an American home, obtaining used and new clothing, and using kitchen appliances or the telephone. In a few programs, native-born and feminist English teachers objected to exclusive reliance on such lessons, and sought to provide sessions on "Women in America" to cover a broader range of issues.[117]

Vocational training for refugee women has been equally out of step with changing American women's lives. Women have received instruction in industrial sewing, cleaning, and electronics assembly; a few programs added training in child care, small business management, and health care. Few suggested that women should prepare themselves for clerical work or service employment, although these are the most important employers of women, perhaps because both require even better English language skills than women's jobs in the past. One result is that welfare dependency among some Southeast Asian migrants has been quite high.[118]

CONCLUSION

How did a woman become American? She did so by first acquiring an American ethnic, class, and gender identity, all with strong implications for her domestic activities. She then transformed the American domesticity she embraced, to weave her own or her parents' memories of the other side into the daily lives of her children and grandchildren. The rate at which this happened, of course, varied widely. Women who came from the rapidly developing parts of the other side in the nineteenth century most quickly claimed American customs (especially American individualism) for themselves, because their proletarianization—begun at home in Ireland, Sweden, or Jewish eastern Europe, and reinforced by their independent migration to the United States—left them little other choice. Popular stereotypes of today's immigrant women—of rapidly adjusting Cubans and lagging Mexicans, of articulate Japanese and unassimilated Hmong—also remind us that their economic starting place in the homeland and the circumstances of migration, as much as culture or race, determine the rate of immigrant women's cultural adaptation.

For immigrant women generally, the creation of an ethnic group or, later, an ethnic identity cannot be separated from women's selective enjoyment of American individualism, their choice of an Americanized domesticity, and their maintenance of family traditions through time. The construction of ethnicity and the construction of identity were intertwined, not conflicting, cultural processes of change. Even in the third generation, women's sense of ethnic identity differed from men's, and was stronger.

By domesticating ethnicity, immigrant women and their daughters also transformed American domesticity into American Jewish,[119] American Catholic, Swedish American, Japanese American, and Italian American versions of it. American domesticity now subsumes a wide variety of traditions, family celebrations, and religious observances. Immigrants' impact on Americans could be seen even in the settlements and missions seeking to change them: Donaldina Cameron's mission among Chinese prostitutes in California, for example, served Chinese food to its American workers; Cameron herself partially adopted Chinese dress over time.[120] Both sides changed during cultural contacts.

Of course, the women and men of the other side often would not have recognized third-generation family celebrations and religious observances as their own, for immigrant women created their own idiosyncratic ethnic American domesticity as they selected old ingredients to cook in new ways, or combined multiethnic elements into "traditional" family rituals.[121] But neither would the Americanizers, public school teachers, and settlement house workers of the early twentieth century have wanted to label women's domestic amalgams as American, for they just as clearly departed from the models outlined by native-born elites in their domestic science textbooks and model apartments. When immigrant women chose domesticity, they made it their own: it was no longer a vehicle of Americanization or of ethnic preservation, but an expression of their individual and evolving sense of themselves as ethnic American women.

Has this complex path to American womanhood been open only to immigrant women from Europe? Increasingly, women and men of European descent have been able to choose whether to accept "the hyphen" of ethnic identity or not; about a third of third-generation women now call themselves simply American.[122] They can choose this identity only because their neighbors now perceive them as "white." The same has not been true for immigrant women or colonized minorities "of color." The daughters of Filipino fathers and white mothers were assigned Filipino American identities because other Americans saw them as physically like their fathers.[123] For them, ethnic womanhood was not chosen, but imposed.

We cannot know if the latest wave of immigrants will help native-born minorities to broaden still further prevailing definitions of who is, or looks, American. In the past, class and economic mobility helped open the door to American status. As the daughters and granddaughters of Catholic, Jewish, and "dark" southern and eastern European immigrants succeeded economically and "became white," they naturalized hyphenated notions of American womanhood. And in the process, they claimed moral distinctiveness for themselves as family-oriented model minorities, presumably in contrast to native-born minorities of African descent.

Does this mean that today's middle-class Asian, Spanish-speaking, and West Indian immigrant women will see their daughters or their daughters' daughters become American women with the option of identifying themselves as Korean Americans or Jamaican Americans? And if they do, will native-born African American women alone remain part of a "racial" minority, destined to be defined by others' perceptions of skin color and culture? Or will they, too, be permitted to see their ethnicity as a beautiful and deeply meaningful element which they may choose to foreground in constructing their individual identities?

The very fact that it is difficult to imagine the latter transformation suggests that it may still be quite some time before immigrant, or other, women "of color" can choose an ethnic identity, rather than having it imposed upon them. Meanwhile, men and women of the African diaspora in the United States have long explored and celebrated a distinctive African American culture, and as a large and vital group, they, too, will seek to influence how new immigrants, especially those of African descent, construct their identities in the U.S. We can be confident only that in the twenty-first century, as in the past, it will be the interactions of native-born and immigrant minorities—with each other, with the "white" majority, and with their own children—that will make American identity anew.

Conclusion

Oscar Handlin once noted that he had set out to study the history of immigrants in America, only to discover that American history was, in fact, the history of immigration. At any time in the nineteenth century, immigrant women and their daughters made up a quarter of the female population of the United States; closer to half the American population had at least one immigrant grandparent. Today, immigrant women and their daughters make up less than ten percent of American womanhood, but including third-generation Americans who embrace ethnic identities would raise the percentage of living female links to the other side substantially. Immigrant minorities are still a highly visible presence in American life, if no longer quite American history itself.

From the Other Side has attempted to offer a portrait of immigrant women and gender in immigrant life that respects cultural diversity, gender ideology, and change over time. It has directed readers' attention to points of contact between immigrant women, immigrant men, and native-born Americans. It has revealed parallel experiences shared by immigrant women past and present, others shared by immigrant men and women of similar backgrounds, and still others shared by immigrant and native-born women. It has noted the ties that have bound women to others—male and female of similar and of differing backgrounds—as well as the forces that have divided woman from woman and woman from man.

Overall, the history of immigrant women in the U.S. points to the flexibility of American identities and the changeableness of ethnic definitions of American womanhood. The peoples of the other side became Americans through gendered transformation: foreign men became ethnic American men and foreign women became ethnic American women. In the third generation, but only among those of European descent, ethnicity has become an option, possibly reversing this earlier process of "ethnicization." Race remains the largest barrier to ethnicization, but even racial understandings have sometimes shifted dramatically in the aftermath of sizeable migrations. *From the Other Side* thus leaves us with a paradox. Immigrant women's lives have showed greater convergence with those of other American women (especially in wage-earning patterns, wages, and life-cycle) than one sees among men (where racial and ethnic differences in wages and occupations are still strong). But they have also showed greater female than male identification with ethnicity and with foreign origins over the generations.

COLONIALISM AND IMMIGRATION: RACIAL AND IMMIGRANT MINORITIES

From the Other Side has argued that distinguishing between racial minorities and immigrant minorities as types, while useful, can also be quite misleading. Both types of minority emerged within a forming world economy that created economic opportunity for some while simultaneously encouraging the institutionalization of inequalities between powerful nations and "the other side." Ethnicity, religion, race, and class defined the boundary separating the two. That boundary ran through the United States—between white majority and colonized minority—as well as around it. The immigrants of the nineteenth century came from the third world of the international economy of their age; today's migrations often appear as third-world empires "striking back." Immigrant men and women sometimes had been colonized minorities in their homelands. Not surprisingly, the experiences of immigrant men and women in the U.S. economy and society—past *and* present—often fall somewhere between those of the native-born minority and those of the native-born majority. The unanswerable question for today's immigrants is, as noted earlier, whether they will become parts of American "racial" minorities or, instead, add to the diversity among Americans who voluntarily embrace ethnic identities.

Gender was not the primary marker of the boundary between the United States and the other side. Women shared with men of their own backgrounds subordination as peasants, the adventure and dangers of migration to the United States, and the experience of being foreign "outsiders." But gender mattered, and in a variety of ways. Gender created distinctive male and female versions of each of these general experiences. Immigrant men's and women's lives diverged sharply—in their labors for wages, and in family and community responsibilities—even while shared languages and religions bound the two in cultural solidarity. Gender also colored men's and women's understanding of social and cultural boundaries, opportunities, and taboos. For both these reasons, it is not really possible to conclude that immigrant women overall became American more slowly and reluctantly or more rapidly and enthusiastically than immigrant men. Structurally they followed different paths to different destinations—ethnic American womanhood and ethnic American manhood.

Attention to gender also reveals some important differences between African Americans and other minorities in the United States. Immigrant women, like colonized women throughout the world and in the U.S., came under intensive pressures to emulate the domestic ideals and behavior of the ruling ethnic group's middle class. Their behavior as sexual beings and as mothers came under especially careful scrutiny. Paradoxically, when women did claim some of the privileges of middle-class domesticity—leisure, consumption, concern with individual appearance, modern clothing, or bourgeois social customs—they sometimes found their efforts the object of mocking humor or scorn from both native-born Americans and the men of their own groups.

But more important, white Americans saw foreign-born women—like Native American and Chicana women—as victims of the men of their own groups rather than as forgers of their own lives. White Americans repeatedly used gender to layer a moral dimension over the fundamentally economic and political boundaries between themselves and the other side. Although they sometimes questioned the morality of women of the other side, they more often viewed women in sympathetic, if condescending terms—as children and sufferers. At the same time, and at least since the end of slavery in the United States, sharply different stereotypes of African American women have repeatedly emerged, to set the descendants of enslaved women apart from most women of the other side. White Americans have singled out African American women as powerful "Mammies" and as matriarchs with enough power at home to deny their brothers, sons, and husbands the manhood they need to succeed in a male-dominated country. And stereotypes of strong, angry, and sexually demanding women—"Jezebels" and "Sapphires"—have not disappeared from contemporary debates about African American communities in the late twentieth century.

RACE, ETHNICITY, AND RELIGION

Structurally, the lives of American women seemed to develop in parallel streams throughout the nineteenth century, before beginning a marked convergence from the 1920s to the present, fueled primarily by the demand for female workers in clerical and service jobs. In the nineteenth century, immigrant and colonized minority women did some of the same jobs, but in different places; today, the working lives of American women of many backgrounds follow more similar trajectories than in the past.

Subjectively, however, cultural diversity among women has proved far more salient and persistent, both now and in the past, than economic and social structures would suggest. Swedish and Irish domestic servants resembled each other in their employment patterns, and in some of their marital and family choices, but they lived in linguistically, ethnically, and religiously separate communities, with little sense of commonality or shared sisterhood. Both foreign-born and African American women gravitated toward entertainment and community service in search of professional work and accomplishment, yet neither a shared religious faith, a common culture, nor personal sympathies united the two groups of women. To discuss the influence of ethnicity or religion on immigrant women thus requires us to accept the parallels, the common experiences, and the striking structural similarities that exist while acknowledging these women's culturally distinctive world views as important sources of division.

Ultimately, religious faith has presented the lowest barriers to immigrant women and men seeking to become American. The religious toleration enshrined in the U.S. Constitution could not prevent harsh religious conflicts—and these were real enough in the nineteenth century when Protestant mobs attacked convents, lay Catholics, or Jews—but it did establish clear limits to American nativism in its early religious expressions. Nativist Protestant Americans had no powerful legal mechanisms for demanding conversion as a requirement of prospective Americans. As Catholics and Jews established their claims as Americans, they created a solid precedent for others hoping to make similar claims in the face of other exclusionary practices.

Today's immigrants are pulled especially sharply by the conflicting dynamics of race and class, which remain the highest barriers to becoming American. In the past, Americans tended to use the terms "ethnicity" and "race" interchangeably, but many saw ethnic and cultural differences as originating in racial or physical ones. By the twentieth century, scholars were drawing a clear distinction between ethnic (that is, cultural) groups and racial (that is, biological) groups. Most recently this dichotomous treatment of race and ethnicity has itself come under attack. Like growing numbers of publications rejecting race as an objective or in any sense scientific category, *From the Other Side* has stressed that racial/ethnic categories changed dramatically over time. For that reason it has viewed all racial categories as in fact cultural ones. For this reason, too, the book has made sparing use of a currently popular category, "Euro-American." Whatever the cultural similarities among Americans of European descent today (and these are significant), European immigrants recently arrived in the nineteenth century shared neither a common religion, a common language, common kinship rules, nor common customs regarding everyday life, gender, or childrearing. Nor did they have a sense of solidarity based on shared history. Similarly, *From the Other Side* has often pointed out the cultural diversity encompassed within American "racial" categories.

Some racial boundaries succumbed to immigrant economic mobility over three generations. As first the Catholic Irish, then Catholic, Orthodox and Jewish southern and eastern Europeans and their children became middle-class, they also, in a very practical sense, became white. The upwardly mobile descendants of Japanese and Chinese did not, however, become white as they became middle-class. The grandchildren and great-grandchildren of Asian immigrants note that white Americans still sometimes ask them where they are from, as if they cannot see that they are English-speaking Americans culturally much like themselves. Indeed, as noted earlier, the great question raised by contemporary migrations is whether the superior class position of a sizeable minority of third world immigrants today will allow them to become Americans in ways apparently reserved for those of European descent in the past.

Religion, race, and ethnicity shaped men and women's lives alike. But this does not mean that gender was irrelevant to immigrant women or that ethnicity (or race) was "more important than gender" in shaping their experiences or those of their daughters. Gender functioned within linguistic and religious groups, within ethnic, racial, and religious categories. As African American women scholars have repeatedly pointed out, women cannot be divided analytically along the several components of their identities. Immigrant women did not act as women in one context and as ethnics in another. Thus it is analytically simplistic to ask whether ethnicity or gender was more important in the histories of immigrant women in the United States. *From the Other Side* has instead pointed to the interaction of gender, class, race, ethnicity, and religion in the lives of the foreign-born.

The best example of this interaction is provided by the perception of ethnicity's importance among the grandchildren of immigrants. These can be traced directly to gendered divisions of labor within the families and communities of immigrants and their children. First as community activists and later as socializers of children and organizers of family and religious rituals, immigrant women reproduced and transformed cultural traditions through their labors. Men at first sought women's help in reproducing ethnicity and then abandoned it increasingly to women and their domestic roles. It is scarcely surprising that women, more than men, continue to view ethnicity and their immigrant "roots" as an important influence on their lives.

CLASS

From the Other Side has traced migration to a world economy in formation, and it has hinted at the parallel consolidation of international classes transcending nation-state borders over time. The adjustment of immigrant women in the United States, the jobs they took, the families and communities they built, and the educational and professional careers they pursued strongly reflected their starting place in the world economy. Women who began their lives in subsistence economies seem to have achieved upward mobility and to have become American more slowly than the women who left the developing peripheries of the world. Furthermore, the best long-term predictor of economic success, education, and community activism in the United States has been middle-class or elite status prior to migration.

Still, Americans have insisted that the American middle-class woman differs from those of other nationalities. In the nineteenth century, they saw middle-class women as uniquely domestic; today, they see them as uniquely autonomous. As Americans' views of themselves have changed, so have their understandings of upwardly mobile or middle-class immigrant women: once chastised as insufficiently domestic, today many seem inappropriately committed to male-dominated families and familial traditions. A look at voluntarism among middle-class women, furthermore, shows that American women have had an easier time working with the poorest of immigrant "girl workers" than they did with their middle-class but foreign-born peers—for example, in the woman's club movement, where ethnic, racial, and religious separatism reigned.

For these reasons, the experiences of past immigrant women allow few sensible predictions about the futures of the many middle-class and elite immigrants arriving in the United States from today's third world. Class, education, and profession would seem to propel such women quickly into the American mainstream. On the other hand, Americans' perception of the foreign-born as necessarily "huddled masses" and their assumption that a large proportion of the newcomers are indistinguishable from native-born African Americans or Hispanics would seem to prohibit just that ending. In the present as in the past, immigrant women may find easier acceptance among those of their own ethnicity—male as well as female—than among native-born American women of their own class.

NATIVITY, NATIONALITY, NATIONALISM

Although United States scholars are accustomed to seeing the transformation of immigrants into Americans as a peculiarly American phenomenon, in fact, there is relatively little that seems unique to the United States about immigrant women's experiences. Crossing the boundary of the United States seems to have been less significant for women than taking jobs for wages, accustoming themselves to urban life, confronting new dialects and languages, or being introduced to new, bourgeois standards of domestic life, mother-child relations, and marital expectations. The Irish country woman who went to Dublin had many of the same experiences as her sister who went to Boston. A Japanese farmer's daughter who ventured off to work in an urban inn in Hiroshima shared many experiences with the picture bride headed for hotel employment in Seattle.

Still, immigration has been central to the United States' conception of its own national identity. Americans continue to this day to refer to their country as a nation of immigrants, and to take pride in that label. Immigration may form only one channel in the wider historical stream of the nationalization of rural, poor peoples throughout the nineteenth and twentieth centuries. But it is an important channel, especially in the United States and in other immigrant nations such as Canada, Argentina, and Australia.

One foundation for Americans' national pride is the assumption that the benefits of the American political system have remained open to all, even foreigners, through naturalization. Of course, we know that this simplifies history. Asians could not become citizens before 1943; those of African descent could not always vote even as citizens. Women, too, and regardless of origin, had no claim to the franchise before 1920. The nationalization of all these outsiders has had a slow, conflictual, and incremental history.

While gender was at most a symbolic marker of the boundary between powerful nations and the other side, it was of the greatest importance in the nationalization of female outsiders. The vast majority of men and women on the other side did not have strong national identities at the time of their arrival in the U.S. They came instead with local, regional, ethnic, religious, and familial loyalties. Increasing numbers of men on the other side had claimed national identities and the privileges of citizenship and political participation for themselves, *as men*, throughout the nineteenth century. In the U.S., many of these men found the path to citizenship, political participation, and national identity still open to them, albeit only as ethnic-bloc voters for ethnic candidates or as soldiers in wars from the Civil War to Vietnam.

The nationalization of immigrant women, like that of Asian immigrants, racial minorities, and white native-born women, followed its own route. White immigrant women gained citizenship initially not as individuals but as family dependents. Citizenship brought them few rewards before 1920 and the enfranchisement of women generally. The Nineteenth Amendment, furthermore, nationalized European naturalized immigrants *as women*—not as foreigners or as members of ethnic groups. Women of African and Asian descent, by contrast, found their access to national life opened along with that of men of their own backgrounds—and usually long after 1920. Of all these women, furthermore, the nation expected service as wives and mothers, not as leaders and governors, for until recently politics remained virtually closed to all women.

In the national patriotic mythology, then, immigrant women scarcely number among the "we" who built the United States. The arrival of several waves of immigrants has reinforced Americans' views of their country as a land actively and voluntarily sought out by ambitious foreigners. Yet as has been shown earlier, U.S. law now guarantees that marriage and family connections, not individual female initiative and the pursuit of economic mobility, bring the largest group of female immigrants to the United States, perpetuating older stereotypes of women immigrants as passive recipients, not active forgers, of their American futures.

"MODERNIZATION" AND FEMALE AUTONOMY

Immigrant women did not—and do not—specifically "Americanize" in the process of becoming an American. Whether the Jamaican nurse today travels to London or New York, she finds herself changing behavior in many parallel ways. In both places, too, the nurse is likely to maintain a connection to her homeland and a sense of identity as a Jamaican. In this sense, scholars are correct in rejecting *Americanization* as a description of immigrants' changing lives; the term they often substitute, however—*modernization*—is equally problematic.

As a description of culture change among immigrant women, "modernization" seems as value-laden as "Americanization." Modernization is usually used to connote the opportunities it opens, not the possibilities it forecloses. These opportunities seem obvious to Americans: they include individual wage-earning, education, free movement, secularism, and participatory politics in a liberal "public" sphere. Thus immigrant women's modernization has meant escape from traditional and negative cultural stereotypes about women, or even from patriarchy itself. Modernity, in other words, has been defined through negative contrasts between the lives of the men and women of the other side and those of the world's most powerful nations. Modernization has not been a value-neutral term, and many social scientists have rejected it for precisely this reason.

Immigrant women did not necessarily see all of their own former lives, or the lives of their immigrant mothers, negatively. They generally did not suffer exceptionally from male domination on the other side, nor did they escape into a modern world free of patriarchal relations in the United States. And they did not accept the lives of modern or American women as unequivocally positive role models. Like anthropologists who document the domestication of third world women under colonialism, or Marxists who trace poverty to proletarianization in capitalist development, immigrant women knew that crossing the boundary from the other side brought losses as well as new opportunities. For them, the main challenge of migration was to claim new forms of power—whether in the form of an individual wage, the choice of a spouse, or leisure time—without losing older female modes of influence within community and kinship networks. For many, it seems, the goal was to be as comfortable and as accepted as any American while still remaining a "mensch." The desire to remain a mensch in a country dominated by individualist values has been central to women's labors in reproducing family and ethnic traditions, as well as to their more tenacious claim (relative to men) to ethnic identities.

By continuing to think of themselves as hyphenated or ethnic American women, immigrant women could behave in new, and modern, ways without casting off the values learned on the other side. In doing so, they could protect themselves as well from the price modernity sometimes extracted, especially from women—notably social isolation, rootlessness, and poverty. They could become, as Maria Zambello put it, "just as good," "just as up to date," and "just as polite," while still remaining "Italian girls." With their skills as "people persons," the women of the other side—now most often speaking through third world feminists and minority feminists in the United States—remind American women, and feminists among them, of some of the limits to modernity's vision. They offer alternative views, not only of female emancipation but of the meaning of a good life for all.

Notes

INTRODUCTION

1. Ewen, *Immigrant Women*, p. 201. Complete citations for works listed in the bibliographical essay are given there and may be located via the index.

2. For varying usages of the term, see Mary Gordon, *The Other Side* (New York: Viking, 1989); Vincent Panella, *The Other Side: Growing Up Italian in America* (Garden City, N.Y.: Doubleday, 1979); Sandra Cisneros, *Woman Hollering Creek and Other Stories* (New York: Random House, 1991), pp. 43, 69.

3. George Sánchez, " 'Go After the Women': Americanization and the Mexican Immigrant Woman, 1915–1929," pp. 250–63 in DuBois and Ruiz, eds, *Unequal Sisters*; Mary Ryan, *Women in Public: Between Banners and Ballots, 1825–1880* (Baltimore: Johns Hopkins University Press, 1990), pp. 34–35.

4. Feminist critiques of migration studies without acknowledgment of gender include Donna Gabaccia, "*The Transplanted*: Women and Family in Immigrant America," *Social Science History* 12, 3 (Fall 1988): 243–52; Betty Bergland, "Immigration History and the Gendered Subject: A Review Essay," *Ethnic Forum* 8, 2 (1988): 24–39; Suzanne Sinke, "A Historiography of Immigrant Women in the Nineteenth and Early Twentieth Centuries," *Ethnic Forum* 9, 1–2 (1989): 122–45; Sydney Stahl Weinberg, "The Treatment of Women in Immigration History," pp. 3–22 in Gabaccia, ed., *Seeking Common Ground*; Silvia Pedraza, "Women and Migration: The Social Consequences of Gender," *Annual Review of Sociology* 17 (1991): 303–25.

5. I use gender here more in its relational, social-historical, or anthropological sense rather than in a post-modernist, linguistic, or deconstructive sense. This is in keeping with its use in most existing writing on immigrant women.

6. E.g., Bodnar, *The Transplanted*; Portes and Rumbaut, *Immigrant America: A Portrait*.

7. I put both terms in quotation marks here to indicate my belief that both racial and sexual differences are socially constructed rather than natural categories. When I use the term race in the text, I refer to contemporary, everyday, American, notions of race as defined by skin color or such standards as "one drop" of "nonwhite blood." As I note in subsequent chapters, other understandings of race and ethnicity prevailed in the past. See Joan W. Scott, *Gender and the Politics of History* (New York: Columbia University Press, 1988); Werner Sollors, ed., *The Invention of Ethnicity* (New York: Oxford University Press, 1989); Kathleen Neils Conzen et al., "The Invention of Ethnicity: A Perspective from the USA," *Altreitalie* 3 (April 1990): 37–62.

8. I borrow this felicitous phrase from Judith Smith, "Our Own Kind: Family and Community Networks in Providence," *Radical History Review* 17 (Spring 1978): 99–120. The phrase may have been first used in this sense by Moses Rischin, *Our Own Kind: Voting by Race, Creed or National Origin* (Santa Barbara: Center for the Study of Democratic Institutions, 1960).

1. WHERE IS THE OTHER SIDE?

1. Heck's story is in Walter D. Kamphoefner, Wolfgang Helbich, and Ulrike Sommer, *News from the Land of Freedom: German Immigrants Write Home*, trans. Susan Carter Vogel (Ithaca: Cornell University Press, 1991), pp. 367–82.

2. Grossman (a pseudonym) told her story to Neil M. Cowan and Ruth Schwartz Cowan, *Our Parent's Lives: The Americanization of Eastern European Jews* (New York: Basic Books, 1989), pp. 8–9, 34, 37–38.

3. Vásquez de Gómez's story is in Marilyn P. Davis, *Mexican Voices, American Dreams: An Oral History of Mexican Immigration to the United States* (New York: Henry Holt, 1990), pp. 43–45.

4. Bodnar, *The Transplanted*, p. 1.

5. As it is in the world-systems analyses on which Bodnar drew, especially Immanuel Wallerstein, *The Modern World System*, 2 vol. (New York: Academic Press, 1976, 1980).

6. Aristide Zolberg, "International Migration Policies in a Changing World System," in *Human Migration: Patterns and Policies*, ed. William H. McNeill and Ruth S. Adams (Bloomington: Indiana University Press, 1978). On U.S. immigration policy, see E. P. Hutchinson, *Legislative History of American Immigration Policy 1798–1965* (Philadelphia: University of Pennsylvania Press, 1981); Michael C. LeMay, *From Open Door to Dutch Door: An Analysis of U.S. Immigration Policy since 1820* (New York: Praeger, 1987).

7. Bodnar, *The Transplanted*, pp. 10, 13–20, passim.

8. Nancie L. Gonzalez and Carolyn S. McCommon, *Conflict, Migration and the Expression of Ethnicity* (Boulder: Westview, 1989), p. 3.

9. Glenn, *Daughters of the Shtetl*, p. 46.

10. Vilhelm Moberg, *The Emigrants* (New York: Simon and Schuster, 1951), pp. 101–108.

11. Robert A. Huttenback, *Racism and Empire: White Settlers and Colored Immigrants in British Self-Governing Colonies, 1830–1910* (Ithaca: Cornell University Press, 1976); Hugh Tinker, *Race, Conflict, and the International Order: From Empire to United Nations* (London: Macmillan, 1977).

12. On the distinction between "colonized minorities" and "immigrant minorities" see Robert Blauner, *Racial Oppression in America* (New York: Harper and Row, 1972), chap. 1.

13. Michael Hechter, *Internal Colonialism: The Celtic Fringe in British National Development, 1536–1966* (London: Routledge and Kegan Paul, 1975); Daniel Chirot, *Social Change in a Peripheral Society: The Creation of a Balkan Colony* (New York: Academic Press, 1976).

14. I have borrowed this phrase from the Centre for Contemporary Cultural Studies, *The Empire Strikes Back: Race and Racism in 70s Britain* (London: Hutchinson, in association with the Centre for Contemporary Cultural Studies, University of Birmingham, 1982).

15. Paul B. Rich, *Race and Empire in British Politics* (Cambridge: Cambridge University Press, 1986).

16. Archdeacon, *Becoming American*, Table I-1; Robert V. Wells, *The Population of the British Colonies in America before 1776* (Princeton: Princeton University Press, 1975).

17. Archdeacon, *Becoming American*, pp. 4–6; Marianne Wokeck, "Harnessing the Lure of the 'Best Poor Man's Country': The Dynamics of German-Speaking Immigration to British North America, 1763–1783," pp. 104–244 in *"To Make America."*

18. A. Roger Ekirch, *Bound for America: The Transportation of British Convicts to the Colonies, 1718–1775* (Oxford: Clarendon, 1987); John Van der Zee, *Bound Over: Indentured Servitude and American Conscience* (New York: Simon and Schuster, 1985); Sharon V. Salinger, *"To Serve Well and Faithfully": Labor and Indentured Servants in Pennsylvania, 1682–1800* (New York: Cambridge University Press, 1987); David W. Galenson, *White Servitude in Colonial America: An Economic Analysis* (Cambridge: Cambridge University Press, 1981).

19. Winthrop Jordan, *White over Black: American Attitudes toward the Negro, 1550–1812* (Chapel Hill: University of North Carolina Press, 1968).

20. Herbert S. Klein, "African Women in the Atlantic Slave Trade," pp. 29–38 in *Women and Slavery in Africa*, ed. Claire C. Robertson and Martin A. Klein (Madison: University of Wisconsin Press, 1983); Farley Grubb, "Servant Auction Records

and Immigration into the Delaware Valley, 1745–1831: The Proportion of Females among Immigrant Servants," *Proceedings of the American Philosophical Society* 133 (June 1989): 154–69.

21. Hutchinson, *Legislative History of American Immigration Policy 1798–1965*, chaps. 2 and 10.

22. Hoerder, "An Introduction to Labor Migrations."

23. Richard Drinnon, *Facing West: The Metaphysics of Indian-Hating and Empire Building* (Minneapolis: University of Minnesota Press, 1980); Reginald Horsman, *Race and Manifest Destiny: The Origins of American Racial Anglo-Saxonism* (Cambridge, Mass.: Harvard University Press, 1981).

24. Rodolfo Acuña, *Occupied America: A History of Chicanos* (New York: Harper and Row, 1981).

25. Daniel M. Johnson and Rex R. Campbell, *Black Migration in America: A Social Demographic History* (Durham: Duke University Press, 1981), pp. 10, 26–27.

26. Eric Foner, *Free Soil, Free Labor, Free Men: The Ideology of the Republican Party before the Civil War* (New York: Oxford University Press, 1970), chap. 7, esp. pp. 236–37.

27. And as David R. Roediger has argued, *not* being black became part of the "wages" of free workers, *The Wages of Whiteness: Race and the Making of the American Working Class* (London: Verso, 1991).

28. Sucheng Chan, ed., *Entry Denied: Exclusion and the Chinese Community in America* (Philadelphia: Temple University Press, 1991). On the Foran Act, see Hutchinson, *Legislative History*, pp. 88–89, 438; LeMay, *From Open Door to Dutch Door*, p. 55.

29. For background to the restriction of Asian immigration, see Elmer Clarence Sandmeyer, *The Anti-Chinese Movement in California* (Urbana: University of Illinois Press, 1991); Gary Okihiro, *Cane Fires: The Anti-Japanese Movement in Hawaii, 1865–1945* (Philadelphia: Temple University Press, 1991); Donald Teruo Hata, *Undesirables: Early Immigrants and the Anti-Japanese Movement in San Francisco, 1892–1893, Prelude to Exclusion* (New York: Arno Press, 1978).

30. Conflicting American views on imperial expansion are summarized in Thomas J. Osborne, *"Empire Can Wait": American Opposition to Hawaiian Annexation, 1893–1898* (Kent, Oh.: Kent State University Press, 1981); Sidney Lens, *The Forging of the American Empire* (New York: Crowell, 1971); Norman Graebner, *Empire on the Pacific: A Study in American Continental Expansion*, 2nd ed. (Santa Barbara: ABC-Clio, 1983).

31. Marcus Lee Hansen, *The Atlantic Migration, 1607–1860* (Cambridge, Mass.: Harvard University Press, 1940); Frank Thistlethwaite, "Migration from Europe Overseas in the Nineteenth and Twentieth Centuries," pp. 32–60 in *Rapports*, XIe Congrès International des Sciences Historiques, vol. 5 (Goteborg, 1960); Dudley Baines, *Emigration from Europe, 1815–1930* (Houndsmill, Basingstoke: Macmillan, 1991).

32. Good general studies of nineteenth-century immigrants are now abundant. Helpful starting surveys include Mack Walker, *Germany and the Emigration, 1816–1885* (Cambridge: Harvard University Press, 1964); Jerre Mangione and Ben Morreale, *La Storia: Five Centuries of the Italian American Experience* (New York: HarperCollins, 1992); Kerby A. Miller, *Emigrants and Exiles: Ireland and the Irish Exodus to North America* (New York: Oxford University Press, 1985); Charlotte Erickson, *Invisible Immigrants: The Adaptation of English and Scottish Immigrants in Nineteenth-Century America* (London: Weidenfeld and Nicolson, 1972); Arthur Hertzberg, *The Jews in America: Four Centuries of an Uneasy Encounter: A History* (New York: Simon and Schuster, 1989); John J. Bukowczyk, *And My Children Did Not Know Me: A History of Polish-Americans* (Bloomington: Indiana University Press, 1986); Hans Norman and Harald Runblom, *Transatlantic Connections: Nordic Migration to the New World after 1800* (Oxford: Oxford University Press, 1988); Takaki, *Strangers from a Different Shore*. Note that totals in this paragraph do not take return migration into account.

33. The best source is Bodnar, *The Transplanted*. But see also Alan Kraut, *The Huddled Masses: The Immigrant in American Society, 1880–1921* (Arlington Heights, Ill.: Harlan Davidson, 1982).

34. Dirk Hoerder, "Immigration and the Working Class: The Remigration Factor," *International Labor and Working Class History* 21 (Spring 1982): 28–41.

35. The best work on nativism remains John Higham, *Strangers in the Land: Patterns of American Nativism, 1896–1925*, 2nd ed. (New Brunswick: Rutgers University Press, 1988).

36. Barbara M. Solomon, *Ancestors and Immigrants: A Changing New England Tradition* (Cambridge: Harvard University Press, 1956); Les Wallace, *The Rhetoric of Anti-Catholicism: The American Protective Association, 1887–1911* (New York: Garland, 1990); Higham, *Strangers in the Land*; Leonard Dinnerstein, *Uneasy at Home: Antisemitism and the American Jewish Experience* (New York: Columbia University Press, 1987); David A. Gerber, ed., *Anti-Semitism in American History* (Urbana: University of Illinois Press, 1986); Gwendolyn Mink, *Old Labor and New Immigrants in American Political Development: Union, Party, and State, 1875–1986* (Ithaca: Cornell University Press, 1986).

37. Roediger, *The Wages of Whiteness*, pp. 133–54.

38. Higham, *Strangers in the Land*, chap. 6.

39. LeMay, *From Open Door to Dutch Door*, pp. 73–86; Archdeacon, *Becoming American*, pp. 167–72; Hutchinson, *Legislative History of American Immigration*, chap. 5, pp. 465–74; Robert A. Divine, *American Immigration Policy, 1924–1952* (New Haven: Yale University Press, 1957), chap. 1.

40. On black migrations, see Florette Henri, *Black Migration: Movement North, 1900–1920* (Garden City, N.Y.: Anchor Press, 1975); James R. Grossman, *Land of Hope: Chicago, Black Southerners and the Great Migration* (Chicago: University of Chicago Press, 1989); Nicholas Lemann, *The Promised Land: The Great Black Migration and How it Changed America* (New York: A. A. Knopf, 1991); Carole Marks, *Farewell, We're Good and Gone: The Great Black Migration* (Bloomington: Indiana University Press, 1989); Johnson and Campbell, *Black Migration in America*, chap. 3. On Puerto Ricans, see Victoria Sánchez-Korrol, *From Colonia to Community* (Westport, Conn.: Greenwood, 1983); Joseph Fitzpatrick, *Puerto Rican Americans: The Meaning of Migration to the Mainland*, 2nd ed. (Englewood Cliffs, N.J.: Prentice-Hall, 1987). On Mexicans, see Carey McWilliams, *North from Mexico* (New York: Greenwood, 1968).

41. Mary Anne Thatcher, *Immigrants and the 1930s: Ethnicity and Alienage in Depression and On-Coming War* (New York and London: Garland Publishing, 1990); Roger Daniels, "Changes in Immigration Law and Nativism Since 1924," *American Jewish History* 76 (December 1986): 159–80.

42. Thatcher, *Immigrants and the 1930s*, chap. 6; Abraham Hoffman, *Unwanted Mexican Americans in the Great Depression: Repatriation Pressures, 1929–1939* (Tucson: University of Arizona Press, 1974).

43. Michael Marrus, *The Unwanted: European Refugees in the Twentieth Century* (New York: Oxford University Press, 1985); Gil Loescher and John A. Scanlan, *Calculated Kindness: Refugees and America's Half-Open Door, 1945-Present* (New York: Free Press, 1986).

44. Robert A. Divine, *American Immigration Policy, 1924–1952* (New Haven: Yale University Press, 1957).

45. Richard B. Craig, *The Bracero Program: Interest Groups and Foreign Policy* (Austin: University of Texas Press, 1971); Ernesto Galarza, *Merchants of Labor: The Mexican Bracero Story; An Account of the Managed Migration of Mexican Farm Workers in California, 1942–1960* (Charlotte, N.C.: McNally and Loftin, 1964).

46. Hutchinson, *Legislative History*, pp. 297–310; LeMay, *From Open Door to Dutch Door*, pp. 103–109; Divine, *American Immigration Policy*, chap. 9.

47. Mark Wyman, *DP: Europe's Displaced Persons, 1945–1951* (Philadelphia: Balch Institute Press, 1989); Amy Zahl Gottlieb, "Refugee Immigration: The Truman Direc-

tive," *Prologue* 13 (Spring 1981): 5–17; see also Alejandro Portes and Robert L. Bach, *Latin Journey: Cuban and Mexican Immigrants in the United States* (Berkeley: University of California Press, 1985); Silvia Pedraza-Bailey, "Cuba's Exiles: Portrait of a Refugee Migration," *International Migration Review* 19, 1 (Spring 1985): 4–34.

48. For discussions of the 1965 law, see LeMay, *From Open Door to Dutch Door*, pp. 111–14; Hutchinson, *Legislative History*, pp. 357–79, David M. Reimers, "An Unintended Reform: The 1965 Immigration Act and Third World Immigration to the United States," *Journal of American Ethnic History* 3 (1983): 9–28.

49. Coming at the same time as the elimination of the bracero program for recruiting temporary workers, the result was a notable increase in illegal migration. See Julian Samora, *Los Mojados: The Wetback Story* (Notre Dame: University of Notre Dame Press, 1971); Daniel James, *Illegal Immigration: An Unfolding Crisis* (Lanham, Md.: University Press of America, 1991).

50. Jasso and Rosenzweig, *The New Chosen People*, pp. 36–38.

51. Jasso and Rosenzweig, *The New Chosen People*, chap. 9.

52. John Cromartie and Carol B. Stack, "Reinterpretation of Black Return and Nonreturn Migration to the South: 1975–1980," *The Geographical Review* 79, 3 (July 1989): 297–311.

53. Mark J. Miller, *Foreign Workers in Western Europe: An Emerging Political Force* (New York: Praeger, 1981); Ronald E. Krane, *International Labor Migration in Europe* (New York: Praeger, 1979).

54. Jasso and Rosenzweig, *The New Chosen People*, Table 1.5.

55. Besides Portes and Bach's *Latin Journey*, see Thomas Muller and Thomas J. Espenshade, *The Fourth Wave: California's Newest Immigrants* (Washington: Urban Institute Press, 1985); Douglas S. Massey and Katherine M. Schnabel, "Recent Trends in Hispanic Immigration to the United States," *International Migration Review* 17 (1983): 212–44. For other groups, see Luciano Mangiafico, *Contemporary American Immigrants: Patterns of Filipino, Korean and Chinese Settlement in the United States* (New York: Praeger, 1988); Illsoo Kim, *New Urban Immigrants: The Korean Community in New York* (Princeton: Princeton University Press, 1981); James P. Allen, "Recent Immigration from the Philippines and Filipino Communities in the United States," *The Geographical Review* 67, 2 (April 1977): 195–208; Virginia R. Dominguez, *From Neighbor to Stranger: The Dilemma of Caribbean Peoples in the United States* (New Haven: Antilles Research Program, Yale University, 1975); Michel S. LaGuerre, *American Odyssey: Haitians in New York City* (Ithaca: Cornell University Press, 1985).

2. THE WOMEN OF THE OTHER SIDE

1. Jacob A. Riis, *How the Other Half Lives* (New York: Hill and Wang, 1957), orig. publ. 1890, p. 18.

2. Bodnar, *The Transplanted*, chap. 2.

3. H. Arnold Barton, ed., *Letters From the Promised Land: Swedes in America, 1840–1914* (Minneapolis: University of Minnesota Press, 1975), pp. 143–56.

4. The slightly fictionalized account of Nathoy is in Ruthanne Lum McCunn, *Thousand Pieces of Gold* (San Francisco: Design Enterprises, 1981).

5. Emma Ciccotosto and Michal Bosworth, *Emma: A Translated Life* (Fremantle: Fremantle Arts Centre Press, 1990).

6. For general background see Robert C. Ostergren, *A Community Transplanted: The Trans-Atlantic Experience of a Swedish Immigrant Settlement in the Upper Middle West, 1835–1915* (Madison: University of Wisconsin Press, 1988), and Jon Gjerde, *From Peasants to Farmers: The Migration from Balestrand, Norway, to the Upper Middle West* (New York: Cambridge University Press, 1985).

7. Orvar Löfgren, "The Potato People: Household Economy and Family Patterns among the Rural Proletariat in Nineteenth Century Sweden," in *Chance and Change: Social and Economic Studies in Historical Demography in the Baltic Area*, ed. Sune Akerman, Hans Christian Johansen, and David Gaunt (Odense: Odense University Press, 1978).

8. John Boli, *New Citizens for a New Society: The Institutional Origins of Mass Schooling in Sweden* (New York: Pergamon, 1989).

9. Sten Carlsson, "Unmarried Women in the Swedish Society of Estates," pp. 220–26 in *Chance and Change*, ed. Akerman et al.; Margareta Matovic, "Swedish Women in the Culture of Origin," in *Peasant Maids, City Women*, ed. Christiane Harzig et al., (Cornell University Press, forthcoming).

10. Matovic, "Swedish Women in the Culture of Origin."

11. Donna Gabaccia, "In the Shadows of the Periphery: Italian Women in the Nineteenth Century," pp. 166–76 in *Connecting Spheres: Women in the Western World, 1500 to the Present*, ed. Jean Quataert and Marilyn Boxer (New York: Oxford University Press, 1987); Simonetta Ortaggi Cammarosano, "Labouring Women in Northern and Central Italy in the Nineteenth Century," in *Society and Politics in the Age of the Risorgimento: Essays in Honour of Denis Mack Smith*, ed. John A. Davis and Paul Ginsborg (New York: Cambridge University Press, 1991); Elda Zappi, *If Eight Hours Seem Too Few: Mobilization of Women Workers in the Italian Rice Fields* (Albany: State University of New York Press, 1991).

12. Marina Warner, *Alone of All Her Sex: The Myth and the Cult of the Virgin Mary* (New York: Vintage, 1983); Michael P. Carroll, *Madonnas That Maim: Popular Catholicism in Italy since the Fifteenth Century* (Baltimore: Johns Hopkins University Press, 1992); Robert Antonio Orsi, *The Madonna of 115th Street: Faith and Community in Italian Harlem, 1880–1950* (New Haven: Yale University Press, 1985).

13. Donna R. Gabaccia, *Militants and Migrants: Rural Sicilians Become American Workers* (New Brunswick: Rutgers University Press, 1988), pp. 55–63.

14. Maurice Freedman, *Family and Kinship in Chinese Society* (Stanford: Stanford University Press, 1970); Freedman, *Lineage Organization in Southeastern China* (New York: Humanities Press, 1965).

15. Judith Stacey, *Patriarchy and Socialist Revolution in China* (Berkeley: University of California Press, 1983), p. 23; Lydia Kung, *Factory Women in Taiwan* (Ann Arbor, Mich.: UMI Research Press, 1983).

16. Rubie S. Watson and Patricia Buckley Ebrey, *Marriage and Inequality in Chinese Society* (Berkeley: University of California Press, 1991).

17. Arthur P. Wolf, "Fertility in Prerevolutionary China," in *Family and Population in East Asian History*, ed. Susan B. Hanley and Arthur P. Wolf (Stanford: Stanford University Press, 1985), p. 178.

18. Arthur P. Wolf, "Adopt a Daughter-in-Law, Marry a Sister: A Chinese Solution to the Problem of the Incest Taboo," *American Anthropologist* 68, 4 (August 1966): 883–98; Arthur P. Wolf and Chieh-shan Huang, *Marriage and Adoption in China, 1845–1945* (Stanford: Stanford University Press, 1980).

19. Margery Wolf, *Women and Family in Rural Taiwan* (Stanford: Stanford University Press, 1972), p. 34; see also Wolf and Huang, *Marriage and Adoption*, pp. 64–65.

20. Sue Gronewald, "Beautiful Merchandise: Prostitution in China, 1860–1936," *Women and History* no. 1 (Spring 1982); also Maria Jaschok, *Concubines and Bondservants: A Social History* (London, Atlantic Highlands: Zed Books, 1988); Gail Hershatter, "Prostitution and the Market in Women in Early Twentieth-Century Shanghai," pp. 256–85 in *Marriage and Inequality*.

21. Sarah Deutsch, *No Separate Refuge: Culture, Class, and Gender on an Anglo-Hispanic Frontier in the American Southwest, 1880–1940* (New York: Oxford University Press, 1987).

22. Louise A. Tilly and Joan W. Scott, *Women, Work and Family* (New York: Holt, Rinehart and Winston, 1978); Bodnar, *The Transplanted*, pp. 71–83.

23. Eric R. Wolf, *Peasants* (Englewood Cliffs, N.J.: Prentice-Hall, 1966); Daniel Thorner, Basile Kerblay, and R. E. F. Smith, eds., *A. V. Chayanov on the Theory of Peasant Economy* (Madison: University of Wisconsin Press, 1986).

24. Daisy Dwyer and Judith Bruce, eds., *A Home Divided: Women and Income in the Third World* (Stanford: Stanford University Press, 1988), p. 7.

25. Susan Carol Rogers, "Women's Place: A Critical View of Anthropological Theory," *Comparative Studies in Society and History* 20 (1978): 123–62.

26. Jane Schneider, "Of Vigilance and Virgins: Honor, Shame, and Access to Resources in Mediterranean Societies," *Ethnology* 10 (1971): 1–24; John Peristiany, *Honor and Shame: The Values of Mediterranean Society* (London: Weidenfeld and Nicolson, 1965).

27. Gita Sen, "The Sexual Division of Labor and the Working-Class Family: Toward a Conceptual Synthesis of Class Relations and the Subordination of Women," *Review of Radical Political Economics* 12 (1980): 76–86; Carole Turbin, "Beyond Dichotomies: Interdependence in mid-Nineteenth Century Working Class Families in the United States," *Gender and History* 2 (Autumn 1989): 293–312.

28. On the Italian case, see Gabaccia, *From Sicily to Elizabeth Street*, pp. 113–14.

29. Barbara Rogers, *The Domestication of Women: Discrimination in Developing Societies* (New York: Tavistock, 1981); Brydon and Chant, *Women in the Third World*, pp. 151, 167.

30. Sydelle Kramer and Jenny Masur, eds., *Jewish Grandmothers* (Boston: Beacon Press, 1976), pp. 103–18.

31. Michiko Tanaka, *Through Harsh Winters: The Life of a Japanese Immigrant Woman* (Novato, Cal.: Chandler and Sharp, 1981).

32. Ide O'Carroll, *Models for Movers: Irish Women's Emigration to America* (Dublin: Attic Press, 1990), pp. 37–38.

33. Diner, *Erin's Daughters in America*, chap. 1; Nolan, *Ourselves Alone*, chap. 1. See also Deirdre Mageean, "Irish Women in the Culture of Origin," in *Peasant Maids, City Women*.

34. Nolan, *Ourselves Alone*, chap. 2; Diner, *Erin's Daughters in America*, pp. 20–26.

35. Deirdre Mageean, "Catholic Sisterhoods and the Immigrant Church," pp. 89–100 in *Seeking Common Ground*.

36. Contrast Diner, *Erin's Daughters in America*, pp. 53–54, and Nolan, *Ourselves Alone*, pp. 73–74.

37. Diner, *Erin's Daughters in America*, p. 26.

38. Charlotte Baum, "What Made Yetta Work? The Economic Role of Eastern European Jewish Women in the Family," *Response* 18 (1973): 32–38.

39. Milton Meltzer, *World of Our Fathers: The Jews of Eastern Europe* (New York: Farrar, Straus and Giroux, 1974); Irving Howe, *World of Our Fathers* (New York: Harcourt Brace Jovanovich, 1976), chap. 1; see also Mark Zborowski and Elizabeth Herzog, *Life Is with People* (New York: Schocken, 1962; orig. publ. 1952).

40. Main sources for this entire section are Ewen, *Immigrant Women*, pp. 38–40; Glenn, *Daughters of the Shtetl*, pp. 9–20; Weinberg, *The World of Our Mothers*, pp. 5–16; Baum, Hyman, and Michel, *The Jewish Woman in America*, chap. 1.

41. See the picture in Howe, *World of Our Fathers*, following p. 140.

42. Howe, *World of Our Fathers*, pp. 29–31.

43. Cowan and Cowan, *Our Parents' Lives*, p. 35.

44. Rose L. Glickman, *Russian Factory Women: Workplace and Society, 1880–1914* (Berkeley: University of California Press, 1984).

45. Howe, *World of Our Fathers*, pp. 20–21; Weinberg, *The World of Our Mothers*, pp. 44–45; Glenn, *Daughters of the Shtetl*, pp. 33–35.

46. Howe, *The World of Our Fathers*, pp. 20–24; Glenn, *Daughters of the Shtetl*, pp. 35–37; see also Ezra Mendelsohn, *Class Struggle in the Pale: The Formative Years of the Jewish Workers' Movement in Tzarist Russia* (Cambridge: Cambridge University Press, 1970), chap. 1.

47. Susan B. Hanley, "Family and Fertility in Four Tokugawa Villages," pp. 196–228 in Family and Population in East Asian History; Takaki, Strangers from a Different Shore, pp. 49–50.

48. Stephen Vlastos, Peasant Protests and Uprisings in Tokugawa Japan (Berkeley: University of California Press, 1986).

49. Robert Y. Eng and Thomas C. Smith, "Peasant Families and Population Control in Eighteenth-Century Japan," pp. 103–32 in Native Sources of Japanese Industrialization, 1750–1920, ed. Thomas C. Smith (Berkeley: University of California Press, 1988).

50. Hanley, "Family and Fertility," pp. 196–228.

51. Takaki, Strangers from a Different Shore, p. 48; E. Patricia Tsurumi, Factory Girls: Women in the Thread Mills of Meiji Japan (Princeton: Princeton University Press, 1990), pp. 137–40, 167–68.

52. Tsurumi, Factory Girls, chaps. 6–7; Takaki, Strangers from a Different Shore, pp. 47–48.

53. Mikiso Hane, Peasants, Rebels and Outcastes: The Underside of Modern Japan (New York: Pantheon, 1982), pp. 207–25.

54. Evelyn Nakano Glenn, Issei, Nisei, War Bride: Three Generations of Japanese American Women in Domestic Service (Philadelphia: Temple University Press, 1986), pp. 43–44.

55. Morawska, For Bread with Butter, p. 53.

56. Maria Hall Ets, Rosa: The Life of an Immigrant Woman (Minneapolis: University of Minnesota Press, 1970), pp. 30–31.

57. Peter Schmidtbauer, "Households and Household Forms of Viennese Jews in 1857," Journal of Family History 5 (Winter 1980): 378.

58. Theresa McBride, The Domestic Revolution: The Modernization of Household Service in England and France 1820–1920 (New York: Holmes and Meier, 1976), p. 34; E. G. Ravenstein, "The Laws of Migration," p. 167.

59. Tilly and Scott, Women, Work and Family, chaps. 2 and 6.

60. Tilly and Scott, Women, Work and Family, part 3.

61. Matovic, "Swedish Women in the Culture of Origin."

62. John Hajnal, "European Marriage Patterns in Perspective," pp. 101–143 in Population in History: Essays in Historical Demography, ed. D. V. Glass and D. E. C. Eversley (Chicago: Aldine, 1965).

63. On the concept of nationalization, see Victoria De Grazia, How Fascism Ruled Women (Berkeley: University of California Press, 1991), chap. 1.

64. Sue Ellen M. Charlton, Women in Third World Development (Boulder: Westview, 1984), p. 14.

65. Al Santoli, New Americans: Immigrants and Refugees in the U.S. Today, An Oral History (New York: Viking, 1988), pp. 208–33.

66. Thomas Kessner and Betty Boyd Caroli, Today's Immigrants, Their Stories: A New Look at the Newest Americans (New York: Oxford University Press, 1981), pp. 194–95.

67. Santoli, New Americans, pp. 43–54.

68. Santoli, New Americans, pp. 146–62.

69. Yolanda Prieto, "Cuban Women in New Jersey: Gender Relations and Change," pp. 185–202 in Seeking Common Ground; Margaret Boone, "The Uses of Traditional Concepts in the Development of New Urban Roles: Cuban Women in the United States," pp. 235–70 in A World of Women, ed. Erika Bourguignon (New York: Praeger, 1980).

70. Grant Evans, Lao Peasants under Socialism (New Haven: Yale University Press, 1990); Geoffrey C. Gunn, Rebellion in Laos: Peasants and Politics in a Colonial Backwater (Boulder: Westview, 1990).

71. Karen L. S. Muir, The Strongest Part of the Family (New York: AMS Press, 1988), pp. 3–63.

72. See the articles collected in Women and Development.

73. Stichter and Parpart, *Women, Employment and the Family*, p. 2.

74. Darmen Diana Deer and Magdalena León de Leal, "Peasant Production, Proletarianization, and the Sexual Division of Labor in the Andes," *SIGNS* 7 (1981): 338–60; Deer, "Changing Relations of Production and Peruvian Peasant Women's Work," *Latin American Perspectives* 4 (1977): 48–69.

75. This was the original insight of Ester Boserup's studies of Africa, *Woman's Role in Economic Development*, Part 1.

76. Suzanne Stiver Lie and Virginia E. O'Leary, eds., *Storming the Tower: Women in the Academic World* (London: Kogan Page, 1990), table 1.3.

77. Bisilliat and Fiéloux, *Women of the Third World*, chap. 4.

78. Elsa M. Chaney and Mary Garcia Castro, *Muchachas No More: Household Workers in Latin America and the Caribbean* (Philadelphia: Temple University Press, 1989); Bissiliat and Fiéloux, *Women of the Third World*, pp. 42–43.

79. Bisilliat and Fiéloux, *Women of the Third World*, p. 49.

80. Ximena Bunster, *Sellers and Servants: Working Women in Lima* (New York: Praeger, 1985); Florence E. Babb, *Between Field and Cooking Pot: The Political Economy of Market Women in Peru* (Austin: University of Texas Press, 1989).

81. Shoshona Tancer, "La Quesqueyana: The Dominican Woman, 1940–1970," in *Female and Male in Latin America*, ed. Ann Pescatello (Pittsburgh: University of Pittsburgh Press, 1973). On Latin American families generally, see Elizabeth Jelin, *Family, Household and Gender Relations in Latin America* (Paris: UNESCO, 1990); Brydon and Chant, *Women in the Third World*, pp. 16–21.

82. Susan E. Brown, "Love Unites Them and Hunger Separates Them: Poor Women in the Dominican Republic," pp. 322–32 in *Toward an Anthropology of Women*, ed. Rayna R. Reiter (New York and London: Monthly Review Press, 1975); Nancie L. González, *Black Carib Household Structure: A Study of Migration and Modernization* (Seattle: University of Washington Press, 1969); Judith Blake, *Family Structure in Jamaica: The Social Context of Reproduction* (New York: The Free Press of Glencoe, 1961).

83. Tracy Backrach Ehlers, *Silent Looms: Women and Production in a Guatemalan Town* (Boulder: Westview, 1990), p. 7.

84. Mayra Buviníc and Sally W. Yudelman, *Women, Poverty and Progress in the Third World* (New York: Foreign Policy Association Headline Series no. 289, Summer 1989), p. 9; see also Brydon and Chant, *Women in the Third World*, pp. 145–46.

85. Saskia Sassen-Koob, "Notes on the Incorporation of Third World Women into Wage-Labor through Immigration and Off-Shore Production," *International Migration Review* 18 (Winter 1984): 1144–67; Diane Elson and Ruth Pearson, "'Nimble Fingers Make Cheap Workers': An Analysis of Women's Employment in Third World Export Manufacturing," *Feminist Review* (Spring 1981): 87–107; Kathryn Ward, *Women Workers and Global Restructuring* (Ithaca: ILR Press, 1990); Annette Fuentes and Barbara Ehrenreich, *Women in the Global Factory* (Boston: South End Press, 1983).

86. Stichter and Parpart, *Women, Employment and the Family*, p. 11.

87. Brydon and Chant, *Women in the Third World*, p. 168.

88. Agreement is strongest on the case of Asian women workers. See Kung, *Factory Women in Taiwan*, p. xiv; Janet W. Salaff, *Working Daughters of Hong Kong: Filial Piety or Power in the Family?* (Cambridge: Cambridge University Press, 1981); Lydia Kung, "Factory Work and Women in Taiwan: Changes in Self-Image and Status," *SIGNS* 2, 2 (Autumn 1976): 35–58.

89. See Susan Tiano, "Maquiladoras in Mexicali: Integration or Exploitation?"; Tiano, "Women's Work and Unemployment in Northern Mexico"; Gay Young, "Gender Identification and Working-Class Solidarity among Maquila Workers in Ciudad Juárez: Stereotypes and Realities"; Peña Devon, "Tortuosidad: Shop Floor Struggles of Female Maquiladora Workers"; all in *Women on the U.S.-Mexico Border: Responses to Change*, ed. Vicki L. Ruiz and Susan Tiano (Boston: Unwin Hyman, 1987). See also

María Patricia Fernández-Kelly, *Women and Industry in Mexico's Frontier* (Albany: State University of New York Press, 1983).

90. Salaff, *Working Daughters of Hong Kong,* pp. 268–69; Brydon and Chant, *Women in the Third World,* pp. 42–44.

91. María Patricia Fernández-Kelly, "Mexican Border Industrialization, Female Labor Force Participation, and Migration," pp. 205–223 in *Women, Men and the International Division of Labor.*

92. See, for example, Margaret Gill and Joycelin Massiah, *Women, Work and Development* (Cave Hill, Barbados: Institute of Social and Economic Research, University of the West Indies, 1984); Keith Hart, *Women and the Sexual Division of Labour in the Caribbean* (Kingston: Consortium Graduate School of Social Sciences, 1989).

3. FROM MINORITY TO MAJORITY

1. Houstoun et al., "Female Predominance of Immigration"; Archdeacon, *Becoming American,* pp. 136–37.

2. John Bodnar, *Workers' World: Kinship, Community, and Protest in an Industrial Society, 1900–1940* (Baltimore: Johns Hopkins University Press, 1982), pp. 43–45.

3. Corinne Azen Krause, *Grandmothers, Mothers and Daughters; Oral Histories of Three Generations of Ethnic American Women* (Boston: Twayne, 1991), pp. 18–20.

4. Glenn, *Issei, Nisei, Warbride,* p. 45.

5. Bodnar, *Workers' World,* pp. 39–40.

6. Hannah Kalajian, *Hannah's Story: Escape from Genocide in Turkey to Success in America* (Belmont, Mass.: American Heritage Press, 1990).

7. Bodnar, *The Transplanted,* pp. 38–43.

8. Paul C. P. Siu, "The Sojourner," *American Journal of Sociology* 58 (July 1952–May 1953): 34–44; Caroline Brettell, *Men Who Migrate, Women Who Wait: Population and History in a Portuguese Parish* (Princeton: Princeton University Press, 1986).

9. On the changing marital, age, and family status among migrants, see Archdeacon, *Becoming American,* p. 135.

10. Jasso and Rosenzweig, *The New Chosen People,* Table 4.3; Houstoun et al., "Female Predominance of Immigration," pp. 932, 935.

11. Gabaccia, "Women of the Mass Migrations."

12. Houstoun et al., "Female Predominance of Immigration," pp. 926, 940–42; see also Monica Boyd, "Occupations of Female Immigrants in North American Immigration Statistics," *International Migration Review* 10 (Spring 1976): 73–80; Katharine Donato and Andrea Tyree, "Family Reunification, Health Professionals, and the Sex Composition of Immigrants to the United States," *Sociology and Social Research* 70, 3 (April 1986): 226–30.

13. Rita J. Simon, "Sociology and Immigrant Women," pp. 25–34 in *Seeking Common Ground;* Houstoun et al., "Female Predominance in Immigration," table 10.

14. Mary Seivwright, "Project Report on Factors Affecting Mass Migration of Jamaican Nurses to the United States," *The Jamaican Nurse* 5 (August and December 1965): 8–13; Richard E. Joyce and Chester L. Hunt, "Philippine Nurses and the Brain Drain," *Social Science and Medicine* 16 (1982): 1223–33; Tomoji Ishi, "International Linkage and National Class Conflict: The Migration of Korean Nurses to the United States," *Amerasia Journal* 14, 1 (1988): 23–50.

15. Donna Gabaccia, "Women of the Mass Migrations."

16. Vol. 1 of the U.S. Census Office's *Statistics of the Population of the United States, 1870* (Washington: Government Printing Office, 1872), also includes statewide data on the numbers of foreign-born men and women for 1850 and 1860. Likewise, the Department of Labor, Bureau of the Census's *Special Reports, Supplementary Analysis and Derivative Tables, Twelfth Census, 1990* (Washington: Government Printing Office,

1906) gives data for 1890 and 1900. For the twentieth century, see U.S. Census Bureau, *Thirteenth Census, 1910, Population: Composition and Characteristics, Preliminary Reports* (Washington: Government Printing Office, 1913) and U.S. Department of Commerce, Bureau of the Census, *Immigrants and their Children, 1920* by Niles Carpenter, Census Monographs 7 (Washington: Government Printing Office, 1927), table 173.

17. Archdeacon, *Becoming American*, pp. 136–37.

18. Bodnar, *The Transplanted*, chap. 1.

19. Suzanne Sinke with Stephen Gross, "The International Marriage Market and the Sphere of Social Reproduction: A German Case Study," pp. 67–87 in *Seeking Common Ground*.

20. Takaki, *Strangers from a Different Shore*, p. 37.

21. Michael Burawoy, "The Functions and Reproduction of Migrant Labor: Comparative Material from Southern Africa and the United States," *American Journal of Sociology* 81 (March 1976): 1076–87.

22. Mary Eleanor Cygan, "Polish Women and Emigrant Husbands," in *Roots of the Transplanted*, vol. 1, ed. Dirk Hoerder and Inge Blank (forthcoming, Eastern Europe Quarterly and Columbia University Press).

23. Susan Ahern et al., "Migration and La Mujer Fuerte," *Migration Today* 13, 1 (1985): 14–20.

24. Nancy J. Pollock, "Women and the Division of Labor: A Jamaican Example," *American Anthropologist* 74 (June 1972): 689–92.

25. Johnson and Campbell, *Black Migration in America*, pp. 70, 78–79.

26. Carl Ross, "Servant Girls, Community Leaders: Finnish American Women in Transition (1910–1920)," pp. 43–44 in *Women Who Dared: The History of Finnish American Women*.

27. Carpenter, *Immigrants and their Children*, p. 162–65.

28. Joseph A. Hill, *Women in Gainful Occupations, 1870–1920* (Washington, D.C.: Government Printing Office, 1929), p. 101.

29. Gabaccia, "Women of the Mass Migrations."

30. On the changing female labor market, see Alice Kessler-Harris, *Out to Work: A History of Wage-Earning Women in the United States* (New York: Oxford University Press, 1982), chap. 5; Valerie Kincade Oppenheimer, *The Female Labor Force in the United States: Demographic and Economic Factors Governing Its Growth and Changing Composition*, Population Monograph 5 (Berkeley: University of California Press, 1970).

31. Easterlin, "Immigration," p. 483; see also Carpenter, *Immigrants and their Children*, p. 160.

32. Dickinson, *The Role of the Immigrant Women*, pp. 209–10; Kessler-Harris, *Out to Work*, pp. 147–49.

33. Dickinson, *The Role of the Immigrant Women*, pp. 22–23.

34. Besides Diner, *Erin's Daughters in America*, and Ross, "Servant Girls," see Joy Lintelman, " 'America is the Woman's Promised Land': Swedish Immigrant Women and American Domestic Service," *Journal of American Ethnic History* 8 (Spring 1989): 9–23.

35. Sinke, "The International Marriage Market," p. 67.

36. Marsha Penti, "Piikajutut: Stories Finnish Maids Told," in *Women Who Dared*, p. 60; Susan Glenn, *Daughters of the Shtetl*, pp. 45–47.

37. See, for example, the transactions of the 1899 meeting of the International Congress for the Suppression of Traffic in Women and Children, *The White Slave Trade* (London: Wertheimer, Lea and Co., 1899); Frederick K. Grittner, *White Slavery: Myth, Ideology, and American Law* (New York: Garland, 1990).

38. Edward J. Bristow, *Prostitution and Prejudice: The Jewish Fight Against White Slavery, 1870–1939* (New York: Schocken, 1983); Donna Guy, *Sex and Danger in Buenos Aires: Prostitution, Family, and Nation in Argentina* (Lincoln: University of Nebraska Press, 1991).

39. Sucheng Chan, "The Exclusion of Chinese Women, 1870–1943," pp. 94–146 in *Entry Denied*, here p. 95; Lucy C. Hirata, "Chinese Immigrant Women in Nineteenth Century California," pp. 224–44 in *Women of America: A History*, ed. Carol R. Berkin and Mary Beth Norton (Boston: Houghton Mifflin, 1979); Lucie Cheng, "Free, Indentured, Enslaved: Chinese Prostitutes in Nineteenth-Century America," pp. 402–34 in *Labor Immigration Under Capitalism: Asian Workers in the United States before World War II*, ed. Lucie Cheng and Edna Bonacich (Berkeley: University of California Press, 1984); Yuji Ichioka, "*Ameyuki-San*: Japanese Prostitutes in Nineteenth-Century America," *Amerasia Journal* 4, 1 (1977): 1–21.

40. Nancie L. González, "Multiple Migratory Experiences of Dominican Women," *Anthropological Quarterly* 49 (January 1976): 36–44; Monica H. Gordon, "Caribbean Migration: A Perspective on Women," pp. 14–55 in *Female Immigrants to the United States*.

41. Besides Kessler-Harris, *Out to Work*, see Lynn Y. Weiner, *From Working Girl to Working Mother: The Female Labor Force in the United States, 1820–1980* (Chapel Hill: University of North Carolina Press, 1985); Claudia D. Goldin, *Understanding the Gender Gap: an Economic History of American Women* (New York: Oxford University Press, 1990); Amott and Matthaei, *Race, Gender and Work*, chap. 8.

42. Donato, "Understanding U.S. Immigration," pp. 172, 181.

43. Elfrieda B. Shukert and Barbara S. Scibetta, *War Brides of World War II* (Novato, Cal.: Presidio, 1988); Teresa K. Williams, "Marriage between Japanese Women and U.S. Servicemen since World War II," *Amerasia Journal* 17, 1 (1991): 135–54; Juliana Kim Haeyun, "Voices from the Shadows: The Lives of Korean War Brides," *Amerasia Journal* 17, 1 (1991): 15–30.

44. William J. Barman, "Korean War Brides, Prostitutes, and Yellow Slavery," *Minerva* 7, 2 (Summer 1989): 31–37; Wanwadee Larsen, *Confessions of a Mail Order Bride: American Life through Thai Eyes* (Far Hills: New Horizon Press, 1989); John Krich, "Here Come the Brides: The Blossoming Business of Imported Love," *Mother Jones* 11 (February/March 1986): 34–37; Bisilliat and Fiéloux, *Women of the Third World*, pp. 57–58.

45. Patricia R. Klausner, "The Politics of Massage Parlor Prostitution: The International Traffic in Women for Prostitution into New York City, 1970-present," Ph.D. diss., University of Delaware, 1987.

46. Isabel Kaprielian, "Creating and Sustaining an Ethnocultural Heritage in Ontario: The Case of Armenian Women Refugees," pp. 139–54 in *Looking into My Sister's Eyes: An Exploration in Women's History*, ed. Jean Burnet (Toronto: Multicultural History Society of Ontario, 1986); Kalajian, *Hannah's Story*; Gary A. Kulhanjian, *The Historical and Sociological Aspects of Armenian Immigration to the United States, 1890–1930* (San Francisco: R and E Research Associates, 1975).

47. Sibylle Quack, "Everyday Life and Emigration: The Role of Women," in *An Interrupted Past: German-Speaking Refugee Historians in the United States after 1933* (Washington, D.C.: German Historical Institute and Cambridge University Press, 1991).

48. Pedraza, "Women and Migration," p. 311.

49. Guillermina Jasso and Mark Rosenzweig, "Family Reunification and the Immigration Multiplier: U.S. Immigration Law, Origin-Country Conditions, and the Reproduction of Immigrants," *Demography* 23, 3 (1986): 291–311.

50. Sinke, "The International Marriage Market," p. 78.

51. Francis A. Kellor, "The Protection of Immigrant Women," *Atlantic* 101 (February 1908): 246–55; Sophonisba P. Breckinridge, *New Homes for Old*, pp. 223–27.

52. It also excluded "Mongolian" contract laborers generally. Chan, "The Exclusion of Chinese Women," pp. 105–109. Some authors believe that the Page Act explains the low migrations of Chinese women to the U.S.; George A. Peffer, "Forbidden Families: Emigration Experiences of Chinese Women under the Page Law, 1875–1882," *Journal of American Ethnic History* 6 (Fall 1986): 28–46.

53. Walter I. Trattner, *From Poor Law to Welfare State: A History of Social Welfare in America* (New York: Free Press, 1974), pp. 19–22.

54. Barbara Welter, "The Cult of True Womanhood," *American Quarterly* 18 (1966): 151–74; Gerda Lerner, *The Majority Finds Its Past* (New York: Oxford University Press 1979), chap. 2.

55. On detainees, see, for example, U.S. Commissioner of Immigration, *Annual Reports*, 1892–1902.

56. Judy Yung, " 'A Bowlful of Tears': Chinese Women Immigrants on Angel Island," *Frontiers* 2 (Summer 1977): 52–55; see also Yung, *Island: Poetry and History of Chinese Immigrants on Angel Island, 1910–1940* (San Francisco: Chinese Culture Foundation, 1980).

57. Miriam King and Steven Ruggles, "American Immigration, Fertility, and Race Suicide at the Turn of the Century," *Journal of Interdisciplinary History* 20 (Winter 1990): 347–70.

58. The classic statement of this dimension of nativist fears is Madison Grant, *The Passing of the Great Race: or, The Racial Basis of European History* (New York: C. Scribner's Sons, 1916). See also Arthur W. Calhoun, *Race Sterility and Suicide*, vol. 3 in *A Social History of the American Family from Colonial Times to the Present* (Cleveland: Arthur H. Clark, 1917–1919).

59. Takaki, *Strangers from a Different Shore*, pp. 40–41, 46–47; Chan, *Entry Denied*; Glenn, *Issei, Nisei, War Bride*, p. 17.

60. Chan, "Exclusion of Chinese Women," pp. 110–11, 114–18.

61. Besides U.S. Commissioner of Immigration, *Annual Report*, 1908, p. 126, and *Annual Report*, 1919, p. 57, see Glenn, *Issei, Nisei, Warbride*, pp. 43–48; Alice Chai, "Picture Brides: Feminist Analysis of Life Histories of Hawaii's Early Immigrant Women from Japan, Okinawa and Korea," pp. 123–38 in *Seeking Common Ground*.

62. U.S. Commissioner of Immigration, *Annual Report*, 1907, p. 100–101.

63. U.S. Commissioner of Immigration, *Annual Reports*, 1917, 1918, 1921, 1928.

64. U.S. Commissioner of Immigration, *Annual Reports*, 1921, pp. 16–17; 1924, p. 28; 1925, p. 3.

65. Houstoun et al., "Female Predominance of Immigration."

66. Barbara Lobodzinska, "A Cross-Cultural Study of Mixed Marriage in Poland and the United States," *International Journal of Sociology and the Family* 15 (Spring-Autumn 1985): 94–117.

67. George J. Borjas, *Friends or Strangers: The Impact of Immigrants on the U.S. Economy* (New York: Basic Books, 1990), p. 51, chap. 12.

68. See coverage of the Houstoun et al. report, "Female Predominance of Immigration," in *New York Times*, September 9, 1985, I, p. 15.

69. Teresa A. Barnes, "The Fight for Control of African Women's Mobility in Colonial Zimbabwe, 1900–1939, "*SIGNS* 17, 3 (Spring 1992): 586–608.

70. Douglas S. Massey and Katherine M. Schnabel, "Background Characteristics of Undocumented Hispanic Migrants to the United States: A Review of Recent Research," *Migration Today* 11 (1983): 9–13; Frank Bean et al., "The Number of Illegal Migrants of Mexican Origin in the United-States: Sex Ratio–Based Estimates for 1980," *Demography* 20 (February 1980): 99–109; Gilberto Cardenas and Estevan T. Flores, *The Migration and Settlement of Undocumented Women* (Austin: Center for Mexican American Studies, University of Texas at Austin, 1986).

4. LIVES OF LABOR

1. Amott and Matthaei, *Race, Gender, and Work*, Table 10–12; Jane Riblett Wilkie, "The Decline of Occupational Segregation between Black and White Women," *Research in Race and Ethnic Relations: A Research Annual*, ed. Cora Bagley Marrett and Cheryl Leggon, 4 (1982): 67–89; Barbara Harris, *Beyond Her Sphere: Women and the Professions in American History* (Westport, Conn.: Greenwood, 1978); Roberta Morse, *The*

Black Female Professional (Washington, D.C.: Mental Health Research and Development Center, Institute for Urban Affairs and Research, Howard University, 1983).

2. For previous uses of this phrase, see Lamphere, *From Working Daughters to Working Mothers*; Lynn Y. Weiner, *From Working Girl to Working Mother: The Female Labor Force in the United States, 1820–1980* (Chapel Hill: University of North Carolina Press, 1985).

3. From a large literature see Christine E. Bose, "Household Resources and U.S. Women's Work: Factors Affecting Gainful Employment at the Turn of the Century," *American Sociological Review* 49 (1984): 474–90.

4. Dickinson, *The Role of the Immigrant Women*, chap. 4; Kessler-Harris, *Out to Work*, chap. 5.

5. Thomas Kessner and Betty B. Caroli, "New Immigrant Women at Work: Italians and Jews in New York City," *Journal of Ethnic Studies* 5 (Winter 1978): 19–32; Barbara M. Klaczynska, "Why Women Work: A Comparison of Various Groups in Philadelphia, 1910–1930," *Labor History* 17 (Winter 1976): 73–87.

6. Compare Stephen Gross, "Domestic Labor as a Life-Course Event: The Effects of Ethnicity in Turn-of-the-Century America," *Social Science History* 15 (Fall 1991): 397–416, and Diane Vecchio, "Italian Women in Industry: The Shoeworkers of Endicott, New York, 1914–1935," *Journal of American Ethnic History* 8 (Spring 1989): 60–86, to Elizabeth H. Pleck, "A Mother's Wages: Income Earning among Married Italian and Black Women, 1896–1911," pp. 367–392 in *The American Family in Social Historical Perspective*, ed. Michael Gordon, 2nd ed. (New York: St. Martin's, 1978).

7. Glenn, *Daughters of the Shtetl*.

8. Ronald T. Takaki, *Pau Hana: Plantation Life and Labor in Hawaii, 1835–1920* (Honolulu: University of Hawaii Press, 1983); Miriam Sharma, "Labor Migration and Class Formation among Filipinas in Hawaii, 1906–1946," pp. 337–58 in Cheng and Bonacich, *Labor Immigration under Capitalism*.

9. Glenn, *Issei, Nisei, War Bride*, Table 1; Gabaccia, *Militants and Migrants*, p. 104.

10. David Montgomery, *The Fall of the House of Labor: The Workplace, the State, and American Labor Activism, 1865–1925* (New York: Cambridge University Press, 1987), p. 243.

11. Carpenter, *Immigrants and their Children*.

12. Virginia Yans-McLaughlin, "A Flexible Tradition: Southern Italian Immigrants Confront a New Work Experience," *Journal of Social History* 7, 4 (Summer 1974): 429–45.

13. Stephen Steinberg, *The Ethnic Myth: Race, Ethnicity and Class in America* (Boston: Beacon, 1981), chap. 6.

14. Evelyn N. Glenn, "Occupational Ghettoization: Japanese American Women and Domestic Service, 1905–1970," *Ethnicity* 8 (1981): 351–86.

15. Diner, *Erin's Daughters in America*, pp. 80–84; Joy K. Lintelman, " 'Our Serving Sisters': Swedish-American Domestic Servants and Their Ethnic Community," *Social Science History* 15 (Fall 1991): 381–96; Inga Holmberg, "Taboos and Morals or Economy and Family Status? Occupational Choice among Immigrant Women in the U.S.," pp. 25–43 in *Swedish Life in American Cities*, ed. Dag Blanck and Harold Runblom (Uppsala, Sweden: Centre for Multiethnic Research, Uppsala University, 1991).

16. Vicki L. Ruiz, *Cannery Women, Cannery Lives: Mexican Women, Unionization, and the California Food Processing Industry, 1930–1950* (Albuquerque: University of New Mexico Press, 1987).

17. Leslie Tentler, *Wage-Earning Women*, (New York: Oxford University Press, 1979), chap. 4; Lamphere, *From Working Daughters to Working Mothers*, chaps. 2–3; Dickinson, *The Role of the Immigrant Women*, chaps. 5–6; Kessler-Harris, *Out to Work*, chap. 5.

18. Tentler, *Wage-Earning Women*, chap. 6; S. J. Kleinberg, *The Shadow of the Mills: Working-Class Families in Pittsburgh, 1870–1907* (Pittsburgh: University of Pittsburgh Press, 1989), chap. 8; Kessler-Harris, *Out to Work*, pp. 191–95.

19. Tentler, *Wage-Earning Women*, chap. 1; Mark Aldrich and Randy Albelda, "Determinants of Working Women's Wages During the Progressive Era," *Explorations in Economic History* 27 (October 1980): 323–41.

20. Tentler, *Wage-Earning Women*, chap. 2; Kessler-Harris, *Out to Work*, chap. 6; Glenn, *Daughters of the Shtetl*, pp. 98–131.

21. Riis, *How the Other Half Lives*, chap. 20.

22. Christine Stansell, "The Origins of the Sweatshop: Women and Early Industrialization in New York City," pp. 78–103 in *Working-Class America: Essays in Labor, Community and American Society*, ed. Michael H. Frisch and Daniel J. Walkowitz (Urbana: University of Illinois Press, 1983); Eileen Boris and Cynthia R. Daniels, eds., *Homework: Historical and Contemporary Perspectives on Paid Labor at Home* (Urbana: University of Illinois Press, 1989).

23. Eileen Boris, "Regulating Industrial Homework: The Triumph of 'Sacred Motherhood,' " *Journal of American History* 71 (1985): 745–63.

24. Barbara Hobson, *Uneasy Virtue: The Politics of Prostitution and the American Reform Tradition* (New York: Basic Books, 1984), pp. 88–94.

25. *Notable American Women: The Modern Period*, pp. 7–8.

26. Ruth Rosen, ed., *The Maimie Papers* (Old Westbury: Feminist Press, 1977).

27. Chan, "The Exclusion of Chinese Women," p. 107; on Ah Toy, see Curt Gentry, *Madams of San Francisco* (Garden City: Doubleday, 1964); Joyce M. Wong, "Prostitution: San Francisco Chinatown, Mid- and Late Nineteenth-Century," *Bridge* 6 (Winter 1978–1979): 23–39.

28. Charlotte B. Borst, "The Training and Practice of Midwives: A Wisconsin Study," *Bulletin of the History of Medicine* 62 (Winter 1988): 606–27.

29. William C. Holden, *Teresita* (Owings Mill, Md.: Stemmer House, 1978); Richard Rodriguez and Gloria C. Rodriguez, "Teresa Urrea: Her Life as It Affected the Mexican-U.S. Frontier," *El Grito: Journal of Contemporary Mexican American Thought* 5 (Summer 1972): 48–68.

30. Sonia Hamburger, "Profile of Curanderos: A Study of Mexican Folk Practitioners," *International Journal of Social Psychiatry* 24 (Spring 1978): 19–25; Oliva M. Espin, "Spiritual Power and The Mundane World: Hispanic Female Healers in Urban U.S. Communities," *Women's Studies Quarterly* 16 (Fall/Winter 1988): 33–47.

31. Charlotte G. Borst, "Wisconsin's Midwives as Working Women: Immigrant Midwives and the Limits of a Traditional Occupation, 1870–1920," *Journal of American Ethnic History* 8 (Spring 1989): 24–59; Eugene Declercq and Richard Lacroix, "The Immigrant Midwives of Lawrence: The Conflict Between Law and Culture in Early Twentieth-Century Massachusetts," *Bulletin of the History of Medicine* 49 (1985): 232–46.

32. Nancy S. Dye, "Modern Obstetrics and Working-Class Women: The New York Midwifery Dispensary, 1890–1920," *Journal of Social History* 20 (1987): 549–64.

33. Nancie L. González, "Giving Birth in America: The Immigrant's Dilemma," pp. 241–53 in Simon and Brettell, *International Migration*.

34. Hill, *Women in Gainful Occupations*, table 75.

35. Ilene DeVault, *Sons and Daughters of Labor: Class and Clerical Work in Turn-of-the-Century Pittsburgh* (Ithaca: Cornell University Press, 1990); Cohen, *Workshop to Office*.

36. Glenn, *Issei, Nisei, War Bride*, pp. 102–105.

37. Valerie Matsumoto, "Japanese American Women during World War II," *Frontiers* 8 (1984): 6–14.

38. Vicki L. Ruiz, "By the Day or Week: Mexican Domestic Workers in El Paso," pp. 269–83 in *"To Toil the Livelong Day;" America's Women at Work, 1780–1980*, ed. Carol Groneman and Mary Beth Norton (Ithaca: Cornell University Press, 1987); Ruiz, " 'And Miles to Go. . . . ': Mexican Women and Work, 1930–1950," pp. 117–36 in *Western Women: Their Land, their Lives*, ed. Lillian Schlissel, Vicki L. Ruiz, and Janice Monk (Albuquerque: University of New Mexico Press, 1988), here p. 118.

39. Marta Tienda et al., "Immigration, Gender, and the Process of Occupational Change in the United States, 1970–1980," *International Migration Review* 18 (Winter 1984): 1021–44.

40. A sampler from an extensive literature includes: Louise Lamphere, "From Working Daughters to Working Mothers: Production and Reproduction in an Industrial Community," *American Ethnologist* 13 (1986): 118–30; M. Patricia Fernández-Kelly, "Delicate Transactions: Gender, Home, and Employment among Hispanic Women," in *Uncertain Terms: Negotiating Gender in American Culture,* ed. Faye Ginsburg and Anna Lowenhaupt Tsing (Boston: Beacon, 1990).

41. Geoffrey Carliner, "Female Labor Force Participation Rates for Nine Ethnic Groups," *Journal of Human Resources* (Spring 1981): 286–93; Paul M. Ong, "Immigrant Wives' Labor Force Participation," *Industrial Relations* 26 (Fall 1987): 296–303.

42. George J. Borjas and Marta Tienda, *Hispanics in the U.S. Economy* (New York: Academic Press, 1985), table 1.4; Morrison G. Wong and Charles Hirschman, "Labor Participation and Socioeconomic Attainment of Asian-American Women," *Sociological Perspectives* 26 (1983): 423–46.

43. David Haines, "Vietnamese Refugee Women in the U.S. Labor Force: Continuity or Change," pp. 62–75 in *International Migration.*

44. Rita J. Simon et al., "The Social and Economic Adjustment of Soviet Jewish Women in the United States," pp. 76–94 in *International Migration.*

45. Barry R. Chiswick, "Immigrant Earnings Patterns by Sex, Race and Ethnic Group," *Monthly Labor Review* 103 (October 1980): 22–25; Suzanne Model, "Caribbean Immigrants: A Black Success Story?" *International Migration Review* 25, 2 (Summer 1991): 248–76.

46. Deborah Woo, "The Socioeconomic Status of Asian American Women in the Labor Force: An Alternative View," *Sociological Perspectives* 28 (July 1985): 307–38.

47. Borjas, *Friends or Strangers,* p. 43.

48. Sonia Jasso and Maria Mazorra, "Following the Harvest: The Health Hazards of Migrant and Seasonal Farmworking Women," pp. 86–99 in *Double Exposure: Women's Health Hazards on the Job and at Home,* ed. Wendy Chavkin (New York: Monthly Review Press, 1984); Alicia Chavira, "Tienes Que Ser Valiente: Mexicana Migrants in a Midwestern Farm Labor Camp," pp. 64–73 in *Mexicanas at Work in the United States,* ed. Margarita B. Melville (Houston: University of Houston Mexican American Studies Program, 1988).

49. Sherrie A. Kossoudji and Susan I. Ranney, "The Labor Market Experience of Female Migrants: The Case of Temporary Mexican Migration to the U.S.," *International Migration Review* 18 (Winter 1984): 1120–1143; Rita J. Simon and Margo C. DeLey, "The Work Experience of Undocumented Mexican Women Migrants in Los Angeles," *International Migration Review* 18 (Winter 1984): 1212–1229; Shellee Colen, " 'With Respect and Feelings': Voices of West Indian Child Care and Domestic Workers in New York City," pp. 46–70 in *All American Women; Lines That Divide, Ties That Bind,* ed. Johnetta B. Cole (New York and London: The Free Press and Collier Macmillan, 1986).

50. Penny Hollander Feldman with Alice M. Sapienza and Nancy M. Kane, *Who Cares for Them? Workers in the Home Care Industry* (New York: Greenwood, 1990); Suvarna Thaker, "The Quality of Life of Asian Indian Women in the Motel Industry," *South Asia Bulletin* 2, 1 (1982): 68–73.

51. Patricia Zavella, *Women's Work and Chicano Families: Cannery Workers of the Santa Clara Valley* (Ithaca, N.Y.: Cornell University Press, 1987).

52. Abeles, Schwartz, Hackel and Silverblatt, Inc., *The Chinatown Garment Study* (New York: International Ladies Garment Workers Union, 1983); Sheldon L. Maram, *Hispanic Workers in the Garment and Restaurant Industries in Los Angeles County: A Social and Economic Profile* (La Jolla: Program in U.S.-Mexican Studies, University of California at San Diego, 1980).

53. Morrison G. Wong, "Chinese Sweatshops in the United States: A Look at the Garment Industry," pp. 357–79 in *Research in the Sociology of Work: A Research Annual*, ed. Ida H. Simpson and Richard L. Simpson (Greenwich, Conn.: JAI Press, 1983).

54. María Patricia Fernández-Kelly, "Economic Restructuring in the United States: Hispanic Women in the Garment and Electronics Industries," *Women and Work: An Annual Review*, 3 (1988): 49–65 (Newbury Park, Calif.: Sage, 1988); María Patricia Fernández-Kelly, "Invisible Amidst the Glitter: Hispanic Women in the Southern California Electronics Industry," pp. 265–90 in *The Worth of Women's Work*, ed. Anne Statham (Albany: State University of New York Press, 1988).

55. See Boris and Daniels, *Homework*, sec. 4.

56. Kamphoefner et al., *News from the Land of Freedom*, p. 226; Osterud, *Bonds of Community*, pp. 284–85.

57. Mary Paik Lee, *Quiet Odyssey: A Pioneer Korean Woman in America* (Seattle: University of Washington Press, 1990), pp. 86–88.

58. L. DeAne Lagerquist, *In America the Men Milk the Cows: Factors of Gender, Ethnicity, and Religion in the Americanization of Norwegian-American Women* (Brooklyn, NY: Carlson Publishing, 1992); Klaus Hoffman, "Sewing Is for Women, Horses Are for Men: The Role of German Russian Women," pp. 131–44 in *Germans from Russia in Colorado*, ed. Sidney Heitman (Ann Arbor: Western Social Science Association, 1978).

59. Kathie Friedman Kasaba, " 'A Tailor Is Nothing without a Wife, and Very Often a Child': Gender and Labor-Force Formation in the New York Garment Industry, 1880–1920," in *Racism, Sexism and the World System*, ed. Joan Smith (New York: Greenwood, 1988); see also Evelyn N. Glenn, "Women, Labor Migration and Household Work: Japanese American Women in the Pre-War Period," pp. 93–114 in *Ingredients for Women's Employment Policy*, ed. Christine Bose and Glenna Spitze (Albany: State University of New York Press, 1987).

60. Evelyn N. Glenn, "Split Household, Small Producer and Dual Wage Earner: An Analysis of Chinese-American Family Strategies," *Journal of Marriage and the Family* 45 (February 1983): 35–46.

61. Parvin Abyaneh, "Post-Migration Economic Roles of Females and Patriarchy in Immigrant Iranian Families," Ph.D. diss., University of California, Riverside, 1986.

62. Chung Y. Kay, "At the Palace: Work, Ethnicity and Gender in a Chinese Restaurant," *Studies in Sexual Politics* 3 (1985): 1–83.

63. Chai, "Picture Brides," p. 129.

64. Laurence A. Glasco, "The Life Cycles and Household Structure of American Ethnic Groups: Irish, German and Native-Born Whites in Buffalo, New York, 1855," *Journal of Urban History* 1 (May 1975): 339–64; John Modell and Tamara K. Hareven, "Urbanization and the Malleable Household: An Examination of Boarding and Lodging in American Families," *Journal of Marriage and the Family* 35 (August 1973): 467–79.

65. Virginia Yans-McLaughlin, "Italian Women and Work: Experience and Perception," pp. 101–19 in *Class, Sex, and the Woman Worker*, ed. Milton Cantor and Bruce Laurie (Westport, Conn.: Greenwood Press, 1977).

66. Ogden, *The Great American Housewife*, pp. 86–90; Strasser, *Never Done*, chap. 12; Breckinridge, *New Homes*, pp. 150–53.

67. Cowan, *More Work for Mother*, pp. 71–73; Strasser, *Never Done*, chap. 1.

68. Susan G. Davis, "Women's Roles in a Company Town: New York Mills, 1900–1951," *New York Folklore* 4 (Summer/Winter 1978): 35–47; Maria Susanna Garroni, "Coal Mines, Farm and Quarry Frontiers: The Different Americas of Italian Immigrant Women," *Studia Nordamericana* 5, 2 (1988): 115–36.

69. Ewen, *Immigrant Women*, pp. 172–76; Gabaccia, *From Sicily to Elizabeth Street* p. 92; Weinberg; *The World of Our Mothers*, pp. 140–41; Cowan and Cowan, *Our Parents' Lives*, pp. 116–17.

70. Gabaccia, *From Sicily to Elizabeth Street*, pp. 95–96; Cowan, *More Work for Mother*, pp. 165–67; Ewen, *Immigrant Women*, chap. 9; Strasser, *Never Done*, chaps. 5 and 6; Breckinridge, *New Homes*, pp. 60–61.

71. Cowan, *More Work for Mother*, pp. 164–66; Strasser, *Never Done*, chaps. 2 and 3.

72. Gretchen A. Condran and Ellen A. Kramarow, "Child Mortality among Jewish Immigrants to the United States," *Journal of Interdisciplinary History* 22 (Autumn 1991): 223–54.

73. Ronald L. William et al., "Pregnancy Outcomes among Spanish Surnamed Women in California," *American Journal of Public Health* 76 (April 1986): 387–91.

74. Barbara Valanis, "Relative Contribution of Maternal Social and Biological Characteristics to Birth Weight and Gestation among Mothers of Different Childhood Socioeconomic Status," *Social Biology* 26 (Fall 1979): 211–25; S. J. Ventura and S. M. Taftel, "Childbearing Characteristics of United States and Foreign-Born Hispanic Mothers," *Public Health Reports* 100 (November/December 1985): 647–652; Ingrid Swenson, "Birth Weight, Apgar Scores, Labor and Delivery Complications and Prenatal Characteristics of Southeast Asian Adolescents and Older Mothers," *Adolescence* 21 (Fall 1986): 711–22; Wendy Chavkin et al., "Reproductive Health: Caribbean Women in New York City, 1980–1984," *International Migration Review* 21 (Fall 1987): 609–25.

75. Carmen A. Johnson, "Breast-feeding and Social Class Mobility: The Case of Mexican Migrant Mothers in Houston, Texas," pp. 66–82 in *Twice a Minority: Mexican American Women*, ed. Margarita B. Melville (St. Louis: C. V. Mosby, 1980); Adela de la Torre and Lynda Rush, "The Determinants of Breastfeeding for Mexican Migrant Women," *International Migration Review* 21 (Fall 1987): 728–44.

76. Ewen, *Immigrant Women*, pp. 154–57; Ogden, *The Great American Housewife*, pp. 119–21; Breckinridge, *New Homes for Old*, chap. 3.

77. Kay F. Turner, "Mexican American Home Altars: Towards Their Interpretation," *Aztlán* 13 (Spring/Fall 1982): 309–26; Turner, "La Vela Prendida: Mexican-American Women's Home Altars," *Folklore Women's Communication* 25 (1981): 5–6.

78. Lizabeth A. Cohen, "Embellishing a Life of Labor: An Interpretation of the Material Culture of American Working-Class Homes, 1885–1915," *Journal of American Culture* 3 (Winter 1980): 752–75.

79. Gabaccia, *From Sicily to Elizabeth Street*, p. 93.

80. Mary G. Castro, "Work Versus Life: Columbian Women in New York," pp. 231–59 in *Women and Change in Latin America*, ed. June Nash and Helen Safa (South Hadley, Mass.: Bergin and Garvey, 1986); Patricia Pessar, "The Dominicans: Women in the Household and the Garment Industry," pp. 103–29 in *New Immigrants in New York*, ed. Nancy Foner (New York: Columbia University Press, 1987).

81. Dorothee Schneider, " 'For Whom Are All the Good Things in Life?': German American Housewives Discuss Their Budgets," pp. 145–62 in *German Workers in Industrial Chicago, 1850–1910*, ed. Hartmut Keil and John B. Jentz (DeKalb, Ill.: Northern Illinois University Press, 1983).

5. ALL HER KIN

1. Ewen, *Immigrant Women*, p. 86.

2. Scholarly refutations of the "disorganization" hypothesis began with Yans-McLaughlin, *Family and Community*, pp. 18–22.

3. Sharon Harley, "For the Good of Family and Race: Gender, Work, and Domestic Roles in the Black Community, 1880–1930," *SIGNS* 15, 2 (Winter 1990): 336–49.

4. John S. MacDonald and Leatrice D. MacDonald, "Chain Migration, Ethnic Neighborhood Formation and Social Networks," *Milbank Memorial Fund Quarterly* 42, 1 (1964): 82–97.

5. M. Estellie Smith, "Networks and Migration Resettlement: Cherchez la Femme," *Anthropological Quarterly* 49 (January 1976): 20–27.

6. Donna R. Gabaccia, "Kinship, Culture and Migration: A Sicilian Example," *Journal of American Ethnic History* 3 (1984): 39–53. Compare to Robert C. Ostergren, "Kinship Networks and Migration: A Nineteenth-Century Swedish Example," *Social Science History* 6, 3 (Summer 1982): 293–320.

7. Vivian Garrison and Carol I. Weiss, "Dominican Family Networks and United States Immigration Policy: A Case Study," *International Migration Review* 13 (Summer 1979): 264–83; Isa María Soto, "West Indian Child Fostering; Its Role in Migrant Exchanges," pp. 131–49 in *Caribbean Life in New York City: Sociocultural Dimensions,* ed. Constance R. Sutton and Elsa M. Chaney (New York: Center for Migration Studies, 1987).

8. See "The Boarder Problem" in Pehotsky, *The Slavic Immigrant Woman;* Ewen, *Immigrant Women,* pp. 119–21.

9. Weinberg, *The World of Our Mothers,* pp. 135–36.

10. Andrew Vázsonyi, "The *Cicisbeo* and the Magnificent Cuckold: Boardinghouse Life and Lore in Immigrant Communities," *Journal of American Folklore* 91 (April-June 1978): 641–56.

11. Gabaccia, *From Sicily to Elizabeth Street,* pp. 77–79.

12. Simon, *Bronx Primitive: Portraits in a Childhood* (New York: Harper Colophon, 1983).

13. Herbert J. Gans, *The Urban Villagers: Group and Class in the Life of Italian-Americans* (New York: Free Press, 1982, orig. pub. 1962); Arlene Mancuso, "Women of Old Town," pp. 312–23 in *The Italian Immigrant Woman.*

14. Chai, "Picture Brides," p. 131.

15. Alice Y. Chai, "Freed from the Elders but Locked into Labor: Korean Immigrant Women in Hawaii," *Women's Studies* 13, 2 (1987): 223–34.

16. Donna R. Gabaccia, "Sicilians in Space: Environmental Change and Family Geography," *Journal of Social History* 16, 2 (1984): 53–66; Muir, *The Strongest Part of the Family,* pp. 145–46.

17. Di Leonardo, *The Varieties of Ethnic Experience.*

18. Yanagisako, *Transforming the Past.*

19. For early views, see Breckinridge, *New Homes for Old,* pp. 98–105. See also Alvena V. Seckar, "Slovak Wedding Customs," *New York Folklore Quarterly* 3 (Autumn 1947): 189–205; Colleen Leahy Johnson, "Celebrating the Family Cycle," pp. 90–105 in Colleen Leahy Johnson, *Growing Up and Growing Old in Italian-American Families* (New Brunswick: Rutgers University Press, 1985).

20. Micaela Di Leonardo, "The Female World of Cards and Holidays: Women, Families, and the Work of Kinship," *SIGNS* 12 (Spring 1987): 440–53; Carroll Smith Rosenberg, "The Female World of Love and Ritual: Relations Between Women in Nineteenth-Century America," *SIGNS* 1 (1975): 1–29.

21. Susan E. Keefe et al., "The Mexican-American Extended Family as an Emotional Support System," *Human Organization* 38 (Summer 1979), 144–52; Louise Lamphere et al., "Kin Networks and Strategies of Working-Class Portuguese Families in a New England Town," pp. 219–49 in *The Versatility of Kinship,* ed. Linda Cordell and Stephen Beckerman (New York: Academic Press, 1980).

22. Young I. Song, "A Study of Asian Immigrant Women Undergoing Postpartum Depression," pp. 203–15 in *Seeking Common Ground.*

23. Patricia D. Rose and Gretchen Van Boemel, "The Psychological Effects of War Trauma and Abuse on Older Cambodian Refugee Women," *Women and Therapy* 8, 4 (1989): 23–50.

24. Ewen, *Immigrant Women,* pp. 98–106.

25. Glenn H. Elder, Jr., *Children of the Great Depression* (Chicago: University of Chicago Press, 1974), pp. 88–89.

26. Gloria Romero et al., "Latinas without Work: Family, Occupational, and Economic Stress Following Unemployment," *Psychology of Women Quarterly* 12, 3 (1988): 281–97.

27. Ari L. Fridkis, "Desertion in the American Jewish Immigrant Family: The Work of the National Desertion Bureau in Cooperation with the Industrial Removal Office," *American Jewish History* 71 (December 1981): 285–99; Reena S. Friedman, " 'Send Me My Husband Who Is in New York City': Husband Desertion in the American Jewish Immigrant Community, 1900–1926," *Jewish Social Studies* 44 (Winter 1982): 1–18.

28. Lillian Brandt, *Five Hundred and Seventy-Four Deserters and Their Families* (New York: Charity Organization Society, 1905).

29. R. Griswold del Castillo, "La Familia Chicana: Social Changes in the Chicano Family of Los Angeles, 1850–1880," *Journal of Ethnic Studies* 3 (Spring 1975): 41–58.

30. W. Parker Frisbie, "Variations in Patterns of Marital Instability among Hispanics," *Journal of Marriage and the Family* 48 (February 1986): 99–106.

31. Marta Tienda and R. Angel, "Headship and Household Composition among Blacks, Hispanics, and Other Whites," *Social Forces* 6 (December 1982): 508–31.

32. Susan H. Buchanan, "Haitian Women in New York City," *Migration Today* 7 (September 1979): 19–25, 39.

33. Kleinberg, *Shadow of the Mills*, chap. 8; Helena Znaniecki Lopata, "Widowhood in Polonia," *Polish American Studies* 34, 2 (Autumn, 1977): 7–25.

34. Harvey Williams, "Social Isolation and the Elderly Immigrant Woman," *Pacific Historian* 26 (Summer 1982): 15–24.

35. Lucy C. Yu, "Acculturation and Stress within Chinese American Families," *Journal of Comparative Family Studies* 15 (Spring 1984): 77–94.

36. Christine Stansell, "Women, Children, and the Uses of the Streets: Class and Gender Conflict in New York City, 1850–1860," *Feminist Studies* 8 (1982): 309–35.

37. Ellen Gray and John Cosgrove, "Ethnocentric Perception of Childrearing Practices in Protective Services," *Child Abuse and Neglect* 9, 3 (1985): 389–96.

38. Seong H. Park, "The Identification of Factors Related to Childbearing Expectations of Korean-American Immigrant Parents of Preschool Children," Ph.D. diss., North Texas State University, 1983.

39. John W. Briggs, "Fertility and Cultural Change among Families in Italy and America," *American Historical Review* 91 (December 1986): 1129–45.

40. See *After Ellis Island: A 1910 Census Monograph* (New York: Russell Sage Foundation, 1994), chap. 7.

41. Leslie J. Reagan, " 'About to Meet Her Maker': Women, Doctors, Dying Declarations, and the States' Investigation of Abortion, Chicago, 1867–1940," *Journal of American History* 77 (March 1991): 1240–64.

42. Watkins et al., *After Ellis Island.*

43. Margaret Sanger, *An Autobiography* (New York: W. W. Norton, 1938, repr. Dover Publications, 1971), pp. 86–92.

44. Avery Guest, "Fertility Variation among the U.S. Foreign Stock Population in 1900," *International Migration Review* 16 (Fall 1982): 577–96.

45. Tamara Hareven and Maris A. Vinovskis, "Patterns of Childbearing in Late Nineteenth-Century America," pp. 85–125 in *Family and Population in Nineteenth-Century America*, ed. Tamara K. Hareven and Maris A. Vinovskis (Princeton: Princeton University Press, 1978).

46. Kathleen Ford, "Declining Fertility Rates of Immigrants to the United States (With Some Exceptions)," *Sociology and Social Research* 70, 1 (1985): 68–70.

47. Rita Simon, "Sociology and Immigrant Women," in *Seeking Common Ground*, table 2.5.

48. Frank D. Bean and Gary Swicegood, *Mexican American Fertility Patterns* (Austin: University of Texas Press, 1985); Elizabeth H. Stephen, *At the Crossroads: Fertility of Mexican American Women* (New York: Garland, 1989).

49. Rubén G. Rumbaut and John R. Weeks, "Fertility and Adaptation: Indochinese Refugees in the United States," *International Migration Review* 20 (1986): 428–65.

50. H. Aviaro, "Latina Attitudes towards Abortion," *Nuestro* 5 (August/September 1981): 43–44.

51. Frank D. Bean and Gary Swicegood, "Generation, Female Education, and Mexican-American Fertility," *Social Science Quarterly* 63 (1982): 1311–44; Nancy A. Fischer and John P. Marcum, "Ethnic Integration, Socioeconomic Status and Fertility among Mexican Americans," *Social Science Quarterly* 65 (June 1984): 583–93.

52. Tamara K. Hareven and Maris A. Vinovskis, "Marital Fertility and Occupation in Urban Families: An Analysis of South Boston and South End in 1880," *Journal of Social History* 8 (Spring 1975): 69–93.

53. David Heer, "The Marital Status of Second-Generation Americans," *American Sociological Review* 26, 2 (1961): 233–41.

54. Frank D. Bean et al., "Generational Differences in Fertility among Mexican Americans: Implications for Assessing Immigration Effects," *Social Science Quarterly* 65 (June 1984): 573–82.

55. Letters of Barbro Ramseth, in *"In Their Own Words": Letters from Norwegian Immigrants*, ed. Solveig Zempel (Minneapolis: University of Minnesota Press, 1991).

56. Rosina M. Becerra and Diane De Anda, "Pregnancy and Motherhood among Mexican American Adolescents," *Health and Social Work* 9 (Spring 1984): 106–23.

57. Pearlina B. Namerow and J. E. Jones, "Ethnic Variation in Adolescent Use of a Contraceptive Service," *Journal of Adolescent Health Care* 3 (1982): 165–72; C. S. Aneshensel et al., "Fertility and Fertility-Related Behavior among Mexican-American and Non-Hispanic White Female Adolescents," *Journal of Health and Social Behavior* 30 (March 1989): 56–76.

58. Colleen Leahy Johnson, "Sibling Solidarity: Its Origin and Functioning in Italian-American Families," *Journal of Marriage and the Family* 44, 1 (February 1982): 155–67.

59. David Nasaw, *Children of the City, At Work and At Play* (New York: Oxford University Press, 1985), chap. 7.

60. M. Joselyn Armstrong, "Ethnicity and Sex Role Socialization: A Comparative Example Using Life History Data from Hawaii," *Sex Roles: A Journal of Research* 10 (February 1984): 157–81.

61. Josefina J. Card, "The Malleability of Fertility-Related Attitudes and Behavior in a Filipino Migrant Sample," *Demography* 15, 4 (1978): 459–76.

62. Ewen, *Immigrant Women*, pp. 96–97.

63. See Baum et al., *The Jewish Woman in America*, pp. 235–37.

64. Sydney S. Weinberg, "Jewish Mothers and Immigrant Daughters: Positive and Negative Role Models," *Journal of American Ethnic History* 6 (Spring 1987): 39–55; Sharon Hartman Strom, "Italian American Women and Their Daughters in Rhode Island: The Adolescence of Two Generations, 1900–1950," pp. 191–205 in *The Italian Immigrant Woman*; Judith E. Smith, "Italian Mothers, American Daughters: Changes in Work and Family Roles," ibid., pp. 206–21.

65. Song, "A Study of Asian Immigrant Women," p. 211.

66. Marvin K. Opler and Jerome L. Singer, "Ethnic Differences in Behavior and Psychopathology: Italian and Irish," *International Journal of Social Psychiatry* 2 (July 1956–April 1957): 11–23.

67. Armine Proudian, "Perceived Parental Power and Parental Identification among Armenian-American Adolescents," *Psychological Reports* 53 (December 1983): 1101–02.

68. Elizabeth G. Messina, "Narratives of Nine Italian American Women: Childhood, Work and Marriage," *Italian Americana* 10, 2 (Spring/Summer 1992): 186–202; Joseph J. Parot, "The 'Serdeczna Matko' of the Sweatshops: Marital and Family Crises of Immigrant Working-Class Women in Late Nineteenth-Century Chicago,"

pp. 155–84 in *The Polish Presence in Canada and America,* ed. Frank Renkiewicz (Toronto: Multicultural Society of Ontario, 1982).

69. Ellen Lewin, *Mothers and Children: Latin American Immigrants in San Francisco* (New York: Arno Press, 1980).

70. Charlotte Ikels, "Parental Perspectives on the Significance of Marriage," *Journal of Marriage and the Family* 47 (May 1985): 253–64.

71. Keum-Young Chung Pan, *Korean Elderly Women in America: Everyday Life, Health, and Illness* (New York: AMS Press, 1991).

72. Ewen, *Immigrant Women,* pp. 97–98.

73. Smith, *Family Connections,* pp. 60–61.

74. Weinberg, *The World of Our Mothers,* pp. 122–23.

75. Peiss, *Cheap Amusements,* pp. 69–71.

76. Tentler, *Wage-Earning Women,* pp. 8–9; Lamphere, *From Working Daughters to Working Mothers,* p. 36.

77. Glenn, *Daughters of the Shtetl,* pp. 157–159; Glenn, *Issei, Nisei, Warbride,* pp. 226–27; Ruiz, "The Flapper and the Chaperone," pp. 141–57 in *Seeking Common Ground,* here pp. 141, 148.

78. Ewen, *Immigrant Women,* pp. 232–33.

79. Prieto, "Cuban Women in New Jersey," pp. 196–98; Beverly Sewell-Coker et al., "Social Work Practice with West Indian Immigrants," *Social Casework* 66 (November 1985): 563–68.

80. Musab U. Siddiqui and Earl Y. Reeves, "A Comparative Study of Mate Selection Criteria among Indians in India and the United States," *International Journal of Comparative Sociology* 27 (September-December 1986): 226–33.

81. Strom, "Italian-American Women," p. 195.

82. Janet E. Rasmussen, " 'I Met Him at Normanna Hall': Ethnic Cohesion and Marital Patterns among Scandinavian Immigrant Women," *Norwegian-American Studies* 32 (1989): 71–92.

83. Peter Adler et al., "Familiar Correlates of Gang Membership: Exploratory Study of Mexican-American Youth," *Hispanic Journal of Behavioral Sciences* 6 (March 1984): 65–76; Mary G. Harris, *Cholas, Latino Girls and Gangs* (New York AMS Press, 1988).

84. Phyllis Deutsch, "Theater of Mating: Jewish Summer Camps and Cultural Transformation," *American Jewish History* 75 (1986): 307–21.

85. Peiss, *Cheap Amusements,* pp. 51–55; Stansell, *City of Women,* pp. 83–101.

86. Meyerowitz, *Women Adrift,* p. 7; Tentler, *Wage-Earning Women,* chap. 5.

87. Mary Lou Locke, "Out of the Shadows and into the Western Sun: Working Women of the Late Nineteenth-Century Urban Far West," *Journal of Urban History* 16 (February 1990): 175–204.

88. Louise Levitas Henriksen, *Anzia Yezierska: A Writer's Life* (New Brunswick, N.J.: Rutgers University Press, 1988); see Yezierska's fictionalized account of her early life in her novel, *Breadgivers;* Kate Simon, *A Wider World: Portraits in an Adolescence* (New York: Harper & Row, 1986).

89. Sinke, "The International Marriage Market," p. 76.

90. Lintelman, " 'America is the Woman's Promised Land,' " p. 19; contrast Diner, *Erin's Daughters,* pp. 63–64, and Nolan, *Ourselves Alone,* pp. 76–77.

91. Paul R. Spickard, *Mixed Blood: Intermarriage and Ethnic Identity in Twentieth-Century America* (Madison: University of Wisconsin Press, 1989), chap. 6.

92. Ira DeAugustine Reid, *The Negro Immigrant: His Background, Characteristics, and Social Adjustment, 1899–1937* (New York: Columbia University Press, 1939), p. 143.

93. Karen Leonard and Bruce LaBrack, "Conflict and Compatibility in Punjabi-Mexican Immigrant Families in Rural California, 1915–1965," *Journal of Marriage and the Family* 46 (1984): 527–37; Juan L. Gonzales, Jr., "Exogamous Marriage Patterns among the Sikhs of California: 1904–1905," *International Journal of Sociology of the Family* 16, 2 (Autumn 1986): 181–96.

94. Barbara Posadas, "Crossed Boundaries in Interracial Chicago: Filipino American Families since 1925," *Amerasia Journal* 8, 2 (1981): 31–52.

95. Harry H. Kitano et al., "Asian-American Interracial Marriage," *Journal of Marriage and the Family* 46 (February 1984): 179–90.

96. Deanna L. Pagnini and S. Philip Morgan, "Intermarriage and Social Distance among U.S. Immigrants at the Turn of the Century," *American Journal of Sociology* 96 (September 1990): 405–32; Richard N. Bernard, *The Melting Pot and the Altar* (Minneapolis: University of Minnesota Press, 1980).

97. Kwang Chung Kim and Won Moo Hurh, "The Burden of Double Roles: Korean Wives in the USA," *Ethnic and Racial Studies* 11 (April 1988): 151–67.

98. Kyriakos S. Markides and S. K. Hoppe, "Marital Satisfaction in Three Generations of Mexican Americans," *Social Science Quarterly* 66 (March 1985): 147–54.

99. Lillian Betts, "Italian Peasants in a New Law Tenement," *Harper's Bazaar* 38 (1904): 802–05.

100. Lamphere, *From Working Daughters to Working Mothers,* chap. 6.

101. Harriet Bloch, "Changing Domestic Roles among Polish Women," *Anthropological Quarterly* 49 (1976): 3–10.

102. Sylvia Guendelman and Auristela Pérez-Itriago, "Double Lives: The Changing Role of Women in Seasonal Migration," *Women's Studies* 13 (1987): 81–104.

103. Patricia R. Pessar, "The Linkage Between the Household and the Workplace of Dominican Women in the U.S.," *International Migration Review* 18 (Winter 1984): 1188–1211; Grasmuck and Pessar, *Between Two Islands,* chap. 6 and pp. 194–95.

104. Sandra M. J. Wong, "For the Sake of Kinship: The Overseas Family," Ph.D. diss., Stanford University, 1987.

105. Myra Marx Ferree, "Employment without Liberation: Cuban Women in the United States," *Social Science Quarterly* 60, 1 (June 1979): 35–35; Kwang Chung Kim and Won Moo Huhr, "Employment of Korean Immigrant Wives and the Division of Household Tasks," pp. 199–218 in *Korean Women in Transition.*

106. See chapter on sexuality in Louis Berman, *Sex Role Patterns in the Jewish Family* (New York: Thomas Yoseloff, 1968).

107. Oliva M. Espin, "Cultural and Historical Influences on Sexuality in Hispanic/Latin Women: Implication for Psychotherapy," pp. 149–64 in *Pleasure and Danger: Exploring Female Sexuality,* ed. Carole S. Vance (Boston: Routledge and Kegan Paul, 1984).

108. Rosalinda M. González, "Chicanas and Mexican Immigrant Families, 1920–1940: Women's Subordination and Family Exploitation," pp. 59–84 in *Decades of Discontent: The Women's Movement, 1920–1940,* ed. Lois Scharf and Joan M. Jensen (Westport, Conn.: Greenwood, 1983); Maxine B. Zinn, "Chicano Family Research: Conceptual Distortions and Alternative Directions," *Journal of Ethnic Studies* 7 (Fall 1979): 59–71.

109. Sanger, *An Autobiography,* pp. 86–92.

110. Bernard Wong, "Family, Kinship and Ethnic Identity of the Chinese in N.Y. City, with Comparative Remarks on the Chinese in Lima, Peru and Manila, Philippines," *Journal of Comparative Family Studies* 16 (Summer 1985): 231–54; Safia F. Haddad, "The Women's Role in the Socialization of Syrian-Americans in Chicago," pp. 84–101 in *The Arab Americans: Studies in Assimilation,* ed. Elaine C. Hagopian and Ann Paden (Wilmette, Ill.: Medina University Press, 1969).

111. Ruby B. Rich and Lourdes Arguelles, "Homosexuality, Homophobia and Revolution: Notes toward an Understanding of the Cuban Lesbian and Gay Male Experience, Part II," *SIGNS* 11 (Autumn 1985): 120–36; Pamela H., "Asian American Lesbians: An Emerging Voice in the Asian American Community," in Asian Women United, *Making Waves,* (Boston: Beacon Press, 1989).

112. Elizabeth H. Pleck, *Domestic Tyranny; The Making of American Social Policy against Family Violence from Colonial Times to the Present* (New York: Oxford University Press, 1987); Linda Gordon, *Heroes of Their Own Lives: The Politics and History of Family Violence* (New York: Viking Press, 1988), p. 9.

113. Gordon, *Heroes of Their Own Lives*, p. 9.

114. Karen M. Jacques, "Perceptions and Coping Behaviors of Anglo-American and Mexican Immigrant Battered Women: A Comparative Study," Ph.D. diss., United States International University, 1981; Young I. Song, *Silent Victims: Battered Women in Korean Immigrant Families* (San Francisco: Oxford Press, 1987).

115. Elizabeth H. Pleck, "Challenges to Traditional Authority in Immigrant Families," pp. 504–17 in *The American Family*.

116. Gordon, *Heroes of Their Own Lives*, p. 9; Diner, *Erin's Daughters in America*, pp. 113–15.

117. Mabel R. Fernald, *A Study of Women Delinquents in New York State* (New York: The Century, 1920); Elizabeth H. Pleck, "The Old World, New Rights, and the Limited Rebellion: Challenges to Traditional Authority in Immigrant Families," *Research in the Interweave of Social Roles* 3 (1983): 91–112.

118. " 'Die, My Daughter, Die!' " *People Magazine*, January 20, 1992, pp. 71–75.

119. Gordon, *Heroes of Their Own Lives*, p. 9.

120. John Bodnar, *Workers' World*, chap. 4.

121. See Patricia Morton, *Disfigured Images: The Historical Assault on Afro-American Women* (Westport, Conn.: Greenwood, 1991).

122. bell hooks, *Ain't I a Woman? Black Women and Feminism* (London: Pluto Press, 1981), pp. 55–56, 70–71.

6. WORKING TOGETHER

1. Milton M. Gordon, *Assimilation in American Life: The Role of Race, Religion and National Origins* (New York: Oxford University Press, 1964), pp. 70–71.

2. Kathleen Neils Conzen, "Immigrants, Immigrant Neighborhoods, and Ethnic Identity: Historical Issues," *Journal of American History* 66, 3 (December 1979): 603–15.

3. On distribution patterns, see James Paul Allen and Eugene James Turner, *We the People: An Atlas of America's Ethnic Diversity* (New York: Macmillan, 1988).

4. Kathleen N. Conzen, "Historical Approaches to the Study of Rural Ethnic Communities," pp. 1–18 in *Ethnicity on the Great Plains*, ed. Frederick C. Luebke (Lincoln: University of Nebraska Press, 1980).

5. David Ward, "The Emergence of Central Immigrant Ghettoes in American Cities: 1840–1920," *Annals of the Association of American Geographers* 58 (1968): 343–59; Sam Bass Warner, Jr., and Colin B. Burke, "Cultural Change and the Ghetto," *Journal of Contemporary History* 4 (October 1969): 173–87.

6. Santoli, *New Americans*, p. 309.

7. Kessner and Caroli, *Today's Immigrants*, chap. 4.

8. Louis Winnick, *New People in Old Neighborhoods: The Role of New Immigrants in Rejuvenating New York's Communities* (New York: Russell Sage Foundation, 1990).

9. Cited in Ewen, *Immigrant Women*, p. 189.

10. Weinberg, *The World of Our Mothers*, pp. 142–43; Liucija Baskaukas, "Multiple Identities: Adjusted Lithuanian Refugees in Los Angeles," *Urban Anthropology* 6, 2 (Summer 1977): 141–54.

11. Jon M. Kingsdale, "The 'Poor Man's Club': Social Functions of the Urban Working-Class Saloon," *American Quarterly* 25, 4 (October 1973): 472–89.

12. Beside Nasaw, *Children of the City*, pp. 32–34, see Cary Goodman, *Choosing Sides: Playground and Street Life on the Lower East Side* (New York: Schocken, 1979).

13. Gwen Kinkead, *Chinatown: A Portrait of a Closed Society* (New York: Harper-Collins, 1992), p. 52.

14. Quoted in Weinberg, *World of Our Mothers*, p. 142.

15. Ole E. Rolvaag, *Giants in the Earth* (New York: Harper and Brothers, 1929); Deborah Fink, "Ann Oleson: Rural Family and Community in Iowa, 1880–1920," *Annals of Iowa* 48, 5/6 (Summer/Fall 1987): 251–63.

16. Compare Linda Schelbitzki Pickle, "Rural German-Speaking Women in Early Nebraska and Kansas: Ethnicity as a Factor in Frontier Adaptation," *Great Plains Quarterly* 9 (Fall 1989): 239–51, to H. Elaine Lindgren, "Ethnic Women Homesteading on the Plains of North Dakota," *Great Plains Quarterly* 9 (Summer 1989): 157–73.

17. Jane Addams, *Democracy and Social Ethics* (New York: Macmillan, 1902), pp. 19–22; Sharlene Hesse-Biber, "The Ethnic Ghetto as Private Welfare," *Urban and Social Change Review* 12, 2 (Summer 1979): 9–15.

18. Dana Frank, "Housewives, Socialists, and the Politics of Food: The 1917 New York Cost-of-Living Protests," *Feminist Studies* 11 (Summer 1985): 255–85; Paula Hyman, "Immigrant Women and Consumer Protest: New York City Kosher Women's Meat Boycott of 1902," *American Jewish History* 70 (1980): 91–105.

19. George Schrode, "Mary Zuk and the Detroit Meat Strike of 1935," *Polish American Studies* 48 (Autumn 1986).

20. Jenna W. Joselit, "The Landlord as Czar: Pre-World War I Tenant Activity," pp. 39–50 in *The Tenant Movement in New York City, 1904–1984,* ed. Ronald Lawson with Mark Naison (New Brunswick, N.J.: Rutgers University Press, 1986).

21. Ewen, *Immigrant Women*, p. 143.

22. Temma Kaplan, "Female Consciousness and Collective Action: The Case of Barcelona, 1910–1918," *SIGNS* 7, 3 (1982): 545–66.

23. Montgomery, *The Fall of the House of Labor*, chap. 2.

24. Yans-McLaughlin, *Family and Community*, chap. 2; Bodnar, *The Transplanted,* chaps. 4–5; Victor Greene, *American Immigrant Leaders, 1800–1910: Marginality and Identity* (Baltimore: Johns Hopkins University Press, 1987); Raymond Breton, "Institutional Completeness of Ethnic Communities and the Personal Relations of Immigrants," *American Journal of Sociology* 70, 2 (September 1964): 193–205.

25. Takaki, *Strangers from a Different Shore*, pp. 118–119; L. Eve Armentrout Ma, "Chinatown Organizations and the Anti-Chinese Movement, 1882–1914," pp. 149–50 in *Entry Denied*.

26. William E. Mitchell, *Mischpokhe: A Study of New York City Jewish Family Clubs* (The Hague: Mouton, 1978); Johnson, *Growing Up and Growing Old*, pp. 102–104.

27. George E. Pozzetta, ed., *Immigrant Institutions: The Organization of Immigrant Life* (New York: Garland, 1991).

28. Bodnar, *The Transplanted*, pp. 124–25.

29. George Pozzetta, ed., *Immigrant Radicals: The View from the Left* (New York: Garland, 1991).

30. Randall M. Miller and Thomas D. Marzik, eds., *Immigrants and Religion in Urban America* (Philadelphia: Temple University Press, 1977); George E. Pozzetta, ed., *The Immigrant Religious Experience* (New York: Garland, 1991).

31. Bodnar, *The Transplanted*, pp. 117–120.

32. Mary Ann Clawson, *Constructing Brotherhood: Class, Gender and Fraternalism* (Princeton: Princeton University Press, 1989).

33. Robert F. Harney, "Religion and Ethnocultural Communities," *Polyphony* 1 (Summer 1978): 1–10; see also Martin E. Marty, "Ethnicity: The Skeleton of Religion in America," *Church History* 41, 1 (March 1972): 5–21; Harry S. Stout, "Ethnicity: The Vital Center of Religion in America," *Ethnicity* 2, 2 (June 1975): 204–24.

34. Hasia Diner, *A Time for Gathering: The Second Migration, 1820–1880,* vol. 2 of *The Jewish People in America* (Baltimore: Johns Hopkins University Press, 1992).

35. Jenna Weissman Joselit, "The Special Sphere of the Middle-Class American Jewish Woman: The Synagogue Sisterhood, 1890–1940," pp. 206–30 in *The American Synagogue,* ed. Jack Wertheimer (New York: Cambridge University Press, 1987); June Sochen, *Consecrate Every Day: The Public Lives of Jewish American Women, 1880–1890* (Albany: State University of New York Press, 1981).

36. Deborah G. Golomb, "The 1893 Congress of Jewish Women: Evolution or Revolution in American Jewish Women's History?" *American Jewish History* 70 (1980): 68–90.

37. Faith Rogow, " 'Gone to Another Meeting': A History of the National Council of Jewish Women," Ph.D. diss., State University of New York, Binghamton, 1989; Linda Gordon Kuzmack, *Women's Cause: the Jewish Woman's Movements in England and the United States, 1881–1933* (Columbus: Ohio State University, 1990).

38. From a large literature on Hadassah and its founder, see Joan Dash, *Summoned to Jerusalem: The Life of Henrietta Szold* (New York: Harper and Row, 1979).

39. Beth W. Wenger, "Jewish Women and Voluntarism: Beyond the Myth of Enablers," *American Jewish History* 74 (Autumn 1989): 16–36.

40. Lenore Salvaneschi, "Die Frau Pastor: The Life of a Missouri Synod Lutheran Pastor's Wife in the First Half of the Twentieth Century," *Palimpsest* 67 (1986): 53–68.

41. Gracia Grindal, "The Americanization of the Norwegian Pastors' Wives," *Norwegian-American Studies* 32 (1989): 199–207; Erik Luther Williamson, " 'Doing What Had to be Done': Norwegian Lutheran Ladies Aid Societies of North Dakota," *North Dakota History* 57 (Spring 1990): 2–13.

42. Martha Reishus, *Hearts and Hands Uplifted: A History of the Women's Missionary Federation of the Evangelical Lutheran Church* (Minneapolis: Augsburg Publishing House, 1958).

43. Evelyn Shakir, "Good Works, Good Times: The Syrian Ladies Aid Society of Boston, 1917–1932," pp. 133–146 in *Crossing the Waters: Arabic-Speaking Immigrants to the United States before 1940*, ed. Eric H. Hooglund (Washington, D.C.: Smithsonian Institution Press, 1987).

44. From a large literature on Catholic sisterhoods, see Elizabeth Komer, "Women Religious in the United States: A Survey of Recent Literature," *U.S. Catholic Historian* 10, 1/2 (1992): 87–92; Margaret Susan Thompson, "Women, Feminism, and the New Religious History: Catholic Sisters as a Case Study," in *Belief and Behavior: Essays in the New Religious History*, ed. Philip R. Vandermeer and Robert P. Swierenga (New Brunswick: Rutgers University Press, 1991).

45. Susan C. Peterson and Courtney A. Vaughn-Robertson, *Women with Vision: The Presentation Sisters of South Dakota, 1880–1985* (Urbana: University of Illinois Press, 1988).

46. Mary J. Oates, "Organized Volunteerism: The Catholic Sisters of Massachusetts, 1870–1940," in *Women in American Religion*, ed. Janet W. James (Philadelphia: University of Pennsylvania Press, 1980).

47. Florence J. Deacon, "Handmaids or Autonomous Women: The Charitable Activities, Institution Building and Communal Relationships of Catholic Sisters in Nineteenth Century Wisconsin," Ph.D. diss., University of Wisconsin, Madison, 1989.

48. For an introduction to the histories of the many immigrant orders in the U.S., see Evangeline Thomas, C.S.J., *Women Religious History Sources: A Guide to Repositories in the United States* (New York: R. R. Bowker, 1983).

49. Mageean, "Catholic Sisterhoods."

50. Mary E. Brown, "The Making of Italian-American Catholics: Jesuit Work on the Lower East Side, New York, 1890's–1950's," *Catholic Historical Review* 73 (April 1987): 285–303; Ann Taves, *The Household of Faith: Roman Catholic Devotions in Mid-Nineteenth Century America* (South Bend, Ind.: University of Notre Dame Press, 1986).

51. Smith, *Family Connections*, pp. 140–41; Diner, *Erin's Daughters in America*, pp. 125–26.

52. Sirkka T. Lee, "The Finns," *Cultural Correspondence* 6 (1978): 41–49.

53. *Peasant Maids, City Women*; the best general introduction remains Breckinridge, *New Homes for Old*.

54. K. Marianne Wargelin Brown, "A Closer Look at Finnish American Women's Issues," pp. 83–102 in *Women Who Dared*.

55. Alice Chai, "Korean Women in Hawaii, 1903–1945: The Role of Methodism in Their Liberation and Their Participation in the Korean Independence Movement," pp. 328–44 in *Women in New Worlds: Historical Perspectives on the Wesleyan Tradition,*

ed. Hilah F. Thomas and Rosemary S. Keller (Nashville: Abingdon, 1981); Robert Szymczak, "An Act of Devotion: The Polish Gray Samaritans and the Relief Effort in Poland, 1919–1921," *Polish American Studies* 43 (Spring 1986): 13–36; William J. Galush, "Purity and Power: Chicago Polonian Feminism, 1880–1914," *Polish American Studies* 47 (1990): 5–24; Thaddeus Radzialowski, "Immigrant Nationalism and Feminism: Glos Polek and the Polish Women's Alliance in America, 1898–1930," *Review Journal of Philosophy and Social Science* 2 (1972): 183–203.

56. *Peasant Maids, City Women.*

57. Mari Jo Buhle, *Women and American Socialism, 1870–1920* (Urbana: University of Illinois Press, 1980), pp. 127–28.

58. Christiane Harzig, "The Roles of German Women in the German-American Working-Class Movement in Late Nineteenth-Century New York," *Journal of American Ethnic History* 8 (Spring 1989): 87–107.

59. Breckinridge, *New Homes for Old*, pp. 210–11.

60. Chai, "Picture Brides," p. 129; Yanagisako, *Transforming the Past*, pp. 45–46.

61. Ruth K. Rafael, "The YMHA and the YWHA in San Francisco," *Western States Jewish History* 19 (April 1987): 208–16.

62. Martha K. Norkunas, "Women, Work and Ethnic Identity: Personal Narratives and the Ethnic Enclave in the Textile City of Lowell, Mass.," *The Journal of Ethnic Studies* 15, 3 (Fall 1987): 27–48.

63. From a large literature, see Kessler-Harris, *Out to Work*, pp. 156–71; Foner, *Women and the American Labor Movement*, vol. 1, chaps. 16–27; Maxine S. Seller, "The Uprising of the Twenty Thousand: Sex, Class, and Ethnicity in the Shirtwaist Makers' Strike of 1909," pp. 280–303 in *Struggle a Hard Battle—Working-Class Immigrants*, ed. Dirk Hoerder (DeKalb, Ill.: University of Northern Illinois Press, 1986).

64. Ruiz, *Cannery Women*, chap. 5.

65. Ross, "Servant Girls," p. 47.

66. Glenn, *Daughters of the Shtetl*, chap. 4.

67. Colomba Furio, "The Cultural Background of the Italian Immigrant Woman and Its Impact on Her Unionization in the New York City Garment Industry, 1880–1919," pp. 81–98 in *Pane e Lavoro: The Italian American Working Class*, ed. George Pozzetta (Staten Island: American Italian Historical Association, 1980).

68. Tentler, *Wage-Earning Women*, p. 181.

69. Carole Turbin, "Beyond Conventional Wisdom: Women's Wage Work, Household Economic Contribution, and Labor Activism in a Mid-Nineteenth-Century Working-Class Community," pp. 47–67 in *"To Toil the Livelong Day."*

70. Carole Turbin, "Reconceptualizing Family, Work and Labor Organizing: Working Women in Troy, 1860–1890," *Review of Radical Political Economics* 16 (1984): 1–16.

71. Alice Kessler-Harris, "Organizing the Unorganizable: Three Jewish Women and Their Union," *Labor History* 17 (1976): 5–23.

72. Altagracia Ortiz, "Puerto Ricans in the Garment Industry of New York City, 1920–1960," pp. 105–128 in *Labor Divided: Race and Ethnicity in United States Labor Struggles, 1835–1960*, ed. Robert Asher and Charles H. Stephenson (Albany: State University of New York Press, 1990).

73. Alice Kessler-Harris, "Where are the Organized Women Workers?" *Feminist Studies* 3 (Fall 1975): 5–14.

74. From a large literature, see Ardis Cameron, "Landscapes of Subterfuge: Working-Class Neighborhoods and Immigrant Women," pp. 56–77 in *Gender, Class and Reform in the Progressive Era*, ed. Noralee Frankel and Nancy Schrom Dye (Lexington: University of Kentucky Press, 1991); Robert E. Snyder, "Women, Wobblies, and Workers' Rights: The 1912 Textile Strike in Little Falls, New York," *New York History* 60 (January 1979): 29–57.

75. Ardis Cameron, "Bread and Roses Revisited: Women's Culture and Working-Class Activism in the Lawrence Strike of 1912," pp. 42–61 in *Women's Work and Protest:*

A Century of U.S. Women's Labor History, ed. Ruth Milkman (Boston: Routledge and Kegan Paul, 1985); Priscilla Long, "The Women of the Colorado Fuel and Iron Strike, 1913–14," pp. 62–85 in *Women's Work and Protest;* Irene Ledesma, "Unlikely Strikers: Mexican-American Women in Strike Activity in Texas, 1919–1974," Ph.D. diss., Ohio State University, 1992.

76. Nancy S. Dye, *As Equals and as Sisters: Feminism, Unionism, and the Women's Trade Union League of New York* (Columbia: University of Missouri Press, 1980).

77. Nancy S. Dye, "Creating a Feminist Alliance: Sisterhood and Class Conflict in the New York Women's Trade Union League," *Feminist Studies* 2, 2/3 (1975): 24–38; Colette A. Hyman, "Labor Organizing and Female Institution-Building: The Chicago Women's Trade Union League, 1904–24," pp. 22–41 in *Women's Work and Protest;* Mary J. Bularzik, "The Bonds of Belonging: Leonora O'Reilly and Social Reform," *Labor History* 24 (1983): 60–84.

78. Meredith Tax, *The Rising of the Women: Feminist Solidarity and Class Conflict, 1880–1917* (New York: Monthly Review Press, 1980), pp. 20–21.

79. Janet E. Rasmussen, "Sisters across the Sea: Early Norwegian Feminists and Their American Connections," *Women's Studies International* 5, 6 (1982): 647–54.

80. Elinor Lerner, "Immigrant and Working-Class Involvement in the New York City Woman Suffrage Movement, 1905–1917: A Study in Progressive-Era Politics," Ph.D. diss., University of California, Berkeley, 1981.

81. Elinor Lerner, "Jewish Involvement in the New York City Woman Suffrage Movement," *American Jewish History* 70 (June 1981): 442–61; Ellen Carol DuBois, "Working Women, Class Relations, and Suffrage Militance: Harriet Stanton Blatch and the New York Woman Suffrage Movement, 1894–1909," *Journal of American History* 74, 1 (June 1987): 34–58.

82. Carol Ross, "The Feminist Dilemma in the Finnish Immigrant Community," *Finnish Americana* 1 (1978): 71–83.

83. Mirandé, *La Chicana,* chap. 7.

84. Hilda Karvonen, "Three Proponents of Woman's Rights in the Finnish-American Labor Movement from 1910–1930: Selma Jokela McCone, Maiju Nurmi and Helmi Mattson," pp. 123–35 in *Women Who Dared.*

85. I am grateful to Linda Reeder for calling my attention to this quote, in Seller, *Immigrant Women,* p. 241.

86. Elisabeth I. Perry, *Belle Moskowitz: Feminine Politics and the Exercise of Power in the Age of Alfred E. Smith* (New York: Oxford University Press, 1987); Susan Duffy, *Shirley Chisholm: A Bibliography of Writings by and about Her* (Metuchen, N.J.: Scarecrow, 1988).

87. Janet Zandy, "Our True Legacy: Radical Jewish Women in America," *Lilith* 22 (Winter 1989): 8–13; Sochen, *Consecrate Every Day,* chap. 3.

88. Margaret Marsh, *Anarchist Women, 1870–1920* (Philadelphia: Temple University Press, 1981).

89. Buhle, *Women and American Socialism,* pp. 125–31; Sally M. Miller, "Other Socialists: Native-Born and Immigrant Women in the Socialist Party of America, 1901–1917," *Labor History* 24 (1983): 84–102.

90. Harvey Klehr, "Female Leadership in the Communist Party of the United States of America," *Studies in Comparative Communism* 10 (Winter 1977): 394–402.

91. Vicki Ruiz, "Dead Ends or Gold Mines? Using Missionary Records in Mexican-American Women's History," *Frontiers* 12, 1 (1991): 33–56; Elizabeth Rose, "From Sponge Cake to Hamentashen: Jewish Identity in a Jewish Settlement House, 1885–1952," *Journal of American Ethnic History* (forthcoming). The most famous such settlement was operated by the German Jewish nurse Lillian Wald. From a large literature, see Clare Coss, *Lillian D. Wald: Progressive Activist* (New York: Feminist Press, 1989).

92. Of several biographies, see Mildred C. Martin, *Chinatown's Angry Angel: The Story of Donaldina Cameron* (Palo Alto, Calif.: Pacific Books, 1977).

93. Peggy Pascoe, *Relations of Rescue: The Search for Female Moral Authority in the American West, 1874–1939* (New York: Oxford, 1990), pp. 73–76.

94. Gordon, *Heroes of Their Own Lives*, pp. 292–95.

95. Pleck, *Domestic Tyranny*, chaps. 4, 10.

96. Steven Gregory, "Afro-Caribbean Religions in New York City: The Case of Santería," pp. 307–24 in *Caribbean Life in New York City*.

97. Karen Brown, *Mama Lola* (Berkeley: University of California Press, 1991).

98. From a large literature, see Elizabeth Weiner and Hardy Green, "A Stitch in Our Time: New York's Hispanic Garment Workers in the 1980s," pp. 278–96, and Laurie Coyle, Gail Gershatter, and Emily Honig, "Women at Farah: An Unfinished Story," pp. 227–77 in *A Needle, A Bobbin, A Strike; Women Needleworkers in America*, ed. Joan M. Jensen and Sue Davidson (Philadelphia: Temple University Press, 1984).

99. Louise Lamphere, "Bringing the Family to Work: Woman's Culture on the Shop Floor," *Feminist Studies* 11 (Fall 1985): 519–40; Patricia Zavella, "Abnormal Intimacy: The Varying Networks of Chicana Cannery Workers," *Feminist Studies* 11 (1985): 541–57.

100. Margaret Rose, "From the Fields to the Picket Lines: Huelga Women and the Boycott, 1965–1975," *Labor History* 31 (Summer 1990): 271–93.

101. Brettell and de Berjeois, "Anthropology and the Study of Immigrant Women," pp. 41–64 in *Seeking Common Ground*.

102. Leo R. Chavez, Wayne Cornelius and Oliver William Jones, "Utilization of Health Services by Mexican Immigrant Women in San Diego," *Women and Health* 11, 2 (1986): 3–19.

103. Ellen Matthews, *Culture Clash* (Chicago: Intercultural Press, 1982).

104. Stacey G. H. Yap, *Gather Your Strength, Sisters: The Emerging Role of Chinese Women Community Workers* (New York: AMS Press, 1989). For the point of view of minority activists, see Cheryl Townsend Gilkes, "Going up for the Oppressed: The Career Mobility of Black Women Community Workers," *Journal of Social Issues* 39, 3 (1983): 115–39.

105. Roxana Ng, *The Politics of Community Services: Immigrant Women, Class, and State* (Toronto: Garamond, 1988).

106. Kinkead, *Chinatown*, pp. 67–68.

107. Esther N. Chow, "The Development of Feminist Consciousness among Asian American Women," *Gender and Society* 1 (September 1987): 284–99.

108. Donna Shai and Ira Rosenwaike, "Violent Deaths among Mexican-, Puerto Rican- and Cuban-Born Migrants in the United States," *Social Science and Medicine* 26, 2 (1988): 269–76.

109. Carlos Vásquez, "Women in the Chicano Movement," pp. 17–18 in *Mexican Women in the United States: Struggles Past and Present*, ed. Magdalena Mora and Adelaida R. Del Castillo (Los Angeles: University of California, Chicano Studies Research Center Publications, 1980); Adaljiza Sosa Riddell, "Chicanas and el Movimiento," *Aztlán* 5 (Spring/Fall 1974): 155–65.

110. Marta Cotera, "Feminism: The Chicana and Anglo Versions, a Historical Analysis," pp. 217–34 in *Twice a Minority*.

111. Elizabeth Lindsey Davis, *"Lifting as They Climb": A History of the National Association of Colored Women* (Washington, D.C.: Howard University Center, 1933).

112. Nancy A. Hewitt, "Charity or Mutual Aid? Two Perspectives on Latin Women's Philanthropy in Tampa, Florida," in *Lady Bountiful Revisited: Women, Philanthropy, and Power*, ed. Kathleen D. McCarthy (New Brunswick: Rutgers University Press, 1990).

7. MIDDLE-CLASS IMMIGRANTS

1. Andre Gunder Frank, *Lumpenbourgeoisie and Lumpendevelopment: Dependence, Class, and Politics in Latin America*, trans. Marion Davis Berdecio (New York: Monthly Review Press, 1972).

2. Charlotte L. Brancaforte, ed., *The German Forty-Eighters in the United States* (New York: P. Lang, 1989).

3. From a sizeable literature, see Annette P. Bus, "Mathilde Anneke and the Suffrage Movement," pp. 79–92 in *The German Forty-Eighters*.

4. An introduction to a large literature is Herbert A. Strauss, ed., *Jewish Immigrants of the Nazi Period in the USA*, 6 vols. (New York: K. G. Saur, 1978–1987).

5. May Derwent, *Hannah Arendt* (New York: Penguin Books, 1986); Elisabeth Young-Bruehl, *Hannah Arendt: For Love of the World* (New Haven: Yale University Press, 1982).

6. Coser, *Refugee Scholars in America: Their Impact and Experiences* (New Haven: Yale University Press, 1984), pp. 37–41.

7. Unless otherwise indicated, the source for biographical information on women named in the text is either *Notable American Women* or *Notable American Women, The Modern Period*.

8. Susan Quinn, *A Mind of Her Own: The Life of Karen Horney* (New York: Summit, 1987); Marcia Westcott, *The Feminist Legacy of Karen Horney* (New Haven: Yale University Press, 1986).

9. Marion Kaplan, *The Making of the Jewish Middle Class: Women, Family, and Identity in Imperial Germany* (New York: Oxford University Press, 1991).

10. Joan Dash, *A Life of One's Own: Three Gifted Women and the Men They Married: Margaret Sanger, Edna St. Vincent Millay, Maria Goeppert-Mayer* (New York: Harper and Row, 1973).

11. See Quack, "Everyday Life and Emigration."

12. Sibylle Quack, "Changing Gender Roles and Emigration: The Example of German Jewish Women after 1933 and Their Emigration to the United States," unpublished paper in author's possession.

13. Christine Backhaus-Lautenschläger, . . . *Und Standen Ihre Frau: Das Schicksal Deutschsprachiger Emigrantinnen in den USA nach 1933* (Pfaffenweiler: Centaurus, 1991).

14. Maxine L. Margolis, "From Mistress to Servant: Downward Mobility Among Brazilian Immigrants in New York City," *Urban Anthropology* 19, 3 (Fall 1990): 215–32.

15. Eui Hang Shin and Kyung-Sup Chang, "Peripheralization of Immigrant Professionals: Korean Physicians in the United States," *International Migration Review* 22 (Winter 1988): 609–26.

16. Joan Ablon, "Samoans in Stateside Nursing," *Nursing Outlook* 18 (December 1970): 33–34.

17. Lisandro Perez, "Immigrant Economic Adjustment and Family Organization: The Cuban Success Story Reexamined," *International Migration Review* 20 (1986): 4–20; Yolanda Prieto, "Cuban Women in the U.S. Labor Force," *Cuban Studies* 17 (1987): 73–91.

18. Yolanda Prieto, "Cuban Women and Work in the United States: A New Jersey Case Study," pp. 95–112 in *International Migration*.

19. Mike Gold, cited in Baum et al., *The Jewish Woman in America*, p. 200; see also chap. 7.

20. Janice Reiff Webster, "Domestication and Americanization: Scandinavian Women in Seattle, 1888 to 1900," *Journal of Urban History* 4 (1978): 275–90.

21. Rivka Lissak, "Myth and Reality: The Patterns of Relationship between the Hull House Circle and the 'New Immigrants' on Chicago's West Side, 1890–1919," *Journal of American Ethnic History* 2, 2 (Spring 1983): 31–32.

22. Peggy Pascoe, "Gender Systems in Conflict: The Marriages of Mission-Educated Chinese-American Women, 1874–1939," *Journal of Social History* 22 (Summer 1989): 631–52.

23. Alexander Grinstein, "Profile of a 'Doll'—A Female Character Type," pp. 79–94 in *The Psychodynamics of American Jewish Life*, ed. Norman Kiell (New York: Twayne, 1967).

24. Ewen, *Immigrant Women*, pp. 158, 197–201.

25. Rachel Josefowitz, "Antisemitism and Sexism in Stereotypes of Jewish Women," *Women and Therapy* 5, 2/3 (Summer/Fall 1986): 249–57.

26. Boone, "The Uses of Traditional Concepts," pp. 263–64.

27. Carlos E. Cortes, *The Latin American Brain Drain to the United States* (New York: Arno, 1980); Tai K. Oh, *The Asian Brain Drain: A Factual and Causal Analysis* (San Francisco: R & E Research Associates, 1977).

28. Barbara M. Barker, "The American Careers of Rita Sangalli, Giuseppina Morlacchi and Maria Bonfanti: Nineteenth Century Ballerinas," Ph.D. diss., New York University, 1981.

29. Alice M. Robinson, Vera Mowry Roberts, and Milly S. Barranger, *Notable Women in the American Theater: A Biographical Dictionary* (New York: Greenwood, 1989).

30. John D. Barry, *Julia Marlowe* (Boston: E. H. Beacon, 1907); Penny M. Landau, "The Career of Mary Ann Duff, the American Siddons, 1810–1839," Ph.D. diss., Bowling Green State University, 1979.

31. From a large literature, see J. C. Furnas, *Fanny Kemble, Leading Lady of the Nineteenth-Century Stage: A Biography* (New York: Dial, 1982).

32. Maxine Schwartz Seller, *Ethnic Theater in the United States* (Westport: Greenwood, 1983).

33. Tetrazzini, *My Life of Song* (London: Cassell, 1921).

34. Carlos Gil, "Lydia Mendoza: Houstonian and First Lady of Mexican American Song," *The Houston Review* 3 (Summer 1981): 249–60.

35. Beaumont Glass, *Lotte Lehmann: A Life in Opera and Song* (Santa Barbara: Capra, 1988).

36. Diana Souhami, *Gluck: Her Biography* (Winchester: Unwin Hyman, 1990).

37. Ruth Brandon, *Being Divine: A Biography of Sarah Bernhardt* (London: Secker and Warburg, 1991); Arthur Gold, *The Divine Sarah: A Life of Sarah Bernhardt* (New York: Knopf, 1991).

38. David A. Gerber, "The First African Woman Graduate of an American University," *Negro History Bulletin* 36 (April 1973): 84–85.

39. Mehri Hekmati-Tehrani, "Alienation, Family Ties, and Social Position as Variables Related to the Non-Return of Foreign Students," Ph.D. diss., New York University, 1970.

40. *Chronicle of Higher Education* 38 (March 18, 1992), p. A35.

41. Nelly P. Stromquist, *Daring to Be Different: The Choice of Nonconventional Fields of Study by International Women Students* (New York: Institute of International Education, 1991); Stanley L. M. Fong and Harvey Peskin, "Sex Role Strain and Personality Adjustment of China-Born Students in America: A Pilot Study," *Journal of Abnormal Psychology* 74 (October 1969): 563–67.

42. Melba J. T. Vasquez, "Confronting Barriers to the Participation of Mexican American Women in Higher Education," *Hispanic Journal of Behavioral Sciences* 4, 2 (1982): 147–65; Norma Varisco de Garcia, "Education and the Spanish Speaking Woman: A Sad Reality," *NABE: The Journal of the National Association for Bilingual Education* 1, 1, (May 1976): 55–60.

43. I have chosen historical examples to avoid violating the privacy of living women in *Who's Who of American Women*.

44. Gabaccia, "Women of the Mass Migrations."

45. Simon, "Sociology of Immigrant Women," Table 4.

46. Bernard Weiss, ed., *American Education and the European Immigrant, 1840–1940* (Urbana: University of Illinois Press, 1982); Joel Perlmann, *Ethnic Differences: Schooling and Social Structure among the Irish, Italians, Jews, and Blacks in an American City* (New York: Cambridge University Press, 1988).

47. DeVault, *Sons and Daughters of Labor*, Table 8–10.

48. Sydney Stahl, "Longing to Learn: The Education of Jewish Immigrant Women in New York City, 1900–1934," *Journal of American Ethnic History* 3 (Spring 1989): 108–26.

49. Michael R. Olneck and Marvin Lazerson, "The School Achievement of Immigrant Children, 1900–1930," *History of Education Quarterly* 14, 4 (Winter 1974): 453–82, table 9; John Rury, "Urban Structure and School Participation: Immigrant Women in 1900," *Social Science History* 8, 3 (Summer 1984): 219–41.

50. Sydney S. Weinberg, "The World of Our Mothers: Family, Work and Education in the Lives of Jewish Immmigrant Women," *Frontiers* 7 (1983): 71–79.

51. Richard D. Alba, *Ethnic Identity: Transformation of White America* (New Haven: Yale University Press, 1990), table 1.1.

52. Richard D. Alba, *Italian Americans: Into the Twilight of Ethnicity* (Englewood Cliffs: Prentice-Hall, 1985), pp. 124–28.

53. Margaret A. Gibson, *Accommodation without Assimilation: Sikh Immigrants in an American High School* (Ithaca: Cornell University Press, 1988), p. 167.

54. E.g., Nathan Caplan, John K. Whitmore and Marcella H. Choy, *The Boat People and Achievement in America: A Study of Family Life, Hard Work, and Cultural Values* (Ann Arbor: University of Michigan Press, 1989).

55. Rita J. Simon, "Refugee Families' Adjustment and Aspirations: A Comparison of Soviet Jewish and Vietnamese Immigrants," *Ethnic and Racial Studies* 6 (October 1983): 492–504; Maxine B. Zinn, "Employment and Education of Mexican-American Women: The Interplay of Modernity and Ethnicity in Eight Families," *Harvard Educational Review* 50, 1 (1980): 47–62.

56. Sylvia Valverde, "A Comparative Study of Hispanic High School Dropouts and Graduates: Why Do Some Leave School Early and Some Finish?," *Education and Urban Society* 19, 3 (1987): 320–29.

57. Besides Gibson, *Accommodation without Assimilation*, pp. 173–89, see Harriett Romo, "The Mexican-Origin Population's Differing Perceptions of Their Children's Schooling," *Social Science Quarterly* 65 (1984): 635–50.

58. Maria Eugenia Matute-Bianchi, "Ethnic Identities and Patterns of School Success and Failure among Mexican-Descent and Japanese-American Students in a California High School: An Ethnographic Analysis," *American Journal of Education* 95, 1 (1986): 233–55.

59. See Judith Theresa Gonzalez, "Dilemmas of the High-Achieving Chicana: The Double-Bind Factor in Male/Female Relationships," *Sex Roles* 18, 17–18 (April 1988): 367–80.

60. Manuel Casas and Joseph G. Ponterott, "Profiling an Invisible Minority in Higher Education: The Chicana," *Personnel and Guidance Journal* 62, 6 (February 1984).

61. See also Simon, "Sociology and Immigrant Women," tables 7–8.

62. From a considerable literature, see Wil A. Linkugel and Martha Solomon, *Anna Howard Shaw: Suffrage Orator and Social Reformer* (Westport, Conn.: Greenwood, 1991).

63. Yuri Suhl, *Ernestine Rose and the Battle for Human Rights* (New York: Reynal and Hitchcock, 1959), new ed., Biblio Press, 1991.

64. Beth S. Wenger, "Radical Politics in a Reactionary Age: The Unmaking of Rosika Schwimmer, 1914–1930," *Journal of Women's History* 2, 2 (Fall 1990): 66–99.

65. Celia M. Eckhardt, *Fanny Wright: Rebel in America* (Cambridge: Harvard University Press, 1984).

66. Janet E. Rasmussen, " 'The Best Place on Earth for Women': The American Experience of Aasta Hansteen," *Norwegian-American Studies* 31 (1986): 245–68.

67. Donald Bogle, *Brown Sugar: Eighty Years of America's Black Female Superstars* (New York: Harmony, 1980).

68. Linda Dahl, *Stormy Weather: The Music and Lives of a Century of Jazzwomen* (New York: Pantheon, 1984).

69. Robert W. Snyder, *The Voice of the City: Vaudeville and Popular Culture in New York* (New York: Oxford University Press, 1989); Neal Gabler, *An Empire of Their Own: How the Jews Invented Hollywood* (New York: Crown, 1988).

70. Martha Gil-Montero, *Brazilian Bombshell: The Biography of Carmen Miranda* (New York: D. I. Fine, 1989).

71. From a sizeable, if idiosyncratic, literature, see Marion Meade, *Madame Blavatsky: The Woman behind the Myth* (New York: Putnam, 1980).

72. Dora Askowith, *Three Outstanding Women* (New York: Bloch Publishing Co., 1941), pp. 11–25.

73. Reverend Joseph B. Code, *Great American Foundresses* (New York: Macmillan, 1929).

74. Kenneth J. Chandler, "Rose Philippine Duchesne: An American Saint," *Gateway Heritage* (Summer 1988): 20–31.

75. The most recent scholarly biography is Mary Louise Sullivan, M.S.C., *Mother Cabrini: "Italian Immigrant of the Century"* (New York: Center for Migration Studies, 1992).

76. Harold J. Taub, *Waldorf-in-the Catskills: The Grossinger Legend* (New York: Sterling Publishing Co., 1952).

77. Maxine Fabe, *Beauty Millionaire: The Life of Helena Rubinstein* (New York: Crowell, 1972).

78. Carolyn Niethammer, "The Lure of Gold," pp. 71–87 in *The Women Who Made the West*, ed. Western Writers of America (Garden City: Doubleday, 1980).

79. Gary Mormino, *Immigrants on the Hill: Italian-Americans in St. Louis, 1882–1982* (Urbana: University of Illinois Press, 1986), chap. 5.

80. Elaine Shannon, *Desperados: Latin Drug Lords, U.S. Lawmen, and the War America Can't Win* (New York: Viking, 1988); Kinkead, *Chinatown*, Part 2.

81. Clifford Browder, *Madame Restell, the Abortionist: The Wickedest Woman in New York* (Hamden, Conn.: Archon, 1988).

82. From a sizeable literature, see Dale Fetherling, *Mother Jones, the Miners' Angel: A Portrait* (Carbondale: Southern Illinois University Press, 1974).

83. The literature on Emma Goldman is enormous, and still growing. The most recent are Marian Morton, *Emma Goldman and the American Left* (Boston: Twayne, 1992); John Chalberg, *Emma Goldman, American Individualist* (New York: HarperCollins, 1991); Martin Duberman, *Mother Earth: An Epic Drama of Emma Goldman's Life* (New York: St. Martin's, 1991); Alice Wexler, *Emma Goldman in Exile: From the Russian Revolution to the Spanish Civil War* (Boston: Beacon, 1989).

84. M. Brigid O'Farrell and Lydia Kleiner, "Anna Sullivan, Trade Union Organizer," *Frontiers* 2 (1977): 29–36.

85. Herbert Shapiro and David L. Sterling, eds., *"I Belong to the Working Class": The Unfinished Autobiography of Rose Pastor Stokes* (Athens: University of Georgia Press, 1992); Arthur and Pearl Zipser, *Fire and Grace: The Life of Rose Pastor Stokes* (Athens: University of Georgia Press, 1989).

86. Morris U. Schappes, "Three Women"; Paula Scheier, "Clara Lemlich Shavelson," *Jewish Life* 8 (1954): 4–11.

87. Mario T. Garcia, *Mexican Americans: Leadership, Ideology and Identity, 1930–1960* (New Haven: Yale University Press, 1989), chapter 6.

88. Ellen Ritter, "Elizabeth Morgan: Pioneer Female Labor Agitator," *Central States Speech Journal* 21 (1971): 242–51; Ralph Scharman, "Elizabeth Morgan: Crusader for Labor Reform," *Labor History* 14 (Summer 1973): 340–51.

89. Sally M. Miller, "From Sweatshop Worker to Labor Leader: Theresa Malkiel, a Case Study," *American Jewish History* 68 (1978): 189–205.

90. From a sizeable literature, see Rosalyn Baxandall, *Words on Fire: The Life and Writing of Elizabeth Gurley Flynn* (New Brunswick, N.J.: Rutgers University Press, 1987).

91. Elizabeth Payne, *Reform, Labor and Feminism: Margaret Dreier Robins and the Women's Trade Union League* (Urbana: University of Illinois Press, 1988).

92. Kessler-Harris, "Organizing the Unorganizable."

93. Elaine J. Leeder, *The Gentle General: Rose Pesotta, Anarchist and Labor Organizer* (Albany: SUNY Press, 1993).

94. Ann Schofield, " 'To Do and to Be': Mary Frier, Pauline Newman and the Psychology of Feminist Activism," *Psychohistory Review* 18 (Fall 1989): 33–55.

95. Ricki C. Cohen, "Fannia Cohn and the International Ladies' Garment Workers Union," Ph.D. diss., University of Southern California, 1976.

96. Pat C. Scholten, "Militant Women for Economic Justice: The Persuasion of Mary Harris Jones, Ella Reeve Bloor, Rose Pastor Stokes, Rose Schneiderman, and Elizabeth Gurley Flynn," Ph.D. diss., Indiana University, 1979.

97. Nina L. Asher, "Dorothy Jacobs Bellanca: Women Clothing Workers and the Runaway Shops," pp. 195–226 in *A Needle, A Bobbin, A Strike*.

98. Jean A. Scarpaci, "Angela Bambace and the International Ladies Garment Workers Union: The Search for an Elusive Activist," pp. 99–118 in *Pane e Lavoro*.

99. Hope Mendoza Schechter, *Hope Mendoza Schechter—Activist in the Labor Movement, the Democratic Party, and the Mexican-American Community: An Interview* (Berkeley: Regional Oral History Office, Bancroft Library, University of California, Berkeley, 1980).

100. Irene D. Neu, "The Jewish Businesswoman in America," *American Jewish Historical Quarterly* 66 (1976): 137–54.

101. Linda Gordon, "Social Insurance and Public Assistance: The Influence of Gender in Welfare Thought in the United States, 1890–1935," *American Historical Review* 97, 1 (February 1992): 25.

102. See, for example, "Georgiana Emma Drew Barrymore," *Notable American Women*.

103. See "Ada Rehan" in *Notable American Women*.

104. Sister John Marie Daly, "Mary Anderson, Pioneer Labor Leader," Ph.D. diss., Georgetown University, 1968.

105. Diane Kirkby, *Alice Henry: The Power of the Pen and Voice, The Life of an Australian-American Labor Reformer* (New York: Cambridge University Press, 1991).

106. Roy S. Bryce-Laporte, "Obituary to a Female Immigrant and Scholar: Lourdes Casal," pp. 349–55 in *Female Immigrants to the United States*.

107. Nancy A. Sahli, "Elizabeth Blackwell M.D. (1821–1910): A Biography," Ph.D. diss., University of Pennsylvania, 1974; Dorothy C. Wilson, *Lone Woman: The Story of Elizabeth Blackwell, the First Woman Doctor* (Boston: Little, Brown, 1970).

108. For humbler physicians, see Stepanka Andrews Coryta, "Dr. Olga Stasney: Her Service to Nebraska and the World," *Nebraska History* 68 (Spring 1987): 20–27. Gerty Radnitz Cori is discussed in *Notable American Women: The Modern Period*, pp. 165–67.

109. Bernard Wong, "Elites and Ethnic Boundary Maintenance: A Study of the Roles of Elites in Chinatown, New York City," *Urban Anthropology* 6, 1 (Spring 1977): 001–022.

110. Betty Bergland, "Ideology, Ethnicity and the Gendered Subject: Reading Immigrant Women's Autobiographies," pp. 101–22 in *Seeking Common Ground*.

111. From a sizeable literature, see, besides Henriksen's *Anzia Yezierska*, Carol B. Schoen, *Anzia Yezierska* (Boston: Twayne, 1982).

112. Joyce Antler, ed., *America and I: Short Stories by American Jewish Women Writers* (Boston: Beacon, 1990); J. R. Christianson, "Literary Traditions of Norwegian-American Women," pp. 92–110 in *Makers of an American Immigrant Legacy*, ed. Odd S. Lovoll (Northfield: Norwegian American Historical Association, 1980); Helen

Barolini, *The Dream Book: An Anthology of Writings by Italian American Women* (New York: Schocken, 1985); Amy Ling, *Between Worlds: Women Writers of Chinese Ancestry* (Elmsford, NY: Pergamon, 1990).

113. See the chapter on her in Janice Morgan and Colette Hall, eds., *Redefining Autobiography in Twentieth-Century Women's Fictions: An Essay Collection* (New York: Garland, 1991).

114. Jeanne Barker-Nunn, "Telling the Mother's Story: History and Connection in the Autobiographies of Maxine Hong Kingston and Kim Chernin," *Women's Studies* 14 (1987): 55–63.

115. Leslie Garis, "Through West Indian Eyes," *New York Times Magazine,* October 7, 1990, pp. 42–44, 70, 78–80, 91.

116. Timothy L. Smith, "Native Blacks and Foreign Whites: Varying Response to Educational Opportunity in America, 1880–1950," *Perspectives in American History* 6 (1972): 307–35 (see esp. p. 310).

117. Sally Ann Drucker, " 'It Doesn't Say So in Mother's Prayerbook': Autobiographies in English by Immigrant Jewish Women," *American Jewish History* 79 (Autumn 1989): 55–71.

8. PRESERVATION AND INNOVATION

1. Julian H. Steward, *Theory of Culture Change: The Methodology of Multilinear Evolution* (Urbana: University of Illinois Press, 1972). See also the discussion of chapter 8 in the present volume's bibliographical essay.

2. Nancie L. González and Carolyn S. McCommon, *Conflict, Migration and the Expression of Ethnicity* (Boulder: Westview, 1989), pp. 2–3.

3. Thus John Bodnar's revision of Oscar Handlin's metaphor from "Uprooted" into *The Transplanted*; see also Michael Novak, *The Rise of the Unmeltable Ethnics: Politics and Culture in the Seventies* (New York: Macmillan, 1973); Werner Sollors, *The Invention of Ethnicity.*

4. Cited in Ewen, *Immigrant Women,* p. 96.

5. Maxine Seller, "Beyond the Stereotype: A New Look at the Immigrant Woman, 1880–1924," *Journal of Ethnic Studies* 3 (Spring 1975): 59–70.

6. Glenn, *Daughters of the Shtetl,* p. 3.

7. Brydon and Chant, *Women in the Third World,* pp. 151, 167.

8. Kessner and Caroli, *Today's Immigrants,* p. 135.

9. Peter Turton, *José Martí, Architect of Cuba's Freedom* (Totowa, N. J.: Zed Books, 1986), p. 74.

10. Barton, *Letters from the Promised Land,* p. 112.

11. Sinke, "The International Marriage Market," p. 81.

12. I thank Deirdre Mageean for this quote from her unpublished paper, "Irish Women and Catholic Charity Work in Chicago, 1840–1910."

13. Seller, *Immigrant Women,* pp. 3–4.

14. Diner, *Erin's Daughters in America,* p. 139; Maxine Seller, "Defining Socialist Womanhood: The Women's Page of the *Jewish Daily Forward* in 1919," *American Jewish History* 76 (June 1987): 416–38.

15. Reid, *The Negro Immigrant,* p. 206.

16. Oliva Espin, "Cultural and Historical Influences on Sexuality in Hispanic/ Latin Women," pp. 272–84 in *All American Women.*

17. Fedwa Malti-Douglas, "A World of Contrasts," *Women's Review of Books* 9, 1 (October 1991): 27–28.

18. Kessner and Caroli, *Today's Immigrants,* p. 200.

19. Jonah Raskin, *The Mythology of Imperialism: Rudyard Kipling, Joseph Conrad, E. M. Forster, D. H. Lawrence, and Joyce Cary* (New York: Random House, 1971), p. 29.

20. Patricia Ruth Hill, *The World Their Household: The American Woman's Foreign Mission Movements and Cultural Transformation, 1870–1920* (Ann Arbor: University of Michigan Press, 1985); Pascoe, *Relations of Rescue*, pp. 39–40, 51–56.

21. Malti-Douglas, "A World of Contrasts," p. 27.

22. Janet Sims-Wood, "The Black Female: Mammy, Jemima, Sapphire, and Other Images," pp. 235–56 in *Images of Blacks in American Culture: A Reference Guide to Information Sources*, ed. Jessie Carney Smith (Westport, Conn.: Greenwood, 1988); Catherine Silk, *Racism and Anti-Racism in American Popular Culture: Portrayals of African-Americans in Fiction and Film* (New York: St. Martin's, 1990).

23. Mimi Chan, *Through Western Eyes: Images of Chinese Women in Anglo-American Literature* (Hong Kong: Joint Publishing Co., 1989).

24. Carlos E. Cortes, "Chicanas in Film: History of an Image," pp. 94–108 in *Chicano Cinema: Research, Reviews, and Resources*, ed. Gary D. Keller (Binghamton: Bilingual Review Press, 1985); Maryann Oshana, *Women of Color: Filmography of Minority and Third World Women* (New York: Garland, 1985).

25. Connie S. Chan, "Asian-American Women: Psychological Responses to Sexual Exploitation and Cultural Stereotypes," in *The Politics of Race and Gender in Therapy*, ed. Lenora Fulani (New York: Haworth, 1988).

26. Gabriel K. Osei, "Caribbean Women at Home and Abroad," pp. 117–128 in *Caribbean Women: Their History and Habits*, ed. G. K. Osei (London: African Publication Society, 1979).

27. Alba, *Ethnic Identity*, chap. 1.

28. Jerre Mangione, quoted in Ewen, *Immigrant Women*, p. 197. See Thanh V. Tran, "Sex Differences in English Language Acculturation and Learning Strategies among Vietnamese Adults Aged 40 and Over in the United States," *Sex Roles* 19, 11/12 (December 1988): 747–58.

29. Ewen, *Immigrant Women*, pp. 196–97.

30. Joshua A. Fishman et al., *Bilingualism in the Barrio* (Bloomington: Indiana University Press, 1971).

31. Charles H. Maxson, *Citizenship* (New York: Oxford University Press, 1930), pp. 107–11; "The Citizenship of Married Women," in Sophonisba P. Breckinridge, *The Family and the State* (Chicago: University of Chicago Press, 1934).

32. Reid, *The Negro Immigrant*, p. 143; Elliott R. Barkan, "Whom Shall We Integrate? A Comparative Analysis of Immigrant and Naturalization Trends of Asians Before and After the 1965 Immigrant Act (1951–1978)," *Journal of American Ethnic History* 3 (Fall 1983): 29–57.

33. Reid, *The Negro Immigrant*, p. 143.

34. Wendy Sarvasy, "Beyond the Difference versus Equality Policy Debate: Postsuffrage Feminism, Citizenship, and the Quest for a Feminist Welfare State," *SIGNS* 17 (Winter 1992): 351–55.

35. Ling, *Between Worlds*, pp. 106, 124; Irvin Child, *Italian or American? The Second Generation in Conflict* (New York: Russell and Russell, 1970, orig. publ. 1943); Malve von Hassell, "Issei Women between Two Worlds, 1875–1985," Ph.D. diss., New School for Social Research, 1987; Ruiz, "The Flapper and the Chaperone," p. 151.

36. Webster, "Domestication and Americanization."

37. Kamphoefner et al., *Letters from the Land of Freedom*, p. 596.

38. Alba, *Ethnic Identity*, chap. 2.

39. Herbert Gans, "Symbolic Ethnicity: The Future of Ethnic Groups and Cultures in America," *Ethnic and Racial Studies* 2, 1 (January 1979): 1–20.

40. Alba, *Ethnic Identity*, pp. 314–15; Mary C. Waters, *Ethnic Options: Choosing Identities in America* (Berkeley: University of California Press, 1990), pp. 155–61.

41. Novak, *Rise of the Unmeltable Ethnics*, chap. 1.

42. Alba, *Ethnic Identity*, pp. 69–70, 130–35, 203.

43. Addams, *The Spirit of Youth and the City Streets* (New York: Macmillan, 1909).

44. Birnbaum, "Education for Conformity: The Case of Sicilian American Women Professionals," pp. 243–52 in *Italian Americans in the Professions*, ed. Remigio U. Pane (New York: American Italian Historical Association, 1983).

45. Paula Fass, *Outside In: Minorities and the Transformation of American Education* (New York: Oxford University Press, 1989), pp. 17, 33–34.

46. Stephan F. Brumberg, *Going to America, Going to School: The Jewish Immigrant Public School Encounter in Turn-of-the-Century New York City* (New York: Praeger, 1986).

47. Cowan and Cowan, *Our Parents' Lives*, p. 94.

48. Maxine Seller, "The Education of Immigrant Children in Buffalo, New York, 1890–1916," *New York History* 57 (April 1976): 183–200.

49. Strasser, *Never Done*, chap. 10; Maxine Seller, "The Education of the Immigrant Women: 1900–1935," *Journal of Urban History* 4 (1978): 307–30.

50. Cowan and Cowan, *Our Parents' Lives*, pp. 181–83.

51. Besides Jane Addams, *Twenty Years at Hull-House*, see Mary Lynn McCree Bryan and Allen F. Davis, *100 Years at Hull-House* (Bloomington: Indiana University Press, 1990).

52. Besides Lissak, *Pluralism and Progressives*, chap. 4, see John Daniels, *America via the Neighborhood* (New York: Harper and Brothers, 1920), pp. 175–87.

53. Addams, *Twenty Years at Hull-House*, pp. 172–78.

54. Lissak, *Pluralism and Progressives*, chap. 10.

55. Susan E. Kennedy, "Poverty, Respectability, and the Ability to Work," *International Journal of Women's Studies* 2 (September/October 1979), 401–14.

56. *I Came a Stranger: The Story of a Hull-House Girl*, ed. Dena J. Polacheck Epstein (Urbana: University of Illinois Press, 1989).

57. Bergland, "Ideology, Ethnicity and the Gendered Subject," pp. 112–13.

58. Pascoe, *Relations of Rescue*, chap. 4.

59. Maxine Seller, "The Education of the Immigrant Women."

60. Edith Blicksilver, "The *Bintl Briv* Woman Writer: Torn Between European Traditions and the American Life Style," *Studies in American Jewish Literature* 3 (Winter 1977–78): 36–49; Harvey R. and Rima D. Greenberg, " 'A Bintel Brief': The Editor as Compleat Therapist," *Psychiatric Quarterly* 52 (Fall 1980): 222–30.

61. Monika Blaschke, "German Immigrant Women and Their Press in Comparative Perspective," in *Roots of the Transplanted;* see also Maxine Seller, "The 'Women's Interest Page' of the *Jewish Daily Forward:* Socialism, Feminism and Americanization in 1919," pp. 221–42 in *The Press of Labor Migrants in Europe and North America, 1880s to 1930s*, ed. Christiane Harzig and Dirk Hoerder (Bremen: Publications of the Labor Newspaper Preservation Project, 1985).

62. Ruiz, "The Flapper and the Chaperone," p. 151.

63. Breckinridge, *New Homes for Old*, Appendix.

64. See entries in Dirk Hoerder and Christiane Harzig, eds., *The Immigrant Labor Press in North America, 1840s–1970s: An Annotated Bibliography* (New York: Greenwood, 1987–88).

65. Ruth Siefert, "Women's Pages in the German-American Radical Press, 1900–1914: The Debate on Socialism, Emancipation, and the Suffrage," pp. 122–46 in *The German-American Radical Press: The Shaping of a Left Political Culture, 1850–1940*, ed. Elliott Shore, Ken Fones-Wolf, and James Danky (Urbana: University of Illinois Press, 1992); Harzig, "The Role of German Women," pp. 90–91.

66. Varpu Lindström-Best, "*Toveritar* and Finnish Canadian Women, 1900–1930," in Harzig and Hoerder, *The Press of Labor Migrants;* Seller, "Immigrant Women Journalists as Agents of Change: The Women's Page of the *Jewish Daily Forward* in 1919," pp. 103–16 in *Changing Education: Women as Radicals and Conservators*, ed. Joyce Antler and Sari Knopp Biklen (Albany: SUNY Press, 1990).

67. Nancy B. Sinkoff, "Educating for 'Proper' Jewish Womanhood: A Case Study in Domesticity and Vocational Training, 1897–1926," *American Jewish History* 77 (June 1988): 572–99.

68. Ewen, *Immigrant Women*, chap. 10; Breckinridge, *New Homes for Old*, pp. 88–89.

69. Andrew R. Heinze, *Adapting to Abundance: Jewish Immigrants, Mass Consumption, and the Search for American Identity* (New York: Columbia University Press, 1990), chap. 6.

70. Ewen, *Immigrant Women*, pp. 188–189; Breckinridge, *New Homes for Old*, pp. 135–36.

71. Heinze, *Adapting to Abundance*, pp. 106–108.

72. Harzig, "The Role of German Women," p. 100; Susan Levine, "Workers' Wives: Gender, Class and Consumerism in the 1920s United States," *Gender and History* 3 (Spring 1991): 45–64.

73. Stanley Nadel, *Kleindeutschland, Little Germany: Ethnicity, Religion, and Class in New York City, 1845–80* (Urbana: University of Illinois Press, 1990), p. 105.

74. Elizabeth Ewen, "City Lights: Immigrant Women and the Rise of the Movies," *SIGNS* 5 (1980): 545–65.

75. Glenn, *Daughters of the Shtetl*, pp. 209–16.

76. Ruiz, "The Flapper and the Chaperone," p. 148–51.

77. Lee Rainwater, *Workingman's Wife: Her Personality, World and Life Style* (New York: Oceana Publications, 1959); Betty Friedan, *The Feminine Mystique* (New York: Norton, 1963).

78. Cowan and Cowan, *Our Parents' Lives*, pp. 208–209.

79. Weinberg, *World of Our Mothers*, pp. 142–44; 214–15.

80. On the effect of age: Jose Szapocznik, "Theory and Measurement of Acculturation," *Inter-American Journal of Psychology* 12 (1978): 113–30; Asaye Tsegga, "The Effects of Sex, Socioeconomic Status, and Generation on the Acculturation of Chinese-American Students," Ed.D. diss., University of Southern California, 1983.

81. Chalsa Loo, "Chinatown's Wellness: An Enclave of Problems," *Journal of the Asian American Psychological Association* 7, 1 (1982): 13–18; Thanh Van Tranh and Lauretta Byars, "Sources of Subjective Well-Being among Vietnamese Women in the United States," *Free Inquiry in Creative Sociology* 15 (November 1987): 195–98.

82. Constance Cronin, *The Sting of Change* (Chicago: University of Chicago Press, 1970).

83. Oliva M. Espin et al., *Refugee Women and Their Mental Health: Shattered Societies, Shattered Lives* (New York: Haworth, 1993).

84. Corinne Krause, "Urbanization without Breakdown: Italian, Jewish, and Slavic Women in Pittsburgh, 1900 to 1945," *Journal of Urban History* 4 (May 1978): 291–305; Krause, "Ethnic Culture, Religion, and the Mental Health of Slavic-American Women," *Journal of Religion and Health* 18 (1979): 298–307.

85. William A. Vega, Bohdan Kolody, and Juan Ramon Valle, "The Relationship of Marital Status, Confidant Support, and Depression among Mexican Immigrant Women," *Journal of Marriage and the Family* 48 (August 1986): 597–605; Velia N. Salgado de Snyder, "Mexican Immigrant Women: The Relationship of Ethnic Loyalty, Self-Esteem, Social Support and Satisfaction to Acculturative Stress and Depressive Symptomatology," Ph.D. diss., University of California, 1986.

86. Ellen Lewin, "Nobility of Suffering: Illness and Misfortune among Latin American Immigrant Women," *Anthropological Quarterly* 52 (July 1979): 152–58.

87. Laurel Kendall, "Cold Wombs in Balmy Honolulu: Ethnogynecology among Korean Immigrants," *Social Science & Medicine* 25, 4 (1987): 367–76.

88. Phyllis N. Stern et al., "Culturally Induced Stress during Childbearing: The Filipino-American Experience," *Health Care for Women International* 6, 1–3 (1985): 105–21; Wing Hon Yeung and Michael A. Schwartz, "Emotional Disturbance in Chinese Obstetrical Patients: A Pilot Study," *General Hospital Psychiatry* 8 (July 1986): 258–62.

89. Diana G. Kirby, "Immigration, Stress, and Prescription Drug Use among Cuban Women in South Florida," *Medical Anthropology* 10 (1989): 287–95.

90. Ramon M. Salcido, "Use of Services in Los Angeles County by Undocumented Families: Their Perceptions of Stress and Sources of Support," *California Sociologist* 5, 2 (1982): 119–31.

91. William A. Vega et al., "Marital Strain, Coping, and Depression among Mexican-American Women," *Journal of Marriage and the Family* 50 (May 1988): 391–403; Rogelio Saenz, Willis J. Goudy, and Frederick O. Lorenz, "The Effects of Employment and Marital Relations on Depression among Mexican American Women," *Journal of Marriage and the Family* 51, 1 (February 1989): 39–251.

92. Sonia Hamburger, "Profile of Curanderos: A Study of Mexican Folk Practitioners," *International Journal of Social Psychiatry* 24 (Spring 1978): 19–25; Carolyn Sargent and John Marcucci, "Aspects of Khmer Medicine among Refugees in Urban America," *Medical Anthropology Quarterly* 16 (November 1984): 7–9.

93. Claudia Fishman, Robin Evans, and Eloise Jenks, "Warm Bodies, Cool Milk: Conflicts in Post-Partum Food Choice for Indochinese Women in California," *Social Science and Medicine* 26 (1988): 1125–32.

94. Muir, *The Strongest Part of the Family*, p. 138.

95. Felipe G. Castro et al., "The Health Beliefs of Mexican, Mexican American and Anglo American Women," *Hispanic Journal of Behavioral Sciences* 6 (December 1984): 365–83.

96. Karyl McIntosh, "Folk Obstetrics, Gynecology, and Pediatrics in Utica, New York," *New York Folklore* 4 (Summer/Winter 1978): 49–59; Chester A. Jurczak, "Ethnicity, Status, and Generational Positioning: A Study of Health Practices among Polonians in Five Ethnic Islands," Ph.D. diss., University of Pittsburgh, 1964.

97. Alba, *Ethnic Identity*, pp. 92–93; Waters, *Ethnic Options*, pp. 118–28.

98. This is the finding of many three-generations studies. See, e.g., Mary J. Cappozzoli, *Three Generations of Italian American Women in Nassau County, 1925–1981* (New York: Garland, 1990); John Connor, *Tradition and Change in Three Generations of Japanese Americans* (Chicago: Nelson-Hall, 1977).

99. Yuet-fung Ho, "Women and Creating a Chinese American Culture," *Bu Gao Ban* (Winter/Spring 1985); Yanagisako, *Transforming the Past*, pp. 215–17; Safia F. Haddad, "The Woman's Role in Socialization of Syrian-Americans in Chicago," in *The Arab Americans: Studies in Assimilation*, ed. Elaine C. Hagopian and Ann Paden (Wilmette: Medina University Press International, 1969); Diane Matza, "Sephardic Jews Transmitting Culture across Three Generations," *American Jewish History* 79 (Spring 1990): 336–54.

100. Alba, *Ethnic Identity*, p. 245.

101. Muir, *The Strongest Part of the Family*, p. 157.

102. Elizabeth Mathias and Richard Raspa, *Italian Folktales in America: The Verbal Art of an Immigrant Woman* (Detroit: Wayne State University Press, 1985); Elizabeth Stone, *Black Sheep and Kissing Cousins: How Our Family Stories Shape Us* (New York: Penguin, 1989).

103. Geoffrey Fox, "Honor, Shame and Women's Liberation in Cuba: Views of Working-Class Emigré Men," in *Female and Male in Latin America*, ed. Ann Pescatello (Pittsburgh: University of Pittsburgh Press, 1973); Oliva M. Espin and Beth Warner, "Attitudes towards the Role of Women in Cuban Women Attending a Community College," *International Journal of Social Psychology* 28 (Autumn 1982): 233–39; Roland G. Tharp et al., "Changes in Marriage Roles Accompanying the Acculturation of the Mexican American Wife," *Journal of Marriage and the Family* 30 (August 1980): 404–12; Nancy Foner, "Sex Roles and Sensibilities: Jamaican Women in New York and London," pp. 133–51 in *International Migration*.

104. William M. Meredith and George P. Roue, "Changes in Lao Hmong Marital Attitudes after Immigrating to the United States," *Journal of Comparative Family Studies* 17 (Spring 1986): 117–26; Jean S. Braun and Hilda M. Chao, "Attitudes toward Women: A Comparison of Asian-Born Chinese and American Caucasians," *Psychology of Women Quarterly* 2 (Spring 1978): 195–201.

105. Waters, *Ethnic Options*, pp. 46–47.

106. Lynn Davidman, *Tradition in a Rootless World: Women Turn to Orthodox Judaism* (Berkeley: University of California Press, 1991); Debra R. Kaufman, *Rachel's Daughters: Newly Orthodox Jewish Women* (New Brunswick, N.J.: Rutgers University Press, 1991).

107. Blu Greenberg, *How to Run a Traditional Jewish Household* (New York: Simon and Schuster, 1983).

108. Hermann Bausinger, *Folk Culture in a World of Technology* (Bloomington: Indiana University Press, 1990), pp. 126–27.

109. Connie Young Yu, "The World of Our Grandmothers," in Asian Women United, *Making Waves*, p. 35.

110. Connie A. Maglione and Carmen Anthony Fiore, *Voices of the Daughters* (Princeton: Townhouse, 1989), p. 1.

111. Harold A. Takooshian and Catherine R. Stuart, "Ethnicity and Feminism among American Women: Opposing Social Trends," *International Journal of Group Tensions* 13, 1–4 (1983): 100–105; also Abraham D. Lavender, *Ethnic Women and Feminist Values: Toward a "New" Value System* (Lanham, Md.: University Press of America, 1986).

112. Maglione, *Voices of the Daughters*, preface.

113. Nancy Seifer, *Nobody Speaks for Me*.

114. Lillian D. Anthony-Welch, "A Comparative Analysis of the Black Woman as Transmitter of Black Values, Based on Case Studies of Families in Ghana and among Jamaicans and Afro-Americans in Hartford, Connecticut," Ed.D. diss., University of Massachusetts, 1976.

115. Anna Wong, "A Study of the Initial Adjustment to the American Society of Six Chinese Immigrant Females in High School," Ph.D. diss., Wright Institute, 1980.

116. Margaret Carpenter, "Addressing the Needs of Women Refugees," *World Refugee Survey* 1981: 42–44; Sarah R. Mason, "Training Hmong Women: For Marginal Work or Entry into the Mainstream," pp. 101–20 in Glenn Hendricks, et al., *The Hmong in Transition* (Staten Island: Center for Migration Studies, 1986); Jo Ann Crandall et al., "Existing Programs for Orientation of Women Refugees and Migrants," *Migration Today* 10 (1982): 33–42; Lani Davison, "Women Refugees: Special Needs and Programs," *Journal of Refugee Resettlement* 1 (1981): 1–16.

117. Gail P. Kelly, "Schooling, Gender and the Reshaping of Occupational and Social Expectations: The Case of Vietnamese Immigrants in the United States," *International Journal of Women's Studies* 1 (July/August 1978): 323–35; "The Schooling of Vietnamese Immigrants: Internal Colonialism and Its Impact on Women," in *Comparative Perspectives on Third World Women: The Impact of Sex, Race, and Class,* ed. Beverly Lindsay (New York: Praeger, 1980).

118. Sarah R. Mason, *Training Southeast Asian Refugee Women for Employment: Public Policies and Community Programs, 1975–1985* (Minneapolis: Center for Urban and Regional Affairs, University of Minnesota, 1986), p. 7.

119. Susan L. Braunstein and Jenna Weissman Joselit, *Getting Comfortable in New York: The American Jewish Home, 1880–1950* (Bloomington: Indiana University Press, 1992); see also Deborah Dash Moore, *At Home in America: Second Generation New York Jews* (New York: Columbia University Press, 1981).

120. Pascoe, *Relations of Rescue*, p. 117.

121. Yanagisako, *Transforming the Past*, pp. 217, 226–27.

122. Waters, *Ethnic Identity*, chap. 2.

123. Barbara Posadas, "Mestiza Girlhood: Interracial Families in Chicago's Filipino American Community since 1925," pp. 273–82 in Asian Women United, *Making Waves*.

Bibliographical Essay

As I was writing this book, colleagues repeatedly asked me whether enough had been written about immigrant women to justify a work of synthesis. In fact, the development of women's studies and the resurgence of immigration into the U.S. since 1965 have resulted in an explosion of new research on immigrant women. In the interests of brevity, I have cited less than half the sources I consulted, and I have limited citations (with one exception) to sources in English. I nevertheless wish to note that a book like this one necessarily rests on the work of dozens of scholars, many of whom I do not name individually. Readers are urged to explore Francesco Cordasco, *The Immigrant Woman in North America: An Annotated Bibliography of Selected References* (Metuchen, N. J.: Scarecrow, 1985) and Donna Gabaccia, *Immigrant Women in the United States: A Selectively Annotated Multi-Disciplinary Bibliography* (New York: Greenwood, 1989).

In this bibliographical essay, I refer to works I found useful in formulating individual chapters. I also append two bibliographies of general works on immigrant women of many backgrounds and of works focused on immigrants of particular national and regional origins. These cite works focused specifically on women and works that analyze gender in immigrant life.

INTRODUCTION

The best historical study remains John Bodnar, *The Transplanted: A History of Immigrants in Urban America* (Bloomington: Indiana University Press, 1985). More inclusive ethnic histories are Thomas Archdeacon's *Becoming American: An Ethnic History* (New York: Free Press, 1983); Roger Daniels's *Coming to America: A History of Immigration and Ethnicity in American Life* (New York: HarperCollins, 1990); Lawrence Fuchs's *The American Kaleidoscope: Race, Ethnicity, and the Civic Culture* (Hanover, N.H.: University Press of New England, 1990).

Recent studies of contemporary immigration include David M. Reimers, *Still the Golden Door: The Third World Comes to America* (New York: Columbia University Press, 1985) and Alejandro Portes and Rubén G. Rumbaut, *Immigrant America: A Portrait* (Berkeley: University of California Press, 1990). Quantifiers can usefully consult Guillermina Jasso and Mark R. Rosenzweig, *The New Chosen People: Immigrants in the U.S.* (New York: Russell Sage Foundation, 1990).

Immigrant women sometimes disappear in ethno-cultural categories like "Euro-American" and "African American" in multicultural histories of American women. Helpful nevertheless are Ellen Carol DuBois and Vicki L. Ruiz, eds., *Unequal Sisters: A Multi-Cultural Reader in U.S. Women's History* (New York: Routledge, 1990); and Teresa L. Amott and Julie A. Matthaei, *Race, Gender and Work: A Multicultural Economic History of Women in the United States* (Boston: South End Press, 1991).

1. WHERE IS THE OTHER SIDE?

International approaches to the study of migration have proliferated. Compare Virginia Yans-McLaughlin, ed., *Immigration Reconsidered: History, Sociology, and Politics* (New York: Oxford University Press, 1990) to Nina Glick Schiller, Linda Basch, and Cristina Szanton, eds., *Towards a Transnational Perspective on Migration: Race, Class, Ethnicity, and Nationalism Reconsidered* (New York Academy of Sciences, forthcoming).

For the nineteenth century, consult the "Atlantic" approaches of Dirk Hoerder, "An Introduction to Labor Migration in the Atlantic Economies, 1815–1914," pp. 3–32 in *Labor Migration in the Atlantic Economies: The European and North American Working Classes during the Period of Industrialization*, ed. Dirk Hoerder (Westport, Conn.: Greenwood, 1985); and Walter Nugent, *Crossings* (Bloomington: Indiana University Press, 1992).

Students interested in theories of migration should still begin with E. G. Ravenstein, "The Laws of Migration," *Journal of the Royal Statistical Society* (1889): 241–301. For more recent work see Kingsley Davis, "The Migrations of Human Populations," *Scientific American* 231, 3 (September 1974): 93–105; Marios Nikolinakis, "Notes Towards a General Theory of Migration in Late Capitalism," *Race and Class* 17 (1975): 5–17. Theorists of migration influenced by world systems analysis include Saskia Sassen-Koob, "The International Circulation of Resources and Development: The Case of Migrant Labour," *Development and Change* (October 1978): 509–45.

Early colonial migrations are described in Philip D. Curtin, *The Atlantic Slave Trade: A Census* (Madison: University of Wisconsin Press, 1970); Bernard Bailyn, *Voyagers to the West: A Passage in the Peopling of America on the Eve of the American Revolution* (New York: Knopf/Random House, 1986); Ida Altman and James Horn, eds., *"To Make America": European Emigration in the Early Modern Period* (Berkeley: University of California Press, 1991); David Eltis, "Free and Coerced Transatlantic Migrations: Some Comparisons," *American Historical Review* 88 (1982): 251–80.

For introductions to the enormous literature on immigrants of particular backgrounds, students can still learn much from *The Harvard Encyclopedia of American Ethnic Groups* (Cambridge, Mass.: Belknap, 1980). They can also find useful bibliographies in Bodnar, *The Transplanted*, and Portes and Rumbaut, *Immigrant America*.

2. THE WOMEN OF THE OTHER SIDE

The best starting place for students interested in gender on the other side is a growing literature on women and development. The classic work is Ester Boserup, *Woman's Role in Economic Development* (New York: St. Martin's, 1970). More recent works include Claude Meillassoux, *Maidens, Meal and Money: Capitalism and the Domestic Community* (New York: Cambridge University Press, 1981); Nanneke Redclift and Enzo Mingione, *Beyond Employment: Household, Gender, and Subsistence* (New York: Blackwell, 1985); Zubeida M. Ahmad and Martha R. Loutfi, *Women Workers in Rural Development* (Geneva: International Labour Office, 1985); Lourdes Benería, ed., *Women and Development: The Sexual Division of Labor in Rural Societies* (New York: Praeger, 1982); Eleanor Leacock, Helen I. Safa, et al., *Women's Work: Development and the Division of Labor by Gender* (South Hadley, Mass.: Bergin and Garvey, 1986).

Works that examine gender in a world-systems perspective include Joan Smith, Immanuel Wallerstein and Hans-Dieter Evers, eds., *Households and the World Economy* (Beverly Hills: Sage, 1984); Sharon Stichter and Jane L. Parpart, *Women, Employment and the Family in the International Division of Labour* (Houndsmill, Basingstoke: Macmillan, 1990); Joan Nash and Patrícia Fernández-Kelly, *Women, Men and the International Division of Labor* (Albany: State University of New York Press, 1983).

Studies of third world women and women in colonialism are also helpful. See Mona Etienne and Eleanor Leacock, eds., *Women and Colonization: Anthropological Perspectives* (New York: Praeger, 1980); Mayra Buviníc, Margaret A. Lycette, and William Paul McGreevey, *Women and Poverty in the Third World* (Baltimore: Johns Hopkins University Press, 1983); Jeanne Bisilliat and Michèle Fiéloux, *Women of the Third World: Work and Daily Life* (Rutherford: Fairleigh Dickinson University Press, 1987); Lynne Brydon and Sylvia Chant, *Women in the Third World: Gender Issues in Rural and Urban Areas* (New Brunswick: Rutgers University Press, 1989).

3. FROM MINORITY TO MAJORITY

Studies of immigrant sex ratios include Marion F. Houstoun et al., "Female Predominance of Immigration to the United States since 1930: A First Look," *International Migration Review* 28 (Winter 1984): 908–63; Andrea Tyree and Katharine M. Donato, "A Demographic Overview of the International Migration of Women," pp. 21–44 in Rita J. Simon and Caroline B. Brettell, eds., *International Migration: The Female Experience* (Totowa, N.J.: Rowman and Allanheld, 1985); Roy S. Bryce-Laporte, "Introduction: The New Immigration: The Female Majority," pp. vii–xxxix in *Female Immigrants to the United States*, ed. Delores M. Mortimer and Roy S. Bryce-Laporte (Washington, D.C.: Smithsonian Institution, Research Institute on Immigration and Ethnic Studies, 1981); Andrea Tyree and Katharine M. Donato, "The Sex Composition of Legal Immigrants to the United States," *Sociology and Social Research* 69 (July 1985): 577–84; Katherine Donato, "Understanding U.S. Immigration: Why Some Countries Send Women and Others Send Men," pp. 159–84 in *Seeking Common Ground*. The only historical overview is Donna Gabaccia, "Women of the Mass Migrations: From Minority to Majority, 1820–1930," in *Global Moves, Local Contexts: European Migrants in International Perspective*, ed. Dirk Hoerder and Leslie Moch (forthcoming).

For general introductions to the topic of women and migration see *International Migration*; Silvia Pedraza, "Women and Migration," *Annual Review of Sociology* 17 (1991): 303–325; Mirjana Morokvasic, "Women in Migration: Beyond the Reductionist Outlook," pp. 13–31 in *One Way Ticket: Migration and Female Labour*, ed. Annie Phizacklea (London: Routledge and Kegan Paul, 1983); Elsa M. Chaney, "Women Who Go and Women Who Stay Behind," *Migration Today* 10 (1982): 6–14.

4. LIVES OF LABOR

A large literature on women's work sheds light on the working lives of immigrants. On domestic service, see David M. Katzman, *Seven Days a Week: Women and Domestic Service in Industrializing America* (New York: Oxford, 1978); Daniel E. Sutherland, *Americans and Their Servants: Domestic Service in the United States from 1800 to 1920* (Baton Rouge: Louisiana State University Press, 1981); Phyllis M. Palmer, *Domesticity and Dirt: Housewives and Domestic Servants in the United States, 1920–1945* (Philadelphia: Temple University Press, 1989); Faye E. Dudden, *Serving Women: Household Service in Nineteenth-Century America* (Middletown, Conn.: Wesleyan University Press, 1983).

On agriculture, see Nancy Grey Osterud, *Bonds of Community: The Lives of Farm Women in Nineteenth-Century New York* (Ithaca: Cornell University Press, 1991); Deborah Fink, *Agrarian Women: Wives and Mothers in Rural Nebraska, 1880–1940* (Chapel Hill: University of North Carolina Press, 1992); Linda C. and Theo J. Majka, *Farm Workers, Agribusiness, and the State* (Philadelphia: Temple University Press, 1982); Cletus E. Daniel, *Bitter Harvest: A History of California Farmworkers, 1870–1941* (Ithaca: Cornell University Press, 1981); Carey McWilliams, *Factories in the Field: the Story of Migratory Farm Labor in California* (Santa Barbara: Peregrine Publishers, 1971); Philip L. Martin, *Harvest of Confusion: Migrant Workers in U.S. Agriculture* (Boulder: Westview, 1988).

On factory work, see Tamara K. Hareven and Randolph Langenbach, *Amoskeag: Life and Work in an American Factory City* (New York: Pantheon Books, 1978); Mary Blewett, *The Last Generation: Work and Life in the Textile Mills of Lowell, Massachusetts, 1910–1960* (Amherst: University of Massachusetts Press, 1990); Patricia A. Cooper, *Once a Cigar Maker: Men, Women, and Work Culture in American Cigar Factories* (Urbana: University of Illinois Press, 1987); Turbin, *Working Women of Collar City*. On garments, the best study is still Mabel H. Willett, *Employment of Women in the Clothing Trades* (New York: Columbia University Press, 1902), but see also Glenn, *Daughters of the*

Shtetl, chapter 3. For the present, see Roger Waldinger, *Immigrants in the New York City Garment Industry* (Cambridge: Joint Center for Urban Studies of MIT and Harvard University, 1981).

Far less has been written about women's unpaid work. Helpful are Susan Strasser, *Never Done: A History of American Housework* (New York: Pantheon, 1982); Glenna Matthews, *"Just a Housewife": The Rise and Fall of Domesticity in America* (New York: Oxford University Press, 1987); Ruth Schwartz Cowan, *More Work for Mother: The Ironies of Household Technology from the Open Hearth to the Microwave* (New York: Basic Books, 1983); Annagret Ogden, *The Great American Housewife: From Helpmate to Wage Earner* (Westport, Conn.: Greenwood, 1986). On the domestic work of immigrants see especially Susan J. Kleinberg, "Technology and Women's Work: The Lives of Working Class Women in Pittsburgh, 1870–1900," *Labor History* 17 (Winter 1976): 58–72; Kleinberg, *The Shadow of the Mills*, chapter 3, 7; Gabaccia, "Housing and Household Work: Sicily and New York, 1890–1910," *Michigan Occasional Papers in Women's Studies* 20 (Spring 1981); and the still very useful Sophonisba P. Breckinridge, *New Homes for Old* (New York: Harper and Brothers, Americanization Studies: The Acculturation of Immigrant Groups into American Society, vol. 6, 1921).

On immigrant family businesses see Alixa Naff, *Becoming American: The Early Arab Immigrant Experience* (Carbondale: Southern Illinois University Press, 1985); Roger Waldinger, Howard Aldrich and Robin Ward, *Ethnic Entrepreneurs: Immigrant Business in Industrial Societies* (Newbury Park: Sage Publications, 1990); Bernard P. Wong, *Patronage, Brokerage, Entrepreneurship, and the Chinese Community of New York* (New York: AMS Press, 1988); Ivan H. Light, *Ethnic Enterprise in America; Business and Welfare among Chinese, Japanese, and Blacks* (Berkeley: University of California Press, 1972); Edna Bonacich and John Modell, *The Economic Basis of Ethnic Solidarity: Small Business in the Japanese American Community* (Berkeley: University of California Press, 1980).

Since this chapter emphasizes women's work within family economies, it is fair to note that women's historians sometime question the usefulness of this approach: Florence T. Bloom, "Struggling and Surviving—The Life Style of European Immigrant Breadwinning Mothers in American Industrial Cities, 1900–1930," *Women's Studies International Forum* 8 (1985): 609–20; Charlene Gannage, "Haven or Heartache? Immigrant Women and the Household," *Anthropologica* 26, 2 (1984): 217–53. By examining paid and unpaid work in a family context, one can see that the transition from "working daughter" to "working mother," as well as sharp differences between African American and working-class white women's work in the past, refer to wage-earning work only.

5. ALL HER KIN

There is a large anthropological literature on kinship. Good recent introductions to the traditions of the other side include Andrejs Plakans, *Kinship in the Past: An Anthropology of European Family Life, 1500–1900* (New York: B. Blackwell, 1986); J. G. Peristiany, *Mediterranean Family Structures* (New York: Cambridge University Press, 1976). On Asia, see Paul Chao, *Chinese Kinship* (Boston: Kegan Paul International, 1983); James Watson, "Chinese Kinship Reconsidered: Anthropological Perspectives on Historical Research," *China Quarterly* 92 (December 1982): 589–622; Francis L. K. Hsu, *Iemoto: The Heart of Japan* (Cambridge: Schenkman, 1975). On Caribbean and Latin American kinship systems, see Hugo G. Nutini, Pedro Carrasco, and James M. Taggart, eds., *Essays on Mexican Kinship* (Pittsburgh: University of Pittsburgh Press, 1976); Arnand F. Marks and Rene A. Romer, *Family and Kinship in Middle America* (Willemstad: Institute of Higher Studies in Curaçao, 1970); Raymond T. Smith, *Kinship Ideology and Practice in Latin America* (Chapel Hill: University of North Carolina Press, 1984). For a feminist perspective, see also *Gender and Kinship: Toward a Unified Analysis*, ed. Sylvia Junko Yanagisako and Jane Collier (Stanford: Stanford University Press, 1987).

On American kinship, see David M. Schneider, *American Kinship: A Cultural Account* (Englewood Cliffs: Prentice Hall, 1968); Sylvia J. Yanagisako, "Women-Centered Kin Networks in Urban Bilateral Kinship," *American Ethnologist* 4 (1977): 207–26; Carlene F. Bryant, *We're All Kin: A Cultural Study of a Mountain Neighborhood* (Knoxville: University of Tennessee Press, 1981); Gwen Kennedy Neville, *Kinship and Pilgrimage: Rituals of Reunion in American Protestant Culture* (New York: Oxford University Press, 1987).

For comparison to African American kinship, see Elmer P. Martin and Joanne Mitchell Martin, *The Black Extended Family* (Chicago: University of Chicago Press, 1978); Carol B. Stack, *All Our Kin: Strategies for Survival in a Black Community* (New York: Harper and Row, 1974).

Oral histories, novels of immigrant life, and immigrant autobiographies remain important untapped sources for the study of immigrant families. I am unable to cite all of the works I have read while preparing this book, but refer the interested reader to chapters 10–12 in Gabaccia, *Immigrant Women in the U.S.*

Those interested in sexuality still have little choice but to turn to fiction and autobiography. See, for example, explorations of homosexuality and ethnicity in Dodici Azpadu, *Saturday Night in the Prime of Life* (Iowa City: Aunt Lute Book Co., 1983); Arlene Voski Avakian, *Lion Woman's Legacy: An Armenian-American Memoir* (New York: The Feminist Press, City University of New York, 1992); Rachel Guido de Vries, *Tender Warriors* (Ithaca: Firebrand, 1986); Arturo Islas, *Migrant Souls* (New York: William Morrow, 1990).

While historians have not focused extensively on childrearing, there is a growing literature by social scientists on the most recent immigrants' practices. See Dorothy P. Bryan, "Nigerian Women and Child-Rearing Practices in Washington, D.C.: A Summary of Research Findings and Implications," pp. 157–70 in *Female Immigrants to the U.S;* Robert Strom et al., "The Adjustment of Korean Immigrant Families," *Educational and Psychological Research* 6 (Summer 1986): 213–27; Luis and Peggy Escovar, "Retrospective Perception of Parental Child-Rearing Practices in Three Culturally Different College Groups," *International Journal of Intercultural Relations* 9, 1 (1985): 31–49; Omprakash K. and Savitri Gupta, "A Study of the Influence of American Culture on the Child-Rearing Attitudes of Indian Mothers," *Indian Journal of Social Work* 46 (April 1985): 95–104; John Chavez and Raymond Buriel, "Reinforcing Children's Effort: A Comparison of Immigrant, Native-Born Mexican-American and Euro-American Mothers," *Hispanic Journal of Behavioral Sciences* 8 (June 1986): 127–42; Masanori Higa, "A Comparative Study of Three Groups of 'Japanese' Mothers: Attitudes toward Child Rearing," pp. 16–25 in *Youth, Socialization and Mental Health*, vol. III of *Mental Health Research in Asia and the Pacific*, ed. William P. Lebra (Honolulu: University of Hawaii Press, 1974); Joan R. F. Kuchner, "Chinese-American and European-American: A Cross-Cultural Study of Infant and Mother," Ph.D. dissertation, University of Chicago, 1981; Timothy Law, "Differential Childrearing Attitudes and Practices of Chinese-American Mothers," Ph.D. dissertation, Claremont Graduate School, 1973; Diana C. Li-Repac, "The Impact of Acculturation on the Child-Rearing Attitudes and Practices of Chinese-American Families: Consequences for the Attachment Process," Ph.D. dissertation, University of California at Berkeley, 1981.

Women's historians have focused particularly on immigrant daughters' efforts to free themselves from family oligarchy, largely through studies of single urban working-class women. The most important works for understanding this interpretation are Kathy Peiss, *Cheap Amusements: Working Women and Leisure in Turn-of-the-Century New York* (Philadelphia: Temple University Press, 1986); Christine Stansell, *City of Women: Sex and Class in New York, 1789–1860* (New York: Knopf, 1986); Joanne J. Meyerowitz, *Women Adrift: Independent Wage Earners in Chicago, 1880–1930*

(Chicago: University of Chicago Press, 1988); Meyerowitz, "Women and Migration: Autonomous Female Migrants to Chicago, 1880–1930," *Journal of Urban History* 13 (February 1987): 197–206.

6. WORKING TOGETHER

On voluntarism among immigrant men, see Frank Renkiewicz, "The Profits of Non-Profit Capitalism: Polish Fraternalism and Beneficial Insurance in America," in *Self-Help in Urban America*, ed. Scott Cummings (Port Washington: Kennikat Press, 1980); William Toll, "Mobility, Fraternalism, and Jewish Cultural Change: Portland, 1910–1930," pp. 86–106 in *The Jews of the West: The Metropolitan Years*, ed. Moses Rischin (Waltham: American Jewish Historical Society, 1979); John Bodnar, "Ethnic Fraternal Benefit Associations: Their Historical Development, Character and Significance," pp. 5–14 in *Records of Ethnic Fraternal Benefit Associations in the United States: Essays and Inventories* (St. Paul: Immigration History Research Center, 1981); Gary R. Mormino and George E. Pozzetta, "The Cradle of Mutual Aid: Immigrant Cooperative Societies in Ybor City," *Tampa Bay History* 7, 2 (Fall/Winter 1985): 36–58.

On voluntarism among African American and native-born white women, see Anne Firor Scott, *Natural Allies: Women's Associations in American History* (Urbana: University of Illinois Press, 1991); Robyn Muncy, *Creating a Female Dominion in American Reform, 1890–1935* (New York: Oxford University Press, 1991); Lori D. Ginzberg, *Women and the Work of Benevolence: Morality, Politics, and Class in the Nineteenth-Century United States* (New Haven: Yale University Press, 1990); Darlene Clark Hine, ed., *Black Women in America*, vol. 2 (Brooklyn: Carlson, 1990); Nancy A. Hewitt, "Politicizing Domesticity: Anglo, Black, and Latin Women in Tampa's Progressive Movements," in *Gender, Class, Race, and Reform*.

For parallels between the feminism of foreign-born and African American women, see Rosalyn Terborg-Penn, "Discontented Black Feminists: Prelude and Postscript to the Passage of the Nineteenth Amendment," pp. 261–78 in Scharf and Jensen, *Decades of Discontent*; bell hooks, *Feminist Theory: From Margin to Center* (Boston: South End Press, 1984), chapter 1.

Women's neighborhood activism has proved difficult to document. For the present, see Nancy Seifer, *Nobody Speaks for Me! Self-Portraits of American Working Class Women* (New York: Simon and Schuster, 1976); Anne Witte Garland, *Women Activists: Challenges to the Abuse of Power* (New York: Feminist Press, 1988); Ruth Sidel, *Urban Survival: The World of Working-Class Women* (Boston: Beacon, 1978); Kathleen McCourt, *Working-Class Women and Grass-Roots Politics* (Bloomington: Indiana University Press, 1976).

On immigrant women labor activists, see Joan M. Jensen, "The Great Uprising in Rochester," pp. 94–113 in *A Needle, A Bobbin, A Strike: Women Needleworkers in America*; Susan Levine, "Honor Each Noble Maid: Women Workers and the Yonkers Carpet Weavers' Strike of 1885," *New York History* 62 (1981): 153–76; N. Sue Weiler, "Walkout: The Chicago Men's Garment Workers' Strike, 1910–1911," *Chicago History* 8 (Winter, 1979–1980): 238–49; Clementina Duron, "Mexican Women and Labor Conflict in Los Angeles: The ILGWU Dressmakers' Strike of 1933," *Aztlán* 15 (Spring 1984): 145–61; Richard Croxdale, "The 1938 San Antonio Pecan Shellers' Strike," in *Women in the Texas Workforce*, ed. Richard Croxdale and Melissa Hield (Austin: People's History in Texas, 1979).

For voluntarism among today's immigrant women, see Eui-Young Yu, "The Activities of Women in South California Korean Community Organizations," pp. 249–99 in *Korean Women in Transition*; Magdalena Mora, "The Tolteca Strike: Mexican Women and the Struggle for Union Representation," pp. 111–77 in *Mexican Immigrant Workers in the U.S.*, ed. Antonio Rios-Bustamente (Los Angeles: Chicano Studies Research Center Publications, UCLA, 1981); Louise Lamphere, "Fighting the Piece-Rate System:

New Dimensions of an Old Struggle in the Apparel Industry," pp. 257–76 in *Case Studies in the Labor Process*, ed. Andrew Zimbalist (New York: Monthly Review Press, 1979); Nina Shapiro-Perl, "Resistance Strategies: The Routine Struggle for Bread and Roses," pp. 193–208 in *My Troubles are Going to Have Trouble with Me: Everyday Trials and Triumphs of Women Workers*, ed. Karen B. Sacks and Dorothy Remy (New Brunswick: Rutgers University Press, 1984); Nina Shapiro-Perl, "The Piece Rate: Class Struggle on the Shop Floor: Evidence from the Costume Jewelry Industry in Providence, Rhode Island," pp. 277–98 in *Case Studies in the Labor Process*.

7. MIDDLE-CLASS IMMIGRANTS

The question of class has not received the same attention in studies of immigrant Americans as it has recently in African American studies. On women and class relations among Jewish Americans, see the work of Selma C. Berrol, "Class or Ethnicity: The Americanized German Jewish Woman and Her Middle Class Sisters," *Jewish Social Studies* 47 (Winter 1985): 21–32; "Julia Richmond and the German Jewish Establishment: Passion, Arrogance, and the Americanization of the *Ostjuden*," *American Jewish Archives* 38 (November 1986): 137–77; "When Uptown Met Downtown: Julia Richman's Work in the Jewish Community of New York, 1880–1912," *American Jewish History* 70 (September 1985): 35–67.

Much has been written on immigrant female notables, largely as a consequence of women's historians' strong interest in women's contributions to American society (in the 1970s) and the sources of female achievement (in the 1980s). Immigration historians, by contrast, largely abandoned biography along with filiopietism during these same years.

Among the major problems facing those who would study immigrant and ethnic women's achievements are the definitions of "achievement" and "American" used in standard sources. How, for example, could a foreign-born woman (who usually worked within a segregated ethnic community) qualify as a notable American? One has to assume that most community activists did not find their way into the standard biographical dictionaries of female notables. Nevertheless, these will remain the starting place for most studies of immigrant careers. For the past, see Edward T. James, Janet Wilson James, and Paul S. Boyer, *Notable American Women, 1607–1950*, 3 vols. (Cambridge, Mass.: Belknap, 1971). For comparisons with African American women, see Jessie Carney Smith, ed., *Notable Black American Women* (Detroit: Gale Research, 1992).

Scattered studies of ethnic community activists do exist. See Christopher Chow and Russell Leong, "A Pioneer Chinatown Teacher: An Interview with Alice Fong Yu," *Amerasia* 5, 1 (1978): 75–86; Carol Hepokosi, "Milma Lappala: Unitarian Minister and Humanist," *Women Who Dared*, pp. 158–64; K. Marianne Wargelin Brown, "Three 'Founding Mothers' of Finnish America," in *Women Who Dared*, pp. 136–57; Gerda W. Klein, *A Passion for Sharing: The Life of Edith Rosenwald Stern* (Chappaqua: Rossel Books, 1984); interview with Angela Carlozzi-Rosso, Italian Welfare League activist, in Salvatore LaGumina, *The Immigrant Speaks: Italian Americans Tell Their Story* (New York: Center for Migration Studies, 1979), pp. 153–63; on the Irish teacher and reformer Kate Kennedy, see Alice C. Lynch, *The Kennedy Clan and Tierra Redonda* (San Francisco: Marnell, 1935).

Foreign-born women in biographical dictionaries of female notables are heavily biased toward secular activists. Most founders, mother superiors, heads of sisterhoods and sisterhood federations, nuns, and ladies aids do not appear in *Notable American Women*. For women's careers in the religious arena see the surprisingly large, if often adulatory, literature on immigrant nuns. For the Irish founder of the Sisters of Charity of the Blessed Virgin Mary, see M. Jane Coogan, *Mary Frances Clarke* (Dubuque: Mt. Carmel Press, 1977); for the Irish founder of the Dominican Sisters of the Sick Poor, see Anne C. Boardman, *Such Love is Seldom: A Biography of Mother Mary Walsh, O. P.* (New York: Harper, 1950); see also Kathleen Healy, *Frances Warde: American Foundress of the Sisters of Mercy* (New York: Seabury, 1973). For the German founder of the Dominican Sisters in Racine, Wisconsin, see Mary H. Kohler, *Life and Work of Mother Benedicta Bauer* (Milwaukee: Bruce Publishing Co., 1937). For the founder of the Sisters of Saint Francis of Penance and Christian Charity, see Georgia Dunn, *Towers of Montauer* (Derby: Saint Paul's Publications, 1971). And see Sister Marie Therese, *Cornelia Connelly* (Westminster, Md.: Newman Press, 1961) (founder of the Society of the Holy Child); Helen L. Nugent, *Sister Louise, American Foundress* (New York: Benziger Brothers, 1931) (founder of the Sisters of Notre Dame de Namur); Francis B. Rothluebber, *He Sent Two* (Milwaukee: Bruce Publishing, 1965) (founders of the Milwaukee School Sisters of Saint Francis). For information on the Irish founder of the New Jersey Sisters of Charity, see Mary A. Sharkey, *The New Jersey Sisters of Charity* (New York: Longmans, 1933).

For mother superiors, see Mary L. Corcoran, *The Seal of Simplicity: Life of Mother Emilie* (privately printed, 1958); Mary P. Fitzgerald, *Beacon on the Plains* (Leavenworth: St. Mary College, 1939) and Sister M. Lilliana Owens, *Loretto in Missouri* (St. Louis: B. Herder, 1965) (both lives of Mother Mary Hayden) and William W. Graves, *Life and Times of Mother Bridget Hayden* (St. Paul: Journal Press, 1938); Edward A. Lenk, "Mother Marianne Cope (1838–1918): The Syracuse Franciscan Community and Molokai Lepers," Ph.D. dissertation, Syracuse University, 1986; Henry M. Malak, *Theresa of Chicago*, transl. Ann K. Dudzik (Lemont, Ill.: League of the Servant of God, Mother Mary Theresa, 1975); Mary McCrosson, *The Bell and the River* (Palo Alto: Pacific Books, 1956); Lucile McDonald, "Mother Joseph," in Western Writers of America, eds., *The Women Who Made the West* (Garden City: Doubleday, 1980), pp. 120–129; Sisters of the Reparation of the Congregation of Mary, *Blessed Are the Merciful: The Life of Mother May Zita, 1844–1917* (New York: n.p., 1953).

For Protestant activists, see Joseph Stoll, *The Lord is My Shepherd: The Life of Elizabeth Kemp Stutzman* (Aylmer, Ont.: Pathway, 1965) and Mrs. Oscar P. Brauer, trans., "As Thou Leadest Me," *Concordia Historical Institute Quarterly* 28 (Winter 1956): 166–77.

The lives of female community activists can more easily be traced in lists of ethnic notables, and in publications aimed at readers of a particular ethnic or religious background. See, for example, Francis Bolek, ed., *Who's Who in Polish America* (New York: Harbinger House, 1943); Mary C. Donelin, "American Irish Women Firsts," *Journal of the American Historical Society* 24 (1925): 215–21; David C. Gross, *Pride of our People: The Stories of One Hundred Outstanding Jewish Men and Women* (Garden City: Doubleday, 1979); Anita L. Lebeson, *Recall to Life—The Jewish Woman in America* (South Brunswick: Thomas Yoseloff, 1970).

8. PRESERVATION AND INNOVATION

I prefer the term culture change to both cultural assimilation (Milton Gordon's term, *Assimilation in American Life*, pp. 70–71; see chap. 6, n. 1) and acculturation, the term preferred recently by many immigration historians. I believe the term leaves open the direction change took and the possibility that Americans also changed in response to their contacts with immigrants.

Given its centrality to immigrant culture, surprisingly little has been written on language usage. See Joshua Fishman et al., *Language Loyalty in the United States: The Maintenance and Perpetuation of Non-English Mother Tongues by American Ethnic and Religious Groups* (The Hague: Mouton, 1966); Nancy Faires Conklin and Margaret A. Lourie, *A Host of Tongues: Language Communities in the United States* (New York: Free Press, 1983). Studies of bilingualism in the U.S. focus mainly on Spanish speakers; e.g.,

Joshua A. Fishman et al., *Bilingualism in the Barrio* (Bloomington: Indiana University Press, 1971). Studies of bilingual education often lack historical perspective, but see Carolyn R. Toth, *German-English Bilingual Schools in America: The Cincinnati Tradition in Historical Context* (New York: P. Lang, 1990).

The most important newspapers aimed at immigrant women include *Dennica* (Slovenian); *Die Deborah* (German-speaking Jewish); *Die Deutsche Hausfrau: Monatschrift für die Deutschen Frauen Amerikas* (German); *Di Froy* (Yiddish-speaking, Jewish, Communist); *Glos Polek* (Polish); *Koti Home* (Finnish); *Kvinden og Hjemmet/Kvinnana och Hemmet* (Swedish/Danish); *L'Operaia* (Italian, union); *Der Leydis Garment Woyrker* (Yiddish, ILWGU); *Misionar* (Ukrainian, religious); *Moteru Balsas* (Lithuanian, Communist); *Nasze Pisemko* (Polish, religious); *Robitnytsia* (Ukrainian, Communist); *Toveritar* (Finnish, Socialist, later Communist); *Di Yidische Froy* (Yiddish-speaking Jewish, Socialist); *Zarja* (Slovenian); *Zenske Listy* (Bohemian); *Zizvena* (Slovak).

The changing literature on settlement houses and social welfare policy remains an important source for the study of cultural change. See Mina Carson, *Settlement Folk: Social Thought and the American Settlement Movement, 1885–1930* (Chicago: University of Chicago Press, 1990); Rivka Shpak Lissak, *Pluralism and Progressives: Hull House and the New Immigrants, 1890–1919* (Chicago: University of Chicago Press, 1989); Ruth H. Crocker, *Social Work and Social Order: The Origins of the Settlement Movement in Two Industrial Cities, 1886–1930* (Champaign/Urbana: University of Illinois Press, 1991); Linda Gordon, *Women, the State, and Welfare* (Madison: University of Wisconsin Press, 1990).

A good introduction to an expanding bibliography on health and medical concerns among today's immigrant women can be found in Caroline Brettell and Patricia De Berjeois, "Anthropology and the Study of Immigrant Women," pp. 41–64 in *Seeking Common Ground*.

IMMIGRANT WOMEN OF MANY BACKGROUNDS

Dickinson, Joan Y. *The Role of the Immigrant Women in the U.S. Labor Force, 1890–1910.* New York: Arno Press, 1980.

Ewen, Elizabeth. *Immigrant Women in the Land of Dollars: Life and Culture on the Lower East Side, 1890–1925.* New York: Monthly Review Press, 1985.

Female Immigrants to the United States. Ed. Delores M. Mortimer and Roy S. Bryce-Laporte. Washington, DC: Smithsonian Institution, Research Institute on Immigration and Ethnic Studies, 1981.

Hareven, Tamara. *Family Time and Industrial Time: The Relationship between the Family and Work in a New England Industrial Community.* New York: Cambridge University Press, 1982.

Immigrant Women. Ed. Maxine Seller. Philadelphia: Temple University Press, 1981.

International Migration: The Female Experience. Ed. Rita J. Simon and Caroline B. Brettell. Totowa, N. J.: Rowman and Allanheld, 1985.

Lamphere, Louise. *From Working Daughters to Working Mothers: Immigrant Women in a New England Industrial Community.* Ithaca: Cornell University Press, 1987.

Manning, Caroline. *The Immigrant Woman and Her Job.* U.S. Department of Labor Women's Bureau Bulletin No. 74. New York: Arno Press, 1970.

Neidle, Cecyle. *America's Immigrant Women: Their Contribution to the Development of a Nation from 1609 to the Present.* New York: Hippocrene Books, 1975.

Peasant Maids, City Women. Ed. Christiane Harzig. Forthcoming.

Seeking Common Ground: Multidisciplinary Studies of Immigrant Women in the United States. Ed. Donna Gabaccia. Westport, Conn.: Praeger, 1992.

Smith, Judith E. *Family Connections: A History of Italian and Jewish Immigrant Lives in Providence, Rhode Island, 1900–1940*. Albany: State University of New York Press, 1985.

Weatherford, Doris. *Foreign and Female: Immigrant Women in America, 1840–1938*. New York: Schocken, 1986.

IMMIGRANT WOMEN OF PARTICULAR BACKGROUNDS

ASIAN

Takaki, Ronald. *Strangers from a Different Shore: A History of Asian-Americans*. Boston: Little, Brown, 1989.

CHINESE

Chih, Ginger. *The History of Chinese Immigrant Women, 1850–1940*. North Bergen, N.J.: by the author, 1977.

Yung, Judy. *Chinese Women of America: A Pictorial History*. Seattle: University of Washington Press, 1986.

CUBAN

Doran, Terry, et al. *A Road Well Traveled: Three Generations of Cuban American Women*. Newton, Mass: Education Development Center, Women's Educational Equity Act Publishing Center, 1988.

DOMINICANS

Grasmuck, Sherri, and Patricia R. Pessar. *Between Two Islands: Dominican Migration*. Berkeley: University of California Press, 1991.

FINNISH

Women Who Dared: The History of Finnish American Women. Ed. Carl Ross and K. Marianne Wargelin Brown. St. Paul, Minnesota: Immigration History Research Center, 1986.

HAITIAN

LaGuerre, Michael S. *American Odyssey: Haitians in New York City*. Ithaca, N.Y.: Cornell University Press, 1984.

IRISH

Diner, Hasia R. *Erin's Daughters in America: Irish Immigrant Women in the Nineteenth Century*. Baltimore: Johns Hopkins University Press, 1983.

Nolan, Janet. *Ourselves Alone: Women's Emigration from Ireland, 1885–1920*. Knoxville: University Press of Kentucky, 1989.

Turbin, Carole. *Working Women of Collar City: Gender, Class, and Community in Troy, New York, 1864–86*. Urbana: University of Illinois Press, 1992.

ITALIAN

Caroli, Betty B., et al. *The Italian Immigrant Woman in North America*. Toronto: Multicultural History Society of Ontario, 1978.

Cohen, Miriam, *Workshop to Office: Two Generations of Italian Women in New York City, 1900–1950.* Ithaca: Cornell University Press, 1992.

Di Leonardo, Micaela. *The Varieties of Ethnic Experience: Kinship, Class and Gender among California Italian-Americans.* Ithaca: Cornell University Press, 1984.

Gabaccia, Donna R. *From Sicily to Elizabeth Street: Housing and Social Change among Italian Immigrants.* Albany: State University of New York Press, 1984.

Yans-McLaughlin, Virginia. *Family and Community: Italian Immigrants in Buffalo, 1880–1930.* Ithaca: Cornell University Press, 1977.

JAPANESE

Glenn, Evelyn Nakano. *Issei, Nisei, War Bride: Three Generations of Japanese American Women in Domestic Service* (Philadelphia: Temple University Press, 1986).

Yanagisako, Sylvia. *Transforming the Past: Tradition and Kinship among Japanese Americans.* Stanford: Stanford University Press, 1985.

JEWISH EASTERN EUROPEAN

Baum, Charlotte, Paula Hyman, and Sonya Michel. *The Jewish Woman in America.* New York: New American Library, 1975.

Cantor, Aviva. *The Jewish Woman, 1900–1980: A Bibliography.* Fresh Meadows: Biblio Press, 1981.

Glanz, Rudolf. *The Jewish Woman in America: Two Female Immigrant Generations, 1820–1929.* 2 vol. New York: KTAV Publishing House and National Council of Jewish Women, 1976.

Glenn, Susan. *Daughters of the Shtetl: Life and Labor in the Immigrant Generation.* Ithaca: Cornell University Press, 1991.

Marcus, Jacob R. *The American Jewish Woman, 1654–1980.* New York: KTAV Publishing House and American Jewish Archives, 1981.

Weinberg, Sydney S. *The World of Our Mothers: Lives of Jewish Immigrant Women.* Chapel Hill: North Carolina University Press, 1988.

KOREAN

Korean Women in Transition: At Home and Abroad. Ed. Eui-Young Yu and Earl H. Phillips. Los Angeles: Center for Korean-American and Korean Studies, California State University, 1987.

LAOTIAN

Muir, Karen L. S. *The Strongest Part of the Family: A Study of Lao Refugee Women in Columbus, Ohio.* New York: AMS Press, 1988.

LATINA

Cotera, Martha P. *Latina Sourcebook: Bibliography of Mexican American, Cuban, Puerto Rican and Other Hispanic Woman: Materials in the U.S.* Austin, Tex.: Information Systems Development, 1982.

MEXICAN

Blea, Irene I. *La Chicana and the Intersection of Race, Class, and Gender.* New York: Praeger, 1992.

Blea, Irene I. *Toward a Chicano Social Science.* New York: Praeger, 1988.

del Castillo, Adelaida R., ed. *Between Borders: Essays on Mexicana/ Chicana History.* Encino: Floricante Press, 1990.

Cotera, Martha P. *Profile on the Mexican American Woman*. Austin, Tex.: National Educational Laboratory, 1976.

Cotera, Martha P. *Diosa y Hembra: The History and Heritage of Chicanas in the United States*. Austin, Tex.: Information Systems Development, 1976.

The Mexican Woman. Ed. Magdalena Mora et al. Los Angeles: Aztlán Publications, Chicano Studies Center, University of California, 1977.

Mirandé, Alfredo, and Evangelina Enriquez. *La Chicana: The Mexican-American Woman*. Chicago: University of Chicago Press, 1979.

Twice a Minority: Mexican American Women. Ed. Margarita B. Melville. St. Louis: The C. V. Mosby Company, 1980.

SLAVIC

Balch, Emily. *Our Slavic Fellow Citizens*. Philadelphia: William F. Fell, 1910.

Morawska, Ewa. *For Bread with Butter: The Life-World of East Central Europeans in Johnstown, Pennsylvania, 1890–1940*. Cambridge: Cambridge University Press, 1985.

Pehotsky, Bessie. *The Slavic Immigrant Woman*. Cincinnati: Powell & White, 1925.

Index

DONNA GABACCIA is Charles H. Stone Professor of American History at the University of North Carolina at Charlotte. She is the author of numerous books and articles on immigration history, including *From Sicily to Elizabeth Street: Housing and Social Change among Italian Immigrants* and *Militants and Migrants: Rural Sicilians Become American Workers.*